DRIVING THE PACIFIC COAST

OREGON AND WASHINGTON

Scenic Driving Tours
along Highway 101

DRIVING THE PACIFIC COAST

OREGON AND WASHINGTON

Scenic Driving Tours along Highway 101

by
Kenn Oberrecht

A Voyager Book

CHESTER, CONNECTICUT

Interior photography by Kenn Oberrecht except where credited otherwise

Library of Congress Cataloging-in-Publication Data

Oberrecht, Kenn.
    Driving the Pacific Coast, Oregon, and Washington : Scenic Driving
    Tours along Highway 101
    / by Kenn Oberrecht.—1st ed.
        p.   cm.
    ISBN 0-87106-475-8
    1. Pacific Coast (U.S.)—Description and travel—Guide-books.
    2. Automobiles—Road guides—Pacific Coast (U.S.) I. Title.
    F852.3.024   1990
    917.9504'43—dc20   89-70657
                                              CIP

Manufactured in the United States of America
First Edition/First Printing

For Trish with love

Contents

Introduction

This is meant to be a book for reading and reference, as well as a tote-along companion when you travel to the coast country. It's a carefully organized volume that's easy to follow and does not require training in advanced vector analysis. Coastal communities are arranged in the book from south to north, but it is equally useful regardless of the direction you travel. A few other essentials, though, will help you get the most out of any trip.

Most people travel with a road atlas, which will serve well in most cases. For more detailed city and county maps, write or stop by any of the chambers of commerce or visitor centers listed under Travel Information in the following pages. National-forest maps, available at ranger stations, are also helpful, especially for exploring off the main highways.

Many recreational activities on the coast depend upon the tides. Beachcombers, for example, like to search for agates, Japanese glass floats, and other treasures on an ebb, or outgoing, tide. Tide-pool exploration calls for low tides. Clam diggers prefer minus tides, and crabbers usually set their gear on the flood, or incoming, tide and continue crabbing through slack high tide. Anglers have all sorts of theories as to which tide is best for catching any given species of fish. Those who hike beaches also must know the tides to avoid being stranded or endangered by rising water. A knowledge of the tides is also crucial for safe boating in salt water.

Engaging in any of these or similar activities requires tide tables. These are published annually in pocket-size booklets that sell for under a dollar at tackle shops, marinas, and department stores along the coast.

Summers on the Northwest Coast are seldom hot. In fact, evenings and foggy or cloudy days can be chilly. Pack appropriate clothing, including a light parka or windbreaker. Winter is the rainy season, but a wet-weather front might come ashore anytime. Bring rainwear, and enjoy the coast regardless of the weather.

No matter what the weather is, we dress casually here—more for comfort than fashion. And if there's one thing we take seriously, it's recreation. So join the fun. Welcome to coast country.

Oregon

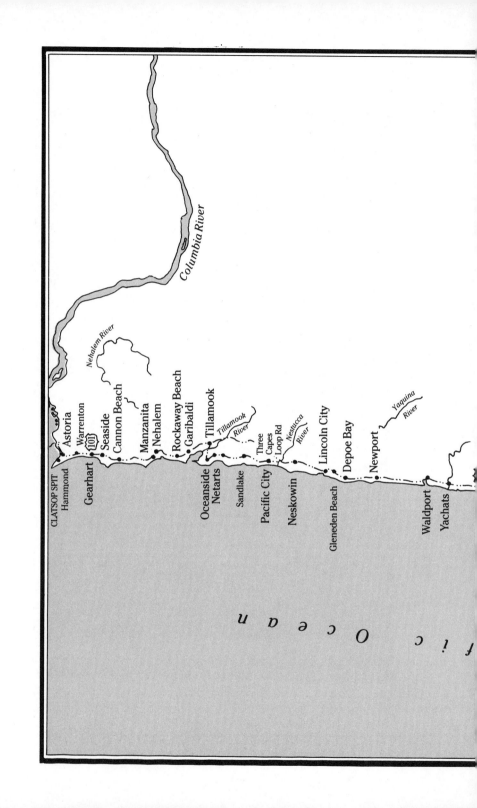

Columbia River

Nehalem River

Tillamook River

Nestucca River

Yaquina River

CLATSOP SPIT
Hammond
Astoria
Warrenton
101
Gearhart
Seaside
Cannon Beach
Manzanita
Nehalem
Rockaway Beach
Garibaldi
Tillamook
Oceanside
Netarts
Sandlake
Three Capes Loop Rd
Pacific City
Neskowin
Lincoln City
Gleneden Beach
Depoe Bay
Newport
Waldport
Yachats

Pacific Ocean

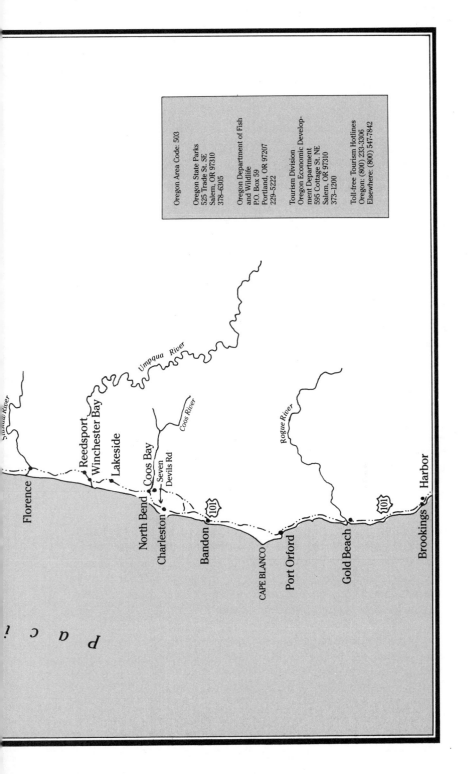

Oregon Area Code: 503

Oregon State Parks
525 Trade St. SE
Salem, OR 97310
378–6305

Oregon Department of Fish
and Wildlife
P.O. Box 59
Portland, OR 97207
229–5222

Tourism Division
Oregon Economic Develop-
ment Department
595 Cottage St. NE
Salem, OR 97310
373–1200

Toll-free Tourism Hotlines
Oregon: (800) 233-3306
Elsewhere: (800) 547-7842

Harris Beach State Park

Brookings/Harbor, Oregon 97415
Population: 3,500/2,856

Location: *On U.S. 101, 5 miles north of the California–Oregon state line, 110 miles south of Coos Bay*

In the vicinity of Brookings, the coastal plain narrows as the Pacific Ocean indents eastward, and the Coast Range mountains quickly slope to the sea. The result is a countryside of spectacular beauty, with rocky headlands intruding on great sweeps of beach where surf and wind and geological upheaval have creafed coves, caves, sea stacks, and vertigo-inducing promontories northward to Port Orford.

Situated on the ocean and along the north bank of the Chetco River, Brookings is the southernmost incorporated city on the Oregon coast. Harbor is an unincorporated community that stretches southward from the Chetco's south bank.

6

Brookings was established in the early 1900s as a company town for the Brookings Lumber and Box Company. Logging and the manufacture of lumber and wood products remain the area's chief industries, although commercial fishing and agriculture are also important.

When not trolling for salmon or seining other species, the commercial fleet is moored at the busy Port of Brookings harbor, on the south side of the river, where there are 281 slips for commercial boats. Visitors can watch the fleet come and go, and photographers will find many worthy subjects.

Among the cash crops here and in nearby northern California are Easter lilies. In fact, a small group of local growers produces about 90 percent of the Easter lilies sold in the United States and Canada. Many other flowers, wild and cultured, grow here in profusion, with some species or another in bloom every month of the year. The area's geology and a meteorological phenomenon known as the "Brookings effect" keep winter temperatures warmer here than anywhere else in Oregon. Ocean breezes temper the summer heat, making the climate moderate, without the seasonal extremes encountered elsewhere. In January, low temperatures are in the forties, with highs in the fifties. July offers temperatures from the low fifties to mid-sixties. Warm spells in the seventies and eighties occur in both July and January.

Lodging

Chetco Inn, 417 Fern Street; P.O. Box 1386; 469–9984. One block east of U.S. 101 in downtown Brookings. Cable TV in 38 units, some with ocean views, most with private baths. Built in 1915 by the California & Oregon Lumber Company. In its heyday it was the center of social activities, with such notable guests as Clark Gable, Carole Lombard, and various other celebrities and dignitaries. It fell into disrepair but was purchased in 1984 and is being restored. Perhaps the best bargain in coastal lodging. Inexpensive.

Holmes Sea Cove Bed & Breakfast, 17350 Holmes Drive; 469–3025. Just north of Harris Beach State Park. Take Dawson Road west off U.S. 101 to Holmes Drive and turn right. Two bedrooms on lower level of Holmes house, as well as a separate guest cottage. Private baths, ocean view, beach access, trail to private park. Continental breakfast brought to rooms. Moderate.

7

The Ward House Bed & Breakfast, 516 Redwood Street; P.O. Box 86; 469–5557. One block east of U.S. 101, overlooking downtown Brookings, near Chetco Inn. Cable TV and shared bath. Full breakfast and evening refreshments. Dinner on request. Walk to shops, movie theater, and restaurants. Moderate.

Campgrounds and RV Parks

Beachfront RV Park, 16024 Boat Basin Drive; P.O. Box 848; 469–5867. On the south bank of the river, west of U.S. 101. Has 173 sites: 43 full hookups, 55 electric. Showers, laundry, cable TV, minimarket, ice. On the ocean and boat basin. Fishing pier for handicapped anglers. Moderate.

Chetco RV Park, 16117 U.S. 101 South; P.O. Box 760; 469–3863. South of Brookings on east side of U.S. 101. Has 121 full-hookup sites, mostly pull-through. Showers, laundry, propane, ice, and bait for sale. Near marina and walking distance to shops. Moderate.

Driftwood RV Park, 16011 Lower Harbor Road; P.O. Box 2066; 469–3213. South of the river, west of U.S. 101, near Port of Brookings harbor. Has 100 full-hookup sites. Cable TV, showers, and laundry. Near river and beaches. Moderate.

Harris Beach State Park, (office) 1655 U.S. 101; 469–2021. Two miles north of Brookings on west side of U.S. 101. Has 151 sites: 34 full-hookup, 51 electric, 66 tent. Showers, tank dump, and firewood. Campground in a beautiful setting, typical of Oregon's coastal parks. Reservations accepted. Moderate.

Food

O'Holleran's Restaurant & Lounge, 1210 Chetco Avenue; 469–9907. In Brookings on east side of U.S. 101, next to the Bonn Motel. Dinner daily. Excellent menu of steaks, chicken, and seafoods, including chinook salmon, prawns, scallops, oysters, frog legs, and abalone. Cocktails, beer, and wine. Moderate.

Pickle Barrel Sandwich & Seafood Company, 702 Chetco Avenue; 469–6401. Downtown Brookings on east side of U.S. 101, opposite Central Mall. Lunch daily, dinner Thursday through Saturday. Great grinders (subs), burgers, soups, clam chowder, and fish and chips. Beer and wine. Inexpensive.

Shopping and Browsing

Great American Smokehouse & Seafood Company, 15657 U.S. 101 South; 469–6903. Located 1.5 miles south of Brookings-Harbor Shopping Center, east side of U.S. 101. Monday through Saturday, 9:00 A.M. to 6:00 P.M.; Sunday, 12:30 to 6:00 P.M. Specializes in gourmet seafoods with gift packs available. Salmon cold-smoked for three days over alder (Indian style). Salmon, albacore, halibut, and other fish and shellfish available. Custom smoking and canning for anglers.

Stateline Myrtlewood, 14377 U.S. 101 South; 469–2307. On east side of U.S. 101 at the California-Oregon line. Daily, 8:00 A.M. to 8:00 P.M. Large selection of myrtlewood products, including many clocks and tables. Also other gift items, homemade fudge, and ice cream. Factory tours. Catalogs available.

Van's Antiques, 15714 U.S. 101 South; 469–3719. South of Brookings on the west side of U.S. 101. Monday through Saturday, 10:00 A.M. to 6:00 P.M. Antiques, furniture, and collectibles. Many old farm implements and tools.

Museum

Chetco Valley Historical Society Museum, 15461 Museum Road; 469–6651. South of Brookings, just off the east side of U.S. 101. Memorial Day to Labor Day: Tuesday through Saturday, 2:00 to 6:00 P.M.; Sunday, noon to 6:00 P.M. Winter: weekends, noon to 5:00 P.M. The building was once the home of a local pioneer family. Displays of antique furniture, old photographs, gold-mining equipment, an old copper still, and many historical objects donated by families of early settlers.

Beaches, Parks, Trails, and Waysides

Beaches stretch north and south from the mouth of the Chetco River, with good access in and out of town. **Azalea State Park** lies within the Brookings city limits, just off North Bank Road. The 76-acre park has an abundance of native azaleas, some of which are 20 feet tall and more than 300 years old. The best time to visit the park is when the azaleas are blooming, from April through June.

9

Brookings/Harbor

Two miles north of Brookings, **Harris Beach State Park** offers camping, picnicking, hiking, beachcombing, and photographic opportunities. Just a half-mile offshore from the picnic area is a bird rookery called Goat Island.

About 2 miles north of Harris Beach State Park, **Samuel H. Boardman State Park** begins and extends north for 11 miles along U.S. 101. Numerous viewpoints offer ample parking and opportunities for hiking, sightseeing, beachcombing, and exploring tide pools.

Hikers and backpackers will find many trails east of Brookings in the **Siskiyou National Forest** and **Kalmiopsis Wilderness.** Trails in the Chetco Ranger District range from a fraction of a mile to 17.1 miles.

Those who don't wish to hike can take a self-guided car tour through the district that covers 42.5 miles and takes about five hours. Maps, brochures, and information are available from the Chetco Ranger Station.

Water Sports and Activities

Fishing centers on the area's two rivers and the ocean, either from beaches and rocks or offshore from boats. With both native and migratory fish species in abundance, there's something to be caught twelve months of the year.

The Winchuck is a small river with headwaters about 15 miles inland. It empties into the ocean south of Brookings near the California–Oregon line. The upper river is good for rainbow and cutthroat trout in the spring and fall. Coho and chinook salmon enter the river in the fall, and steelhead fishing peaks in January. Perch fishing is good near the river's mouth in late winter and spring.

Although not so well known as the Rogue and Umpqua rivers, which were made famous by Zane Grey and other notables, the Chetco, one of Oregon's wild and scenic rivers, is every bit a classic coastal stream. It rises in the Kalmiopsis Wilderness in the Siskiyou Mountains and courses some 40 miles over a rocky bottom and clean gravel beds that are ideal for spawning fishes. It's a good river for both wading and floating, with best access in the lower 20 miles. Coho and chinook fishing is from August through October, and steelheading from mid-December through January.

10

The Chetco is known for big fish, each year giving up steelhead of twenty pounds and chinook weighing more than fifty pounds.

Charter boats are available at the Port of Brookings harbor. Those who tow boats to Brookings will find eight paved launch ramps in the harbor and slips for 610 pleasure craft. Although it is said to be the calmest harbor and safest bar crossing in Oregon, it's the same big ocean beyond; only the experienced and well-equipped boater should head for the offshore grounds.

Brookings Sports Unlimited, 625 Chetco Avenue; 469–4012. Downtown Brookings on west side of U.S. 101. Full line of tackle, crabbing gear, rainwear, and boots. Fishing licenses, tags, and information.

Dick's Sporthaven Marina, 16372 Lower Harbor Road; P.O. Box 2215; 469–3301. Port of Brookings harbor, south side of river, west of U.S. 101. Full-service fishing center, with tackle and bait for sale, crabbing gear for sale or rent. Fishing licenses, custom canning, and smoking. River guide service by day or half day. Ocean charter fishing for salmon and bottomfish. Information on local fishing and crabbing.

Leta-J Charters, 97448 North Bank Chetco River; 469–3452. Office at Port of Brookings harbor. Salmon and bottomfish charters. Two trips daily. All bait and tackle furnished.

Lee Myers Guide Service, 15657 U.S. 101 South; 469–6903. Located at The Great American Smokehouse & Seafood Company. Guided drift boat trips for salmon and steelhead on the Chetco River, fall and winter.

Events

March Beachcomber's Festival, 469–3181
May Azalea Festival, 469–3181
July Fourth of July Celebration and Fireworks, 469–3181

Weather and Tide Information

U.S. Coast Guard, Chetco River harbor; recorded message, 469–4571

Travel Information

Brookings Chamber of Commerce, P.O. Box 940; 469–3181
U.S. Forest Service, Chetco Ranger Station, 555 Fifth Street; 469–2196

Rogue River at Gold Beach

Gold Beach, Oregon 97444
Population: 1,585

Location: *On U.S. 101, 37 miles north of the California–Oregon state line, 83 miles south of Coos Bay*

Gold was once mined from the black-sand beaches of Curry county. In fact, in the mid-nineteenth century, hundreds of placer miners worked the beaches near the present site of Gold Beach, which lies smack on the ocean and along the south bank of the Rogue River. But now the broad, uncrowded beaches, stretching north and south from the mouth of the Rogue, attract whale watchers, beachcombers, clam diggers, kite fliers, hikers, surf fishermen, and windsurfers.

The area's main attraction is the Rogue, a designated wild and scenic river. The canyons and meadows of the Rogue River valley were home to Indians for thousands of years. In the nineteenth century, trappers, miners, and homesteaders came to the Rogue, followed by loggers and ranchers. Although they ultimately settled the land, they never tamed the river.

The lower 52 miles of the river—the scenic section—are traversed mainly by jet sleds: shallow-draft boats powered by hydrojet engines. Anglers use the sleds to reach favorite fishing spots. Jet-powered boats also deliver mail and take countless sightseers up the river and into the scenic Coast Range and Rogue canyons.

Waters above the scenic section are off-limits to powerboats. Here drift boats, kayaks, and inflatable rafts take anglers and adventurers along the wild Rogue. To control traffic in this section, access is limited, and permits are required.

Many miles of trails serve hikers and backpackers, either along the ocean or along the Rogue. Upriver trails take hikers past pioneer ranches and a fishing cabin that belonged to author Zane Grey.

Those who prefer to explore by car will find several routes to their liking. On the north side of the U.S. 101 bridge, turn east and follow North Bank Rogue Road along the river to the bridge near Lobster Creek. Cross the bridge, and turn west on State Route 33, which returns to Gold Beach. The round trip takes less than an hour, unless you decide to stop for fishing or a picnic.

Another loop trip starts just south of town, where you can turn east on Hunter Creek Road (County Route 635) and follow it to the end of the pavement. From there, National Forest Secondary Route 3680 is a good gravel road maintained for auto travel. Take that to National Forest Secondary Route 3313, which goes to the Rogue River, where a turn left on State Route 33 leads back to Gold Beach. Before embarking on this loop, stop by the Gold Beach Ranger Station to check on the latest road conditions and pick up a copy of the excellent Siskiyou National Forest map.

Lodging

Ireland's Rustic Lodges, P.O. Box 774; 247–7718. In town, south of Rogue River on west side of U.S. 101. Private cabins with queen beds, cable TV, fireplaces, ocean view, and beach access. Moderate.

Jot's Resort, P.O. Box J; 247–6676 or 1–800–367–5687. On north bank of the Rogue, west of U.S. 101 bridge. Full-service resort with 140 waterfront rooms and suites. Standard and deluxe units accommodate two to four persons in 1- and 2-bedroom condominiums. Cable TV, fireplaces, river and ocean views. Pool, restaurant and lounge, dancing and entertainment, sport shop and marina, boat launch and dock space, rental boats, fishing licenses. Books ocean-charter trips, jet-boat trips, and salmon and steelhead guides. Moderate.

Shore Cliff Inn, 1100 U.S. 101 South; P.O. Box 615; 247–7091. South of Rogue River on west side of U.S. 101. Comfortably appointed rooms with queen and king beds, cable TV and HBO, ocean view, and beach access. Most rooms have balconies facing the ocean. Moderate.

Upriver Lodges

Along the wild section of the Rogue River are seven lodges that offer travelers a unique wilderness experience. They're spaced just far enough apart so hikers can pack light and enjoy a pleasant pace on the **Rogue River Trail** in the splendor of the **Wild Rogue Wilderness.** At day's end, hikers can slip off their daypacks and enjoy showers, dinner, and comfortable beds. Breakfast and a sack lunch get hikers started in the morning toward the next lodge.

Plan a trip to fit any schedule—overnight, weekend, or week. For nonhikers, a jet boat goes to Paradise Lodge or any of the other lodges downstream.

Spring is the best time for hiking the Rogue River Trail, with fall the next best time. Summers are hot, and the traffic is heavy on both the river and the trail.

Drive and park near the trailhead at Foster Bar. From there, hike upstream to the lodges. Following are the lodges in the order they occur. Write them or phone for more information.

Illahe Lodge, 37709 Agness-Illahe Road; Agness 97406; 247–6111. On the Rogue River Trail, north bank, 1 mile upstream from trailhead at Foster Bar.

Wild River Lodge, 5759 Crater Lake; Medford 97501; 826–9453. On the south bank of the Rogue, 3 miles upstream from trailhead at Foster Bar. Accessible only by boat, but owner will ferry you across the river.

Clay Hill Lodge, Box 5; Agness 97406; 826–9453. On the Rogue River Trail, north bank of the Rogue, 6 miles from trailhead at Foster Bar. A favorite overnight spot for two-day hikes.

Paradise Bar Lodge, Box 456; Gold Beach 97444; 247–6022. On the Rogue River Trail, north bank of the Rogue, 11.7 miles upstream from trailhead at Foster Bar. The upriver terminus for jet-boat tours.

The Lodge at Half Moon Bar, P.O. Box 15; Grants Pass 97526; 476–4002. On the south bank of the Rogue, across the river from Paradise Lodge. Owner will ferry you across the river. Season is from March to November 1. Good place to spend a weekend or several days.

Marial Lodge, Box 1395; Grants Pass 97526; 474–2057. On the Rogue River Trail, north bank of the Rogue, 4 miles above Paradise Lodge, 15.7 miles from trailhead at Foster Bar. On the site of century-old homestead.

Black Bar Lodge, Box 510; Merlin 97532; 479–6507. On the south bank of the Rogue and accessible only by prearrangement. The farthest lodge upstream from trailhead at Foster Bar, at 30.4 miles, but only 9.6 miles downstream from the trailhead at Grave Creek Bridge.

Campgrounds and RV Parks

Four Seasons RV Resort, 96526 North Bank Rogue Road; 247–7959. Located 6.5 miles east of U.S. 101, off North Bank Road— follow the signs. Angler's delight, offering full hookups, showers, laundry, boat launch, dock, tackle shop, licenses and tags, gas and oil, and guide service. Only 6 miles from Cedar Bend Golf Course. Putting green at the resort. Open all year. Moderate.

Indian Creek Recreation Park, 94680 Jerry's Flat Road; 247–7704. East of U.S. 101 a half-mile on the south bank of the Rogue. A full-service RV park and campground with 100 full-hookup and tent sites in a beautiful parklike setting. Showers, laundry, store, horseback trails, outdoor games, recreation room. Restaurant on premises. Moderate.

Food

Grant's Pancake and Omelette House, Jerry's Flat Road; 247–7208. A half-mile east of U.S. 101, at Indian Creek Recreation

15

Park, on south bank of the Rogue. Breakfast and lunch daily. Good selection of pancakes, waffles, eggs, omelets, including Egg Beaters for those on low-cholesterol diets, as well as traditional and specialty sandwiches. Large portions, so bring a big appetite. Moderate.

Rod 'n' Reel Tavern Company, at Jot's Resort; 247–6823. North of the Rogue, west off U.S. 101 at the north end of the bridge. Breakfast, lunch, and dinner daily. Excellent menu includes breakfast specials, specialty sandwiches, soups, salads, steaks, seafood, and such specialties as veal parmigiana and ravioli, chateaubriand, and baked scampi. Cocktails, beer, and wine. Moderate.

Water Sports and Activities

Sportfishing is one of the main attractions in the Gold Beach area, with offshore ocean fishing for salmon and bottomfish and angling in the lower river for salmon, bottomfish, perch, sea-run cutthroat, steelhead, sturgeon, and smelt. Upriver, the Rogue is famous for its superb salmon fishing and angling for summer and winter steelhead, as well as cutthroat trout. Many smaller streams attract fly and spin fishermen, who test their skills on native cutthroat and rainbow trout.

Rogue Outdoor Store, 560 North Ellensburg; 247–7142. East side of U.S. 101, just south of the bridge. Full line of camping gear, fishing tackle, crabbing and clam-digging gear, maps, tide books, and rental gear. Licenses and tags. Good source of information about local outdoor sports.

Rogue Sportfishing Unlimited, Rogue River Reservations; P.O. Box 548; 247–6504 or 247–6022. Year-round fishing and river access via jet boat or drift boat. Coho and chinook salmon, summer and winter steelhead.

Tours and Trips

No visit to the Gold Beach area would be complete without a trip up the Rogue River in a jet boat—an unforgettable experience for travelers of all ages, offered by several companies. The boats are safe, stable craft, piloted by experts with extensive experience on the Rogue. Special provisions allow the handicapped to enjoy the splendors of Rogue River jet-boat trips. Reservations are recommended.

Rogue River Mail Boat Trips, P.O. Box 1165-G; 247–7033 or 1–800–458–3511. On North Bank Rogue Road, east of U.S. 101. May through October, 64-mile trips depart daily at 8:30 A.M. and 2:30 P.M. Mid-June through mid-September, 80-mile trips depart daily at 8:00 A.M. and 2:45 P.M. Mid-May through mid-October, 104-mile trips depart daily at 8:00 A.M. Special, free transportation to and from boat for the handicapped. Latest fleet addition is the *Rogue Queen,* a glass-covered, 43-foot jet boat that carries seventy passengers and will skim over water only 10 inches deep.

Whitewater raft, kayak, and drift boat trips are also popular and exciting ways to see and experience the Rogue. Several outfitters specialize in such trips and can provide everything needed. Advance planning and booking are essential. Write or phone the following outfitters for information.

Orange Torpedo Trips, P.O. Box 1111; Grants Pass 97526; 479–5061. One- to six-day inflatable-kayak trips. Trips designed for novices and families. Camp or stay at river lodges.

Rogue River Raft Trips, 8500 Galice Road; Merlin 97532; 476–3825 or 476–3027. Headquartered at Morrison's Lodge, offering two- to four-day trips in the wild section and one-day trips in the scenic section. Camp or stay at river lodges.

Sundance Expeditions, 14894 Galice Road; Merlin 97532; 479–8508. Raft and kayak trips. "The College of Kayaking" provides instruction, equipment, lodging, and river trips.

Golf

Cedar Bend Golf Course, P.O. Box 1234; 247–6911. Located 11 miles north of Gold Beach, 16 miles south of Port Orford, on Squaw Valley Road off U.S. 101. Only golf course in Curry County. Nine-hole course in low, rolling hills, out of the wind and fog.

Events

For information on any of the following events, phone 247–7526 or 1–800–452–2334.

March Little Reno Night
September Curry County Fair

17

Gold Beach

October   South Coast Quilt Show
November Gold Beach Calico Bazaar
December Community Christmas Bazaar

Travel Information

Gold Beach Chamber of Commerce, City Hall; 247–7526 or 1–800–452–2334

U.S. Forest Service, Gold Beach Ranger District, 1225 South Ellensburg, Box 7; 247–6651.

Port Orford Heads Waysides

Port Orford, Oregon 97465
Population: 1,035

Location: *On U.S. 101, 54 miles north of the California–Oregon state line, 52 miles south of Coos Bay*

Situated on a marine terrace above a protected natural harbor, Port Orford is the westernmost incorporated city in the contiguous United States. In recent years the town has suffered the same financial woes that have befallen many coastal communities, whose economies have depended primarily upon timber and commercial fishing. Port Orford has been slower than most to recover. Nevertheless, the area offers some notable attractions worthy of the traveler's time.

Port Orford's harbor is a coastal cove, not a marine estuary, so vessels have no river bar to cross. In calm weather some commercial boats, sport craft, and sailing vessels anchor in the scenic cove. Most boats, however, rest in unusual berths at this unique waterfront; there are no customary docks, floats, or moorage slips. Instead, boats are cradled on rubber-tired dollies atop a large wharf and are launched and retrieved by a hoist capable of handling vessels up to 42 feet long and weighing up to 26,000 pounds.

Depending on the time of the year, commercial boats return to port with catches of salmon, blackcod (sablefish), bottomfish, shrimp, or crab. Recently Port Orford has also become the center of Oregon's sea urchin fishery.

In the timber world the Port Orford vicinity is well known for a beautiful tree bearing the same name. Port Orford cedar is an aromatic, straight-grained tree, native to a small local range. The durable wood has seen a number of uses over the years, from Indians' canoes and dwellings to battery separators, venetian-blind slats, house siding, and decking.

The tree's beauty, ironically, may lead to its eventual extinction. The attractive cedars have been cultured in nurseries and used as ornamentals for more than sixty-five years. A root fungus, once confined to nurseries, has now spread to the forests and is attacking trees throughout their range. Only the discovery of a way to combat the spreading fungus will save the rest of these exquisite trees from extinction.

Lodging

Home By The Sea Bed & Breakfast, 444 Jackson Street; P.O. Box 606-PC; 332–2855. Just west of U.S. 101, overlooking Battle Rock. Private bath, queen bed, and cable TV in each of 2 guest rooms in this contemporary house. Laundry and kitchen privileges available. Resident cat. Moderate.

Neptune Motel, 545 West Fifth; P.O. Box 844; 332–4502. West of U.S. 101 on a hill overlooking the port. Has 14 units, most with kitchens and ocean view. Some 3-bedroom suites. Cable TV and HBO. Situated on a site once occupied by Fort Orford. Inexpensive to moderate.

Campgrounds and RV Parks

Cape Blanco State Park, 332–6774. About 5 miles west off U.S. 101, 5 miles north of Port Orford. Water and electricity at all

58 sites. Showers and tank dump. Good spot for flying kites and radio-remote gliders. Plenty of hiking in an area rich in history. Great salmon and steelhead fishing, beachcombing, and photography opportunities. Nearby lighthouse and museum. Inexpensive.

Evergreen RV Park, 839 Coast Guard Road; P.O. Box 306; 332–5942. Two blocks west of U.S. 101 on Ninth. Small park in a pleasant residential setting. Pull-through sites, showers, full hookups, laundry, and cable TV. Walking distance to restaurants, shops, parks, port, and lake. Inexpensive.

Humbug Mountain State Park, 332–6774. About 7 miles south of Port Orford on U.S. 101. Has 30 full-hookup RV sites and 77 tent sites. Showers, tank dump, firewood, and laundry. Plenty of hiking opportunities, including a 3-mile trail to the top of 1,756-foot Humbug Mountain. Surf fishing on the beach at Brush Creek for surfperch. Trout fishing in Brush Creek. Moderate.

Food

The Golden Owl Deli, 755 U.S. 101; P.O. Box 136; 332–6595. On the west side of U.S. 101 at the big curve. Lunch and dinner daily. Salads, soups, chili, and chowder, as well as a full menu of great sandwiches and desserts. Fresh-ground coffee, herbal teas, imported beers, and Oregon wines. A local favorite. Inexpensive.

Whale Cove Restaurant, U.S. 101 South; 332–7575. East side of U.S. 101, overlooking Battle Rock Beach. In summer dinner daily, plus Sunday brunch. In winter closed Wednesday. Offers a large selection of appetizers, such soups as lobster bisque and chilled borscht, salads, and vegetarian dinners. Meat dishes include veal piccata, crab-stuffed chicken breast, quail baked in pear halves, pheasant under glass, and various steak and seafood combinations. Sumptuous desserts go well with any of a half-dozen special coffees. Full bar, imported and domestic beers, and large wine list. Moderate.

Shopping and Browsing

The Wooden Nickel, 1205 Oregon Street; 332–5201. West side of U.S. 101, south end of town. Summer: daily, 8:00 A.M. to 7:00 P.M. Winter: daily, 9:00 A.M. to 5:00 P.M. Myrtlewood factory and shop offering a large selection of myrtlewood cutting boards, artworks, dinnerware, and more. Also gifts, souvenirs, kites, and windsocks. Gift wrapping and shipping offered.

Museum

Hughes House, Cape Blanco State Park; 332-2975. West off U.S. 101 at Cape Blanco Road, about 5 miles north of Port Orford. Summer: Thursday, Friday, Saturday, and Monday, 10:00 A.M. to 4:00 P.M.; Sunday, noon to 4:00 P.M. Off-season hours vary (phone for more information). Beautiful old house built in 1898 for Patrick and Jane Hughes, who settled the Cape Blanco area in 1860 and raised dairy cattle here. The house is furnished with many period antiques and displays historical photographs and artifacts.

Beaches, Parks, Trails, and Waysides

In Port Orford the beach is right downtown. Waves nearly lap at the edge of the Battle Rock Wayside parking lot at the south end of town. Another easy access is west off U.S. 101, where signs lead to the port.

Watch for state-park signs in town. Turn west and drive 1 mile to **Port Orford Heads Wayside** on the site of a former Coast Guard lifeboat station. Here are a small picnic spot and a paved trail to a headland that commands some of the most spectacular views on the coast. This is a great place for photography, watching whales, or just relaxing. Parking is limited, and there is no turn-around for trailers.

Just north of town, watch for the sign for **Paradise Point Wayside.** Garrison Lake Road leads 1 mile to the beach parking area. Here are miles of broad beach for combing, hunting agates, flying kites, or hiking.

Five miles north of town and 5 miles west of U.S. 101, Cape Blanco pokes into the Pacific farther than any other point of land in the contiguous states. Here stands the oldest lighthouse in Oregon, the **Cape Blanco Light,** operating since December 20, 1870. Towering 245 feet above the ocean, its million-candlepower light is visible 22 miles out.

The lighthouse is closed to the public, but it is possible to drive within viewing and picture-taking range. Near the light the road is narrow and winding, and there is no trailer turnaround.

Water Sports and Activities

Beaches north and south of town—especially near Rocky Point, 3 miles south of town—offer fair to good clam digging. Surf fishing is good for perch and bottomfish from the beaches and the breakwaters near the port dock. In July smelt move into the port area.

Two tremendously popular rivers empty into the ocean near Port Orford: the Elk River (designated wild and scenic) just south of Cape Blanco, and the Sixes River just north of the cape. Both rivers are wadable most of the year, but best access is via drift boat.

Sea-run cutthroat trout move into both rivers in August and offer good to excellent angling well into September. The first salmon, usually jacks, begin showing up in September as well.

After the first fall rains in October, chinook salmon enter the Elk and Sixes and offer angling opportunities well into December, with November fishing usually best.

Anglers begin taking winter steelhead in December and continue catching them well into February. January is the peak month.

Hannah Fishing Lodges, RR Box 94893; Elk River Road; 332–8585; summer, 584–2611. Guided fishing, including meals and lodging, on the Elk River for fall chinook salmon and winter steelhead.

Events

July Port Orford Jubilee, 332–5201

Travel Information

Port Orford Chamber of Commerce, P.O. Box 637; 332–8055

Bandon Historical Society Museum

Bandon, Oregon 97411
Population: 2,386

Location: *On U.S. 101, 24 miles south of Coos Bay, at the mouth of the Coquille (koh-*keel*) River and along its south bank*

Named after a city in Ireland that is located on the Bandon River in County Cork, this Oregon community, sometimes called Bandon-By-The-Sea, could as fittingly be called Phoenix. Like the mythical bird, Bandon has twice risen from its own ashes after fire consumed it.

In 1914 a fire left a large part of downtown Bandon a smoldering heap. Then on September 26, 1936, fire again swept through the town. This time nearly 2,000 residents were evacuated, and Bandon was reduced to charred rubble.

On that "Black Saturday" the hope that Bandon would become the most prominent port between Portland and San Francisco was forever dashed. The long-term result, however, was the emergence of a seaside hamlet with a relaxed pace and innate charm neither Portland nor San Francisco could even remotely approximate.

Bandon's Old Town area lies a swerve off U.S. 101. Ease into it, find a parking spot, and enjoy its funky shops, fine galleries, and restaurants.

Adjacent to Old Town, just across First Street, is Bandon's newly refurbished waterfront and boat basin, where you can stroll the docks and piers, watch the commercial fleet, charter a fishing boat, take a sternwheeler trip, or fish and crab right off the docks.

One of the most prominent Bandon landmarks—not to mention the most photographed, sketched, and painted—is the **Coquille River Light.** Built in 1896, the lighthouse operated until 1939, when it was replaced by an unmanned light on the south jetty. The squat but attractive lighthouse, with its 47-foot tower, has been restored and is kept in good repair as a historical site. View and photograph it from the south jetty area, just west of Old Town, or drive right to it via Bullards Beach State Park.

In recent years the travel industry has gained importance in Bandon, and the town has grown and improved, attracting a lively lot of artists and artisans. More than three dozen artists live and work in the area, and the city boasts thriving theater and dance groups, as well as enough cowboy philosophers, yarn-spinning old salts, mystics, and iconoclasts to keep things interesting.

Lodging

Harbor View Motel, P.O. Box 1409; 347–4417. West side of U.S. 101, south side of Old Town district. Has 42 units with king and queen beds, cable TV, and Showtime. Stands atop a hill, commanding the best view in Bandon. From the northwest-facing balconies, view the river, ocean, Old Town, lighthouse, and waterfront. Walk to shops, restaurants, performing-arts center, galleries, and boat basin. Continental breakfast. Moderate.

The Inn at Face Rock, 3225 Beach Loop Road; 347–9441. On the east side of the road, south of town. Has 56 units with queen beds and cable TV. Spacious suites have fireplaces, kitchens, two baths, and balconies and can accommodate up to four persons. Wheelchair access. Beautiful golf course adjacent. Top-rated restaurant and cocktail lounge on premises. Private access to beach. Moderate to expensive.

Lighthouse Bed & Breakfast, 650 Jetty Road Southwest; 347–9316. South side of the river, west of Old Town, across from the lighthouse. Four guest rooms with king and queen beds and private baths, 1 with whirlpool. Excellent view of ocean, river bar, jetties, and lighthouse. Short walk to beach. Near Old Town. Cable TV and Showtime. Full breakfast. Moderate to expensive.

The Oldtown Guest House, 370 First Street; 347–9632. On the harbor, across the street from the small-boat basin. Four units, 2 with kitchens, 2 with community-kitchen privileges. Private entrances, private baths, cable TV, and Showtime. Near shops and restaurants. Excellent view. Inexpensive.

Sea Star Hostel, 375 Second Street; 347–9533. In Old Town. Small, carpeted dorms and private rooms for couples and families. Lounge, kitchen, showers, and laundry. Near shops, restaurants, and other attractions. Inexpensive.

Campgrounds and RV Parks

Bullards Beach State Park, 347–2209 (office); 347–3501 (booth, mid-May through Labor Day). Situated along the north bank of the Coquille River, west of U.S. 101, about 2.5 miles north of Bandon. Has 100 electric hookups and 92 full hookups. Showers, tank dump, and firewood. A beautiful park for camping, picnicking, and day use. River and ocean surf fishing, crabbing, clam digging, kite flying, beachcombing, photography, biking, and horseback riding are main attractions. Excellent public boat ramp and parking area. Moderate.

Food

Andrea's Old Town Cafe, 160 Baltimore; 347–3022. In Old Town, between First and Second. Breakfast, lunch, and dinner Monday through Saturday. Brunch and dinner Sunday. Great omelets, muffins, and croissants for breakfast. Homemade pizza, soups, salads, and an assortment of sandwiches for lunch. Dinner menu changes nightly and includes such specialties as Creole, African, Israeli, Italian, French, and American cuisine. Fresh local seafoods and home-grown lamb are featured. Imported and domestic beers and wines. Cheesecakes and chocolate desserts served with freshly brewed coffee. Moderate.

Bandon Boat Works, South Jetty Road; 347–2111. On the south bank of the river, across from the lighthouse. Lunch and dinner Tuesday through Saturday. Brunch and dinner, Sunday. One of Bandon's best restaurants, offering seafoods, pasta dishes, veal, beef, lamb, and, on Sundays, Mexican cuisine. Specialties include cioppino, seafood fettuccine, Mediterranean-style linguine, oysters flambé, rack of lamb, and three kinds of surf 'n' turf. Homemade desserts. Imported and domestic beers and wines. Moderate.

Wheelhouse Restaurant & Crow's Nest Lounge, Chicago and First; 347–9331. Across the street from the boat basin. Breakfast, lunch, and dinner daily. Features fresh seafoods, chicken, lamb, beef, salads, sandwiches, soups, and chowder. Specialties include seafood crepes, award-winning chicken Baja (with cheese and fresh Oregon shrimp), and rack of lamb. The lounge offers excellent atmosphere and a superb view of the harbor. Moderate.

Shopping and Browsing

Bandon's Cheddar Cheese, P.O. Box 1668, 347–2456 or 1–800–548–8961. East side of U.S. 101 at the north end of town. Daily, 9:00 A.M. to 6:00 P.M. Great aged cheeses, gourmet foods, fine wines, and more. Renowned for its excellent cheeses, for which gift packs are available and shipped anywhere.

Gray Whale Gallery, 375 South Jetty Road; 347–3931. Near the south bank of the river, on the way to the south jetty and beach. Summers: daily, 10:30 A.M. to 5:00 P.M. Winter hours vary. A special little gallery that will particularly delight those interested in wildlife and marine art and objects. Features paintings, wood sculpture, metal sculpture, glass, batiks, antiques, collectibles, and decoys.

Northwest Collectors Gallery, Route 1; Box 1310; 347–9332. Seven miles south of Bandon, on west side of U.S. 101. April through December: daily, 10:00 A.M. to 5:30 P.M. One of the finest collections of contemporary art and crafts on the coast. Beautiful gallery featuring many local artists and artisans who work with native woods, glass, metal, oils, and watercolors. Large selection of jewelry and gift items available. Take time to stop here.

Second Street Gallery, 175 East Second Street; 347–4133. In

Bandon

Old Town. Daily, 10:00 A.M. to 5:30 P.M. Great gallery for shoppers and browsers, where you can enjoy artworks free from sales pressure in a large, open, and well-lighted interior. Fine paintings, prints, sculptures, ceramics, bronzes, wall hangings, and handmade furnishings—most created by local and nearby artists and artisans.

Whiskey Run Silver Shop, 265 East Second; 347–9810. In Old Town. Daily, 10:00 A.M. to 5:00 P.M. A little shop crammed with exquisite stained- and leaded-glass works, gold and silver jewelry, charms, mineral specimens, and some of the finest fossils available anywhere, as well as carvings, jewelry boxes, and various gift items.

Museums

Abandoned By-The-Sea in Bandon-By-The-Sea, P.O. Box 1068; 347–3587. Open every day. A great collection of driftwood—every piece unique. The collection, owned by Bill Magness, is certainly the largest on the Oregon coast and is thought to be the largest in the world. Parts of the collection are exhibited at Bigwheel General Store, the rest on Magness's property. Both exhibits are free and open to the public. Phone for appointment to see exhibit at Magness's home.

Bandon Historical Society Museum, P.O. Box 737; 347–2164. In the old Coast Guard Station building on the south bank of the river, just west of Old Town. Tuesday through Sunday, 10:00 A.M. to 4:00 P.M. An ideal location in this historic area. A handsome and well-preserved old Coast Guard structure. Many photographs of the area's maritime heritage and the great fire of 1936. Good displays of pioneer and Indian artifacts. Fine selection of publications. A small museum, but certainly worth a stop.

Beaches, Parks, Trails, and Waysides

Extending northward from the north jetty at the mouth of the Coquille River, **Bullards Beach** offers miles of surf and sand for hiking, horseback riding, and beachcombing. Gravel beds, exposed by storm-tossed seas, offer good hunting for agates, jasper, and petrified wood. This is also an excellent beach for collecting drift-

28

wood. Stout winds, usually every afternoon during the summer, make for great kite flying, here and along the river.

To reach Bullards Beach, watch for the state-park sign about 2.5 miles north of Bandon, just beyond the bridge over the Coquille. Turn west off U.S. 101 and follow the road to the beach parking lot or park near the lighthouse.

The beach stretching southward from the south jetty is distinctly different. Here, great sea stacks punctuate beach and surf and serve as rookeries for many species of birds, including a colony of more than 10,000 murres. Other species include gulls, cormorants, tufted puffins, pigeon guillemots, black oystercatchers, auklets, and murrelets. Along the beaches, sandpipers, sanderlings, plovers, turnstones, and other shorebirds peck and dart and dodge the waves.

Famous Face Rock and Table Rock stand amidst the sea stacks just off the beach. The best vantages for viewing and photography are off Beach Loop Road. The best beach access is via Jetty Road, where there is ample parking near the jetty. To reach either road, drive west on First Street in the Old Town district. Just after the road turns south, follow it up the hill to connect with Beach Loop Road or turn west onto Jetty Road.

Water Sports and Activities

Surfperch are popular with Bandon anglers, who fish the beaches north and south of the Coquille, as well as from the jetties and the rocks near the lighthouse. Smelt move into the river in June and July, and many folks jig for them from the boat-basin docks.

Angling for salmon and bottomfish is good offshore through the summer months. In the early fall, salmon begin moving into the river and provide action until December, which heralds the start of the steelhead season.

The lower Coquille offers superb crabbing, from the bar upstream to the bridge. The best catches are made from boats, but many keepers are taken from the boat-basin docks and piers.

Bandon Bait Shop, 110 First Street; 347–3905. On the waterfront in Old Town. Daily, 8:00 A.M. to 6:00 P.M. The place to buy bait and other fishing essentials. Crab rings for sale or rent.

Coquille River Charters, Prosper Route 2; Box 1080; 347–

Bandon

9093 or 347–4314. At the boat basin. Both ocean fishing and river trolling, as well as crabbing trips. River sightseeing excursions with stops at Bullards Beach State Park and Prosper Village.

Tours and Trips

Dixie Lee Riverboat Trips, Route 2; Box 2485; 347–3942. One of Bandon's main manmade attractions—a chugging sternwheeler to take you on a wonderfully relaxed trip up the Coquille River. During the peak summer season, two two-hour trips a day, plus a three-hour dinner cruise on Saturdays. Two or three times a year, a trip to Coquille is a seven-hour step back in time, complete with barbecue lunch on board. A *Dixie Lee* trip is great family fun. Mark this down as *must do.*

Golf

Bandon Face Rock Golf Course, 3235 Beach Loop Road; 347–3818. South of town. Nine-hole, par-32 course in a scenic setting. Walking distance from the Inn at Face Rock. Open every day. Rental carts available.

Other Attractions

Encore Presenters—Harbor Hall, 325 Second Street; P.O. Box 1740; 347–4404. Billed as *"the* entertainment spot on the south coast." Computerized theatrical lighting system and specially designed acoustics. Regular theater season, late-night theater and special dance shows called Insomni-ACTS, ballet, and musical concerts. In recent years sell-out concerts by such renowned musicians and performers as Mason Williams, Donovan, Taj Mahal, Maria Muldaur, John Lee Hooker, and Laurindo Almeida.

Events

May	Stormwatchers Seafood & Wine Festival, 347–9616
	Sandcastle-Building Contest, 347–9616
July	Fish Fry, Old Time Fiddlers, and Fireworks, 347–9616
September	Bandon Cranberry Festival, 347–9616
December	Festival of Lights, 347–9616

Travel Information

Bandon Chamber of Commerce, P.O. Box 1515; 347–9616

Qualman Oyster Farms

Charleston, Oregon 97420
Population: 700

Location: *West off U.S. 101, 6 miles west of Coos Bay on Cape Arago Highway, 20.6 miles north of Bandon via Seven Devils Road*

Charleston and the nearby parks and beaches must rank among the most overlooked attractions on the Oregon coast, probably because they lie a few miles off U.S. 101. At Charleston are canneries, fish-processing plants, boatbuilding and repair facilities, and one of the largest commercial fishing fleets on the Oregon coast. The area is also popular with sport fishermen, crabbers, and clam diggers. For boaters Charleston has a large launch ramp, moorage, fuel, and repair services.

The busy harbor offers several shops worth a stop and restaurants serving up everything from hearty fishermen's breakfasts to fine seafood dinners.

31

Charleston

One of the best-kept sightseeing and photography secrets in Oregon is the Coast Guard lookout at Charleston, which commands the best view of the bay, jetties, and Coos Bay bar—a place to watch fishing boats and freighters come and go. Take Boat Basin Drive off Cape Arago Highway almost a half-mile to an unmarked road on the left and a small sign for Coast Guard Tower. That road, not recommended for trailers, leads to a small parking area atop a high bluff overlooking the bar.

One of the maritime treasures along this expanse of coast is the **Cape Arago Light Station,** which actually lies 2.5 miles north of the cape. The lighthouse can be seen and photographed from a number of vantages, including several spots along Cape Arago Highway, and from hiking trails along headlands south of the light. But Lighthouse Beach offers the best approach for frame-filling pictures.

Whether traveling north or south on U.S. 101, don't miss the Charleston Loop. After visiting the parks and beaches, northbound travelers should take the Cape Arago Highway into Coos Bay and North Bend. Those heading south should take Seven Devils Road, just south of town, which connects with U.S. 101 about 13 miles later.

Lodging

Capt. John's Motel, 8061 Kingfisher Drive; P.O. Box 5398; 888–4041. On Kingfisher at Boat Basin Drive. Has 40 units with queen beds, cable TV, and some kitchens. Fish house for cleaning and cooking the catch. Nearby charter boats, fishing, crabbing, and clam digging. Across the street from the Portside Restaurant. The only motel in the boat-basin complex. Inexpensive.

Campgrounds and RV Parks

Bastendorf Beach County Park, 888–5353. Just under a half-mile west of Cape Arago Highway, 2 miles southwest of Charleston. Has 81 campsites: 56 with electricity and water to accommodate RVs up to 24 feet, and 25 tent sites. Showers, tank dump, firewood, fish-cleaning station, horseshoe pits, and hiking trails. Beautiful picnic area and great playground for the kids. Spectacular view of the beach, ocean, and jetties from the picnic area parking lot. Inexpensive.

Seaport RV Park, P.O. Box 5750; 888–3122. On Boat Basin Drive, just off Cape Arago Highway. Full hookups at 26 sites. Showers, cable TV, and laundry. Close to charter boats, boat basin, and all water sports. Walk to shops and restaurants. Beaches nearby. Moderate.

Sunset Bay State Park, 13030 Cape Arago Highway; 888–4902. West side of the highway, 3.6 miles south of Charleston. Has 29 full-hookup and 108 tent sites, showers, laundry, and firewood. Beautiful park setting, sheltered from the wind. Shallow bay is popular for swimming, scuba diving, and fishing. Broad beach and bathhouse. Boat launch for small boats. Hiking trails. Rock and surf fishing. Spectacular scenery. Naturalist on duty in summer. Moderate.

Food

Portside Restaurant, 8001 Kingfisher Drive; P.O. Box 5025; 888–5544. In the Charleston marine complex, across the street from Capt. John's Motel. Lunch Monday through Friday, dinner every day. Award-winning restaurant and lounge with superb waterfront view. Fine steaks and prime rib available, but seafoods fresh off the restaurant's own boat are the specialty here. Features live Maine lobster and Dungeness crab, abalone, salmon, halibut, lingcod, shrimp, prawns, oysters, clams, scallops, calamari, and more. Excellent seafood combo dinner. Seafood buffet every Friday evening is highly recommended. Cocktails, imported and domestic beers, house wines, and wine list of imported, domestic, and Oregon wines. Moderate.

Shopping and Browsing

Chuck's Seafoods, P.O. Box 5502; 888–5525. At Cape Arago Highway and Boat Basin Drive. Daily, 9:00 A.M. to 6:00 P.M. Fresh, smoked, fresh-frozen, and locally canned seafoods. Gift packs, shipped anywhere, feature coho and chinook salmon, albacore tuna, Oregon shrimp, Dungeness crab, smoked salmon, and smoked sturgeon. Try their fresh smoked seafood on a beach picnic.

Kinnee's Gifts 'n' Shells, 8031 Cape Arago Highway; P.O. Box 5498; 888–5924. Across the street from Chuck's Seafoods. Summer: daily, 9:00 A.M. to 6:00 P.M. Winter: daily, 10:00 A.M. to 5:30 P.M. A good selection of shells, souvenirs, cards, Oregon products, and nautical items in this snug shop.

Qualman Oyster Farms, 4898 Crown Point Road; Coos Bay 97420; 888–3145. A half-mile east of Cape Arago Highway, just north of Charleston. The fresh oysters here can't get any fresher. The 145 acres of oyster beds on the South Slough produce 3,000 to 6,000 gallons of fresh oysters a year. Drive out at low tide to see the oysters growing on thousands of wooden stakes.

Beaches, Parks, Trails, and Waysides

Just south of Charleston, along Cape Arago Highway, is one of Oregon's finest yet least-used playgrounds—a series of beaches and parks to rival any on the West Coast.

About 2 miles south of Charleston, turn right off Cape Arago Highway to reach Bastendorf Beach and the south jetty. On the west side of the highway, 2.4 miles south of Charleston, begins a short trail leading to Lighthouse Beach. Although the trail is a good one, the slope to the beach is steep and requires caution. Also watch the tides here to avoid being stranded.

A mile farther south is **Sunset Bay State Park,** with its shallow bay protected by sandstone cliffs and an outer reef. Waters here warm faster than elsewhere; it's a popular place for wading and swimming. Currents can be treacherous, however, so swim only on an incoming tide. The splendid picnic area has a kitchen shelter. Hikers will enjoy trails through the forest and along oceanside cliffs from here to Cape Arago.

Shore Acres State Park is west of the highway, 4.5 miles south of Charleston. The parks along this stretch comprise 1,272 acres, all of which once belonged to Louis J. Simpson, a timber tycoon, shipbuilder, and prominent North Bend businessman. Shore Acres was the site of his oceanfront estate.

Simpson developed this property as a summer home and a Christmas gift for his wife in 1906. The house eventually outgrew those plans, however, with such amenities as a huge, heated indoor pool and a ballroom with more than 2,700 square feet of dance floor. Tennis courts and formal gardens enhanced the already spectacular setting.

The mansion burned to the ground in 1921, and although Simpson built another in its place, it was not so elegant as the original and eventually fell into disrepair. The state purchased the property in 1942 and had to raze the house. A glass-enclosed observation building now stands on the site of the mansion.

The formal gardens are still cared for and delight visitors year round. The caretaker's house is still intact in the garden area. A trail leads from the south end of the garden to a secluded beach, then beyond along the cliffs.

A parking area 1.1 miles south of Shore Acres overlooks Simpson Reef. Stop here to examine the rocky islet and reef where seals and sea lions bask and bark.

The highway ends 6 miles from Charleston at **Cape Arago State Park.** The picnic area, with kitchen shelter and restrooms, is unmatched anywhere. There are trails and sites along the cliffs above the pounding surf. Trails also lead to some of the best tide pools on the coast.

Water Sports and Activities

Opportunities for fishing, crabbing, clam digging, boating, and sailing abound in the Charleston area. A public fishing pier extends into South Slough on the waterfront. The pier and docks are popular for crabbing and fishing for a variety of species, including perch, flounder, sole, and smelt.

Minus tides expose many nearby clam-digging flats where diggers find large horseneck (locally called Empire clams) and hard-shell clams, cockles, and littlenecks.

Rock and surf fishing along the coastline south of Charleston produces various bottom species, such as greenling, cabezone, lingcod, and several kinds of rockfish. These same areas are good for gathering mussels at low tide.

The offshore salmon season usually begins in May and runs until Labor Day, unless early quotas call for early closures. Limit coho catches are common early in the season, but by July and August the fish run much bigger. Chinook fishing ranges from fair to outstanding throughout the season, with most fish running to about twenty pounds and occasionally thirty to forty pounds or more.

Offshore bottomfishing is good all year, but it is mainly dependent on weather and water conditions. Some of the best light-tackle fishing for greenling, black rockfish, and others is in August and September.

Betty Kay Charters, P.O. Box 5020; 888–9021. At the small-boat basin. Modern, comfortable boat. Specializes in salmon and bottomfish angling. Also features light-tackle bottomfishing for great sport. Everything furnished. Licenses sold on premises. Five-hour trips leave daily at 5:30 A.M. and 10:45 A.M. Bait and dry ice available.

Charleston Charters, 5100 Cape Arago Highway; P.O. Box 5032; 888–4846. On South Slough, next to Englund Marine Supply. Features fishing for salmon, albacore tuna, bottomfish, and sharks. Two trips daily in season. Check in at 5:15 A.M. and 10:30 A.M. All bait and tackle furnished. Licenses available.

Golf

Sunset Bay Golf Course, 11001 Cape Arago Highway; 888–9301. Just past the Sunset Bay campground entrance. A 9-hole course only about 3.5 miles from Charleston. Follow the signs for the state parks. Pro shop, refreshments, and power carts available.

Other Attractions

South Slough National Estuarine Sanctuary, P.O. Box 5417; 888–5558. Five miles southeast of Charleston on Seven Devils Road. Exit Cape Arago Highway just south of town. September through May: Monday through Friday, 8:30 A.M. to 4:30 P.M. June through August, daily. The nation's first estuarine sanctuary, comprising 3,800 acres of upland forest and 600 acres of tidal lands, including a variety of habitats, such as freshwater marsh, salt marsh, mud flats, and open water. Home to a great array of flora and fauna, including at least twenty-two species of commercially important fish and shellfish. Many songbirds, shorebirds, and waterfowl, as well as deer, elk, black bear, and bobcat use the area. Canoe launch and hiking and study trails. Workshops and canoe trips held during summer months. Pick up trail guides, bird check-list, and canoeing information at the interpretive center.

Events

August Salmon Barbecue, 267–6609

Weather and Tide Information

U.S. Coast Guard, Charleston; recorded message; 888–3102

Travel Information

Charleston Information Center, Boat Basin Drive & Cape Arago Highway; P.O. Box 5735; 888–2311

McCullough Bridge (U.S. 101) over Coos Bay

Coos Bay/North Bend,
Oregon 97420/97459
Population: 14,330/8,770

Location: *On U.S. 101, 120 miles north of the California–Oregon state line, 23 miles south of Reedsport*

The December 1988 issue of *M*, the slick and sophisticated magazine for "The Civilized Man," carried the cover story, "100 Things They Haven't Ruined Yet." On the list, among such disparate notables as the *Queen Elizabeth II*, the Harvard-Yale game, Pepperidge Farm cookies, gold, Guinness Stout, Hardy fly rods, and Morgan sports cars, was none other than Coos Bay, Oregon.

What do the editors of *M* know about Coos Bay that others, particularly the travel writers, don't? Probably somebody from that New York monthly took the time to get off U.S. 101 to find out what the community and surroundings have to offer.

Coos Bay and North Bend share a common boundary and, in places, are impossible to distinguish, creating one metropolitan area—the largest on the Oregon coast. Together with Charleston, they compose what has come to be known as "Oregon's Bay Area."

Ironically, though, the area's greatest asset and most obvious feature is often ignored by visitors and residents alike—the bay itself. Travelers bound north and south zoom through the twin cities on four lanes of U.S. 101, and, before they know it, they're in Reedsport or Bandon, with memories of the bay area already fading. Too many residents just take it all for granted.

Don't make the same mistake. Get off the highway and enjoy the restaurants, accommodations, parks, shops, museums, galleries, theaters, and, above all, the bay. This is the largest deep-water port between San Francisco and Puget Sound, but the adjacent lands aren't nearly so crowded and congested. It's also a sprawling estuary, rich in marine wildlife, and a great place to enjoy a variety of water sports and activities.

Lodging

Best Western Holiday Motel, 411 North Bayshore Drive; Coos Bay; 269–5111. Between northbound and southbound U.S. 101, downtown. Queen and king beds in 76 units, some with kitchens. Two-room suites and in-room whirlpools available. Cable TV, Movie Channel, heated indoor pool, sauna, fitness center. Next to restaurant and near others, shops, and theaters. Moderate to expensive.

Coos Bay Inn, 1445 North Bayshore Drive; Coos Bay; 267–7171 or 1–800–635–0852. On west side of U.S. 101, north of downtown. Newly remodeled. Queen and king beds in 94 units, some with kitchen facilities. Cable TV, in-room VCRs, large rental video library, free wine-and-cheese social (5:00 to 7:00 P.M.), free continental breakfast, in-room whirlpools and fireplaces available, spa, exercise room, laundry, video games adjacent to laundry. Handicapped units available. Inexpensive to moderate.

Sea Gull Summer Hostel, 438 Elrod; P.O. Box 847; Coos Bay; 267–6114. West on Elrod off U.S. 101, downtown. Open summers only. Low rates include breakfast and dinner. No reservations needed, except for groups. Inexpensive.

Sherman House Bed & Breakfast, 2380 Sherman Avenue;

North Bend; 756–3496. One block west of U.S. 101. Built in 1903, furnished with antiques. Three rooms with shared or private bath. Full breakfast. Moderate.

This Olde House Bed & Breakfast Inn, 202 Alder Street; Coos Bay; 267–5224. At the corner of Second and Alder, one block west of northbound U.S. 101 and King's Table Buffet. Built in 1893. Queen and king beds in 4 rooms, 1 with private bath. Victorian furnishings. Full breakfast. Moderate.

Campgrounds and RV Parks

Bluebill Campground, Oregon Dunes National Recreation Area. Located 2.8 miles west of U.S. 101, via Jordan Cove Road (causeway), just north of the McCullough and Haynes Inlet bridges. A pretty little Forest Service camp in a shore pine–forest setting on the edge of Bluebill Lake. Has 19 sites for RVs up to 22 feet. Hiking trail around the lake. Restrooms and water. Inexpensive.

Horsfall Staging Area and Campground, Oregon Dunes National Recreation Area. Located 1.7 miles west of U.S. 101, via Jordan Cove Road (causeway), just north of the McCullough and Haynes Inlet bridges. Seventy paved, striped, and numbered sites for RV rigs with trailers, used mainly by ORV enthusiasts. Three ramps for unloading and loading ORVs. Ample dune access. Restrooms. No water. Nearest water is at Bluebill Campground. Inexpensive.

Lucky Logger RV Park, 250 East Johnson; Coos Bay; 267–6003. West on Johnson off U.S. 101 at the south end of Coos Bay, near Fred Meyer store. New in 1989, top-quality facilities include 78 full-hookup sites for all sizes of RVs, showers, laundry, cable TV, minimart, wheelchair access. Near restaurants and shops. Expensive.

Food

Benetti's Italian Restaurant & Lounge, 260 South Broadway; Coos Bay; 267–6066. On the east side of northbound U.S. 101, downtown, across from the Egyptian Theater. Dinner daily. Fine Italian cuisine and a lounge with a view of the bay. Veal dishes— piccata, scaloppine, parmigiana. Scampi, New York steak, lasagna, cannelloni, ravioli, gnocchi, spaghetti, eggplant parmigiana—all served with soup, salad, and garlic bread. Cocktails, beer, and wine. Moderate.

Dishner's Fine Foods, 2603 Broadway; North Bend; 756–2881. Southeast corner of Broadway at 16th. Breakfast and lunch daily. A local favorite for good food at reasonable prices, and probably the most popular breakfast stop in the bay area. No-frills diner serves up large portions of pancakes, waffles, roll-ups, and all the traditional breakfast fare, as well as twenty-three omelets, superb homemade burgers, sandwich platters, and the biggest and best chicken-fried steak on the coast. Inexpensive to moderate.

1887 Union, 1887 Union Street; North Bend; 756–6752. One block west of southbound U.S. 101, between Connecticut and California. Lunch and dinner daily. A fine restaurant in a restored Victorian house. Specializes in steaks, seafood, poultry, and pasta dishes. Linguine served with choice of eight sauces. Soups made fresh daily. Beer and wine. Moderate.

The Hilltop House Restaurant & Lounge, 166 North Bay Drive; North Bend; 756–4160. Just east of U.S. 101 at the south end of Haynes Inlet Bridge. Lunch and dinner daily. One of the area's finest restaurants. Sandwiches, soups, and salads for lunch. Large list of shellfish appetizers. Superb steaks, prime rib, veal dishes, and seafoods. House specialties include bouillabaisse, stuffed English sole, lobster Thermidor, and salmon Monte Carlo. Cocktails, beer, and wine. Great view of the bay, especially at sunset. Moderate.

Nonni's Italian Delicatessen, 1430 Vermont Street; North Bend; 756–1600. Near the southeast end of Pony Village Mall parking lot, a half-mile west of U.S. 101. Lunch and dinner Monday through Saturday. Large menu of Italian hoagy sandwiches, burgers, and deli-style sandwiches. Soups, salads, and many full dinners, such as homemade lasagna, ravioli, fettuccine, steaks, veal, chicken, seafood, stuffed eggplant, and stuffed mushrooms. Large portions and reasonable prices. Deli foods to go. Beer and wine. Moderate.

Pancake Mill & Pie Shoppe, 2390 Tremont; North Bend; 756–2751. West side of U.S. 101, south of downtown. Breakfast and lunch daily. Pancakes big and tasty, three-egg omelets with fresh fillings, French toast, and waffles are breakfast favorites. Soups, salads, and deli-style sandwiches for lunch, homemade pies and cakes for dessert. Moderate.

Coos Bay/North Bend

Shopping and Browsing

The Frame Stop, 171 South Broadway; Coos Bay; 269–2615. West side of southbound U.S. 101, downtown. Weekdays, 9:30 A.M. to 5:30 P.M.; Saturday, 10:00 A.M. to 5:00 P.M. Limited-edition prints and posters. Large selection of marine and wildlife art. Some originals. Many prints by a nationally renowned local artist, Don Mc-Michael. Exquisite custom matting and framing.

Granny's Hutch, 1964 Sherman Avenue; North Bend; 756–1222. West side of southbound U.S. 101, downtown. Monday through Saturday, 10:00 A.M. to 5:00 P.M. Antiques, collectibles, and secondhand items. Furniture, glassware, kitchenware, tools, dolls, and more.

Griff's Seafood & Deli, 2596 Broadway; North Bend; 756–3784. On northwest corner at 16th. Monday through Saturday, 8:30 A.M. to 6:30 P.M.; Sunday, 10:00 A.M. to 5:30 P.M. Excellent fresh seafoods, such as salmon, lingcod, perch, shrimp, crab, scallops, and oysters. Pickled and smoked seafoods. Also deli-style sandwiches, salads, slaw, and seafood cocktails. Some gift items.

House of Myrtlewood, 1125 South First; P.O. Box 457; Coos Bay; 267–7804. Just west of U.S. 101 at the south end of town, across from Fred Meyer store. Daily, 8:30 A.M. to 6:00 P.M. Gift shop with one of the largest selections of myrtlewood items on the coast, including kitchen items, cribbage boards, candleholders, jewelry boxes, plates and bowls, clocks and weather instruments, cutting boards, furniture, and carvings. Oregon wines, homemade fudge, and other taste treats. Tours of adjacent factory several times a day. Products packaged and shipped anywhere.

Mo's Golden Storehouse, 700 South Broadway; Coos Bay. East side of southbound U.S. 101, downtown. Opens daily at 9:00 A.M. Minimall situated in a refurbished warehouse. Mo's Restaurant and a dozen small shops, including antique, jewelry, clothing, and candy shops.

Peddlers Three, 2048 Sherman Avenue; North Bend; 756–1011. West side of southbound U.S. 101, downtown. Monday through Saturday, 10:00 A.M. to 5:00 P.M. Antiques and collectibles. Specializes in kitchenware and collectibles from the 1920s, 1930s, and 1940s.

Seaborne Gallery, 1656 Sherman Avenue; North Bend; 756–3451. West side of U.S. 101, north end of town. July, August, and

December: daily, 10:00 A.M. to 5:00 P.M. Off-season closed Sundays. Bright and airy gallery featuring Mudlark pottery, paintings, rugs, jewelry, and more.

Wagon Wheel Antiques & Collectibles, 1984 Sherman Avenue; North Bend; 756–7023. West side of southbound U.S. 101, downtown. Daily, 11:00 A.M. to 6:00 P.M. Antiques and small collectibles. Good selection of old and collectible toys and games.

Museums

Coos Art Museum, 235 Anderson; Coos Bay; 267–3901. One block west of southbound U.S. 101, in old post office building, downtown. Tuesday through Friday, 11:00 A.M. to 5:00 P.M.; weekends, noon to 4:00 P.M. Only art museum on the Oregon coast. Large display areas with various exhibits throughout the year—paintings, sculpture, and photography. Gift shop and sales gallery on premises.

Coos County Historical Society Museum, Simpson Park; North Bend; 756–6320. West side of U.S. 101 at north end of town, next to the visitor center. Tuesday through Saturday, 10:00 A.M. to 4:00 P.M. Summer: also open Sunday, noon to 4:00 P.M. Displays include pioneer kitchen, Indian artifacts, Horsfall family parlor, and Dr. Horsfall's desk and medical instruments. Old homestead tools, logging exhibit, and many old photographs. Logging locomotive and tender on premises.

The Marshfield Sun Printing Museum, P.O. Box 783; Coos Bay; 269–1363. Between Front Street and northbound U.S. 101, across from the Timber Lodge. Summer: Monday, Wednesday, and Friday, 1:00 to 4:00 P.M. Phone for tour in off-season. Historic newspaper and job-printing shop, displaying equipment used to publish *The Marshfield Sun* from 1891 to 1944. Museum has an old Washington Hand Press, a Chandler & Price platen press, and nearly 200 type cases and fonts, as well as other equipment.

Water Sports and Activities

The Coos River system, Coos Bay, and the various inlets and tributaries offer abundant recreational opportunities from canoeing, kayaking, powerboating, sailing, and windsurfing to crabbing, clam digging, and fishing for a great variety of species.

43

Private property obstructs bay access along much of the south shore, but elsewhere access is ample and easy. Popular fishing, crabbing, and clam-digging areas are along Jordan Cove Road (causeway), west off U.S. 101, north of town. Take the same road to connect with the Trans-Pacific Parkway and reach the shoreline near Roseburg Forest Products and the T-Dock area. The same causeway leads to the dunes and Horsfall Beach, popular with surf fishermen.

The area offers some kind of angling all year: steelheading, December through February; surfperch and seaperch, February through summer; spring chinook, April to early summer; coho, late spring through fall; sea-run cutthroat, late summer; fall chinook, late September into December; and sturgeon, striped bass, and a variety of bottomfish most of the year.

Coos Bay has some of the best clam beds on the coast. Although razor clams are not so plentiful as they once were, diligent diggers find a few along the ocean beaches. Best digging, however, is for an assortment of succulent bay clams, including horsenecks (locally called Empire clams), hard-shells or quahogs, cockles, and littlenecks, all of which are found on the flats near Charleston and on the South Slough, as well as along the north shore of the bay in the North Spit area. Minus tides are best for digging these species.

Soft-shell clams are found in upper bay areas and can be dug on any low tide. These are bonus clams, meaning that diggers can take thirty-six soft-shells in addition to the limit of bay clams. Haynes Inlet and the area north of Jordan Cove Road are good for soft-shell clams.

Fisherman's Center & Whitewater Experience, 1934 Virginia; North Bend; 756–2721. Monday through Saturday, 8:00 A.M. to 6:00 P.M. Small shop with a large selection of tackle, supplies, waders, and bait.

Fishin' Shack, 818 South Broadway; Coos Bay; 267–3474. East side of U.S. 101, downtown. Daily, 6:00 A.M. to 6:00 P.M.; closes Sunday at 2:30 P.M. Small shop, but good selection of tackle, supplies, and bait for freshwater and saltwater fishing for warm-water, cold-water, and anadromous species. Good source of fishing information and maps. Tackle repair. Tackle and crab ring rental. Licenses and tags. Guide service.

Milicoma Guide Service, c/o Robert L. Hughes; HC Box 52;

Coos Bay; 269–0957. Guides anglers for spring chinook, striped bass, summer steelhead, fall chinook, winter steelhead, and small-mouth bass on coastal rivers. All fishing from McKenzie drift boats.

River Drifter Booking Service, 1333 Bayview Drive; North Bend; 756–6934. Acts as free consultant to match interested parties with guides and outfitters. Books fishing trips for salmon, steelhead, trout, sturgeon, striped bass, smallmouth bass, and more. Wild or mild river trips. Also arranges outdoor ventures for the handicapped.

Surplus Center, 310 South Broadway; Coos Bay; 267–6711. Between northbound and southbound U.S. 101, downtown. Daily, 9:00 A.M. to 6:00 P.M.; Friday until 9:00 P.M. Large selection of fishing tackle and supplies, camping gear, rainwear, boots, waders, inflatable rafts, and canoes. Crabbing and clam-digging gear. Licenses and bait.

Tours and Trips

River Runner Harbor Cruises, at the Port of Coos Bay city dock, east end of Anderson at U.S. 101. Champagne cruises of the bay area aboard the *River Runner.* Departs daily at 1:00, 3:00, and 6:00 P.M. during summer season. Special three-hour upriver cruises on weekends. Ample parking downtown, along the street or in lots between northbound and southbound highway.

Golf

Kentuck Golf Course, Kentuck Inlet; North Bend; 756–4464. Located 3 miles east of U.S. 101 on East Bay Drive at north end of McCullough Bridge. The only 18-hole public golf course on the south coast. Pro shop, club and cart rentals, refreshments. Set in a scenic valley in the foothills at the head of Kentuck Inlet on Coos Bay.

Other Attractions

Little Theater on the Bay, P.O. Box 404; North Bend; 756–4336. On the west side of southbound U.S. 101, at Sherman and Washington. A full season of live theater each year, offering plays, musicals, and "Little Ole Opry On The Bay."

Coos Bay/North Bend

On Broadway Theater, 226 South Broadway; Coos Bay; 269–2501. East side of southbound U.S. 101, downtown. Playwright's American Conservatory Theater presents live performing of plays and musicals each summer.

Events

For information about events listed without phone numbers, phone the Bay Area Chamber of Commerce (see Travel Information).

February	Governors' Seafood Cook-off
March	Dune Mushers' Mail Run, 756–4613
	Festival of the Myrtle Tree, 267–5755
May	Youth Festival, 267–7232
	Whalefest, 267–5755
July	Sandblast in the Dunes
	Fireworks Display, 269–0215
	North Bend Air Show, 756–1723
	North Bend Jubilee, 756–4613
	Oregon Music Festival
August	Empire Community Days, 267–5755
	Blackberry Arts Festival, 267–7232
September	Sand Dune Sashay Square Dance Festival, 269–1069
	Charlie Tuna Festival, 269–0215
	Bay Area Fun Festival
	Tour de Coast Bicycle Race
	Prefontaine Memorial 10K Race
	Oregon Shorebird Festival, Cape Arago Audubon Society, P.O. Box 381, North Bend

Weather and Tide Information

U.S. Coast Guard, Charleston; recorded message, 888–3102

Travel Information

Bay Area Chamber of Commerce, 50 East Central; P.O. Box 210; Coos Bay; 269–0215; Oregon, 1–800–672–6278; elsewhere, 1–800–824–8486

North Bend Chamber of Commerce, 1380 Sherman Avenue; 756–4613

Tenmile Lakes, near Lakeside, on the Oregon coast

Lakeside, Oregon 97449
Population: 1,453

Location: *About 1 mile east of U.S. 101, 12 miles north of North Bend, 9 miles south of Reedsport*

The small community of Lakeside, situated on the northwest shore of Tenmile Lake and along Tenmile Creek, was once a thriving resort town. It still possesses a resort atmosphere, but the pace has slowed considerably. With the recent closure of its only remaining sawmill, however, outdoor recreation will likely become the area's economic mainstay.

Tenmile and North Tenmile lakes are typical of lakes found in hill country. They are sprawling bodies of water with many arms, bays, and coves. The two, joined by a canal at their western ends, offer 42 miles of shoreline to explore by boat. The lakes are among the most popular on the coast for swimming, water-skiing, sailing, and fishing.

Lakeside

Just north of Lakeside and east of U.S. 101 lies Eel Lake. Though smaller than either of the other two, this is still among the largest lakes on the coast. Beautiful **Tugman State Park** is on its west shore, offering excellent picnic and camping facilities, as well as a public boat ramp and beach.

In Lakeside are several restaurants, stores for stocking up on groceries and supplies, and a county park with picnic tables and good boat-launch facilities. To reach the park, turn east on North Lake Road, in downtown Lakeside, then south on 11th.

Campgrounds and RV Parks

Mid Eel Creek Campground, Oregon Dunes National Recreation Area; 271–3611. Located 9.5 miles south of Reedsport, next to North Eel Creek Campground. Has 25 tent and trailer sites and turnarounds to accommodate RVs up to 16 feet. Fire pit and picnic table at each site. Restrooms, water, no hookups. Near dunes and lakes. Inexpensive.

North Eel Creek Campground, Oregon Dunes National Recreation Area; 271–3611. West of U.S. 101 at Lakeside junction, 9 miles south of Reedsport. Has 53 tent and trailer sites and turnarounds to accommodate RVs to 22 feet. Restrooms, water, no hookups. Picnic table and fire pit at each site. Located in the dunes, 2 miles from the beach. Marked trails with scenic viewpoints. Inexpensive.

North Lake Resort & Marina, 2090 North Lake Road; 759–3515. Just east of downtown Lakeside, on the northwest side of the canal bridge and southwest tip of North Lake. Sites available with full hookups, water and electric, or no hookups. Fire pits at all sites. Showers, boat launch, moorage, fuel, boat rentals, groceries, bait, tackle, and propane. Moderate.

William M. Tugman State Park, 365 North Fourth Street (office); Coos Bay 97420; 269–9410; booth, mid-May through Labor Day; 759–3604. Located about a mile north of Lakeside and 7 miles south of Reedsport, east off U.S. 101 on Eel Lake. Has 115 campsites with water and electric hookups. Showers, tank dump, beach, bathhouse, public boat launch. In a beautiful park setting with many trees and wild rhododendrons. Moderate.

Shopping and Browsing

Myrtlewood Chalet, Bayview Manufacturing Company; 3955 Coast Highway; P.O. Box 644; North Bend 97459; 756–2220. West side of U.S. 101, 5 miles north of North Bend. Daily, 10:00 A.M. to 4:00 P.M. A pleasant and well-stocked shop that displays an assortment of myrtlewood furniture, bowls, cutting boards, jewelry boxes, lamps, candlesticks, carvings, cribbage boards, clocks, and more. Tours of adjacent 40,000-square-foot factory.

Water Sports and Activities

Tenmile and North Tenmile lakes are relatively shallow and support populations of warm-water, cold-water, and anadromous fishes. The angling ranges from good to outstanding, depending on the time of year and the species sought.

Warm-water species include bluegill, yellow perch, brown bullhead, largemouth bass, and whiterock or hybrid bass—a cross between white and striped bass. You can catch bluegill by the boatload much of the year. Bullhead fishing is best during the warmer months and at night. Largemouth bass are available all year, but spring and fall are peak times for fish of one to three pounds, with occasional lunkers of five to eight pounds. During the summer, night fishing produces the most and biggest bass. Hybrids are nearly dormant during the winter, but as the waters warm in spring, they become very active, cruising both lakes from near shore to well offshore. The lakes have given up hybrids exceeding ten pounds.

Eel Lake has a similar fishery, but it is deeper and colder, better suited to a cold-water fishery. There are largemouth bass in the lake, and the fishing for them can be good, but rainbow trout are the prime quarry here. Most anglers troll for the trout or still-fish with bait, but the fly fisherman will find great sport when conditions are right. Early mornings in sheltered coves or evenings after the wind has subsided are best for dry-fly action. Spring and early-summer mayfly hatches often spur feeding frenzies.

Lakeside Marina, south end of Eighth Street, in Lakeside; 759–3312. Summer: daily, 6:00 A.M. to 9:00 P.M. Off-season: daily, 7:00 A.M. to 7:00 P.M. Bait, tackle, fuel, marine accessories, service, and repair. Boat and canoe rentals.

Lakeside

Lakeside Tackle & Hardware, 130 South Eighth Street; 759–3448. East side of street, downtown Lakeside. Monday through Saturday, 8:00 A.M. to 8:30 P.M.; Sunday, 8:00 A.M. to 4:00 P.M. Bait, tackle, licenses, and tags. Information on local fishing.

Rentals

Far West Rentals, Hauser Depot Road; North Bend 97459; 756–2322 or 756–4274. About 5 miles north of North Bend, a half-mile west of U.S. 101. Turn at Myrtlewood Chalet. Summer: daily, 8:00 A.M. to 8:00 P.M. Off-season: daily, 11:00 A.M. to 3:00 P.M. Four-wheel ORVs for rent by the hour or by the day. Helmets provided free. Dune and beach access. No deposit required.

Pacific Coast Recreation, 4121 Coast Highway; North Bend 97459; 756–7183. About 5.5 miles north of North Bend on the west side of U.S. 101, opposite the Hauser exit. Daily, 8:00 A.M. to 7:30 P.M. Four-wheel ORVs for rent by the hour or day. Easy access to the dunes.

Spinreel Dune Buggy Rentals, 9122 Wildwood Drive; North Bend 97459; 759–3313. Two miles south of Lakeside, west off U.S. 101. Watch for signs. Four-wheel ORVs for rent by the hour or the day. Small ORVs available for children. Largest selection on the Oregon coast. Deposit required. Free shuttle service to beach or dunes for non-riders in the party. Access to dunes and beach.

Travel Information

Lakeside Chamber of Commerce, P. O. Box 333; 759–3011

ORV riders in Oregon Dunes National Recreation Area

Reedsport/Winchester Bay, Oregon 97467
Population: 4,915/900

Location: *At the junction of U.S. 101 and State Route 38, along U.S. 101 and the south bank of the Umpqua River, about 21 miles north of North Bend*

At the far eastern end of Douglas County in the Cascade Mountains, the North Umpqua River rises and flows westward, gathering the waters of two dozen other rivers and creeks before joining the South Umpqua near Roseburg. From there the mighty river courses north and west through the Coast Range, creating what might be called the Valley of the Green Giant, because that's exactly what the Umpqua is by the time its slate green waters pass beneath the State Route 38 bridge at Scottsburg, the head of tidewater.

Flanked by emerald mountains, the great river parallels State

51

Route 38 for another 16 miles and is joined by the Smith River before passing beneath the U.S. 101 bridge at Reedsport. Beyond, it rounds the big bend just past Gardiner, swings southward, and becomes Winchester Bay. Having traversed the breadth of Douglas County and wended its way through the canyons, gorges, and benchlands of two mountain ranges, the Umpqua has become the largest coastal river between the Columbia and San Francisco Bay.

Once an important transportation and commerce corridor, the Umpqua moved passengers and freight, via riverboat, between the coast and Scottsburg. The Willamette Valley was connected to Scottsburg by roads traveled by stagecoach and wagon. Sawmills in the area sent their lumber on schooners and streamers south to the burgeoning boomtown on the bay, San Francisco.

Today most people travel through this area in their own vehicles. Freight and lumber go by truck and train and, if destined for some distant port, eventually get loaded aboard freighters at the Port of Portland or Coos Bay. The Umpqua and Smith rivers and Winchester Bay are no longer merely modes of conveyance; they now provide a more important commodity to residents and visitors alike—fun.

This watery world has become a coastal playground, attracting campers, boaters, crabbers, clam diggers, anglers, beachcombers, wildlife watchers, photographers, artists, and folks who would just as soon sit back, relax, and let it all happen.

Great beaches, the longest in the state, sprawl northward and southward from the mouth of the estuary. And for 20 miles in the same directions, huge dunes provide yet more recreational opportunities.

To the east is some of the most scenic inland country on the coast, where you can follow the course of the Umpqua or Smith River along paved highways, or venture off into the Coast Range on graveled Forest Service roads.

In 1988, a contest sponsored by Harley-Davidson named State Route 38 one of "America's 10 Best Roads." It closely follows the course of the Umpqua through the Coast Range to Elkton and beyond. Smith River Road exits east off U.S. 101 just north of Reedsport and carries travelers along another beautiful river and into the forested mountains.

Lodging

Tropicana Motel, 1593 U.S. 101; 271–3671. East side of U.S. 101, downtown. Has 41 units with cable TV and HBO. Heated pool. Adjacent restaurant and lounge. Inexpensive to moderate.

Winchester Bay Motel, P.O. Box 37B; Winchester Bay; 271–4871. West of U.S. 101, 3 miles south of Reedsport. Has 52 units with queen beds, cable TV, and HBO. Near restaurants, shops, charter boats, beaches, and dunes. Moderate.

Campgrounds and RV Parks

Surfwood Campground, Route 4; Box 268; 271–4020. East side of U.S. 101, half-mile north of Winchester Bay, 2.5 miles south of Reedsport. Has 163 sites: 141 full-hookup, 22 tent. Pull-throughs, showers, tank dump, firewood, cable TV, laundry, heated and covered pool and sauna, store, ice, car wash, shuffleboard, tennis court, horseshoes, and playground. Moderate.

Tahkenitch Campground, Oregon Dunes National Recreation Area; 271–3611. On west side of U.S. 101, 7 miles north of Reedsport. Has 36 campsites with picnic tables and fire pits. Restrooms, trailer sites for RVs to 22 feet, and turnaround. Water available May 15 to September 15. Hiker access to dunes and beach. No ORV access. Wooded setting, half-mile south of Tahkenitch landing and boat ramp. Inexpensive.

Tahkenitch Landing, Oregon Dunes National Recreation Area; 271–3611. Seven miles north of Reedsport on east side of U.S. 101. Fire pits and picnic tables at 26 sites for RVs up to 22 feet. Graveled road and pads. Trailer turnaround, but sites are narrow and brushy. No hookups or water. Closed in winter. Boat ramp. Fishing dock with wheelchair access. Inexpensive.

Umpqua Lighthouse State Park; 271–4118. West off U.S. 101, 6 miles south of Reedsport. Has 41 tent sites and 22 full-hookup sites for RVs to 44 feet. Showers, laundry, firewood. Beach and swimming at small lake. Hiking trails. Near ocean beaches and dunes. Moderate.

Windy Cove County Park, P.O. Box 265; Winchester Bay; 271–4138 or 271–5634. Three miles south of Reedsport, west off U.S. 101, across from Salmon Harbor boat basin. Has 75 full-hookup sites for RVs to 30 feet. Showers, picnic tables, and playground. An attractive park near beaches, dunes, charter boats, restaurants, and stores. Moderate.

Food

The Seafood Grotto, Winchester Bay; 271–4250. Just west of U.S. 101, 3 miles south of Reedsport. Lunch and dinner daily. Soups, salads, sandwiches, steaks, and superb seafood dishes. Homemade clam chowder, oyster stew, cioppino, fish and chips, salmon, halibut, razor clams, shrimp, fresh local oysters. A favorite dining spot of local residents. Beer and wine. Moderate.

Windjammer Restaurant, 1280 Highway Avenue; 271–5415. On west side of U.S. 101, downtown Reedsport. Breakfast, lunch, and dinner daily. Traditional breakfast fare and great omelets. Sandwiches are extraordinary—barbecued beef, barbecued turkey and bacon, and shrimp and crab stuffers, grilled on sourdough bread with cheese. Dinners include steaks, chicken, pork chops, halibut, scallops, oysters, and clam fritters. Locally popular. Moderate.

Shopping and Browsing

Captain Bly's Gift & Art Gallery, Winchester Bay; 271–3406. By **C** Dock, on the waterfront. West off U.S. 101, 3 miles south of Reedsport. Summer: daily, 9:00 A.M. to 7:00 P.M. Winter: daily, 10:00 A.M. to 5:30 P.M. Wood carvings, metal sculpture, brass, pottery, oil paintings, pen-and-ink drawings, and limited-edition prints. Marine and wildlife art, myrtlewood, jewelry, candles, and cards.

Sportsman's Cannery, P.O. Box 11; Winchester Bay; 271–3293. Between **B** and **C** docks, on the waterfront. West of U.S. 101, 3 miles south of Reedsport. Summer: daily, 7:00 A.M. to 7:00 P.M. Winter: daily, 9:00 A.M. to 6:00 P.M. Fresh, smoked, and canned seafoods. Gift packs shipped anywhere. Phone and mail orders. Salmon, albacore, sturgeon, halibut, and crab. Custom canning for anglers. "Catch what you can—we can what you catch." Daily cannery tours.

Museum

Douglas County Coastal Historical and Information Center, Winchester Bay. In the former Umpqua River U.S. Coast Guard

Station, 1.5 miles south of Winchester Bay, near the lighthouse, or west off U.S. 101, 6 miles south of Reedsport. May through September: Wednesday through Saturday, 10:00 A.M. to 5:00 P.M.; Sunday, 1:00 to 5:00 P.M. Built in 1939 and occupied by the Coast Guard until 1971. Now houses historical displays, photographs, and information about early life on the Umpqua River—transportation, logging, shipping, and more.

Beaches, Parks, Trails, and Waysides

The **Oregon Dunes National Recreation Area** (N.R.A.) might be considered Oregon's largest park, because in many respects it certainly is a park, complete with trails, beaches, campgrounds, lakes, ponds, streams, and many recreational opportunities. It is managed by the U.S. Forest Service as part of the **Siuslaw National Forest** and has its headquarters in Reedsport, on the west side of U.S. 101 at the State Route 38 junction. N.R.A. Headquarters are open weekdays from 8:00 A.M. to 4:30 P.M. all year and weekends during the summer.

The N.R.A. stretches some 42 miles from North Bend to Florence and comprises 32,000 acres. Here, dunes rise to heights of 700 feet and lengths of nearly a mile, making them the largest oceanside dunes in the world. Also within this vast area are 41 miles of broad beaches, thirty-two lakes and numerous ponds and marshes, 247 species of birds, fifty land mammals, four marine mammals (as well as twenty-five species of whales and dolphins offshore), twelve amphibians, three reptiles, and eighty-three fishes, not to mention coniferous and deciduous softwood and hardwood trees, shrubs, grasses, ferns, berries, and wildflowers. It's enough to boggle the mind of any nature lover.

An abbreviated glimpse of the dunes is offered to U.S. 101 travelers about 10 miles north of Reedsport at the **Oregon Dunes Overlook.** Boardwalks and ramps lead to two viewing platforms overlooking six typical wildlife habitats and ten dune landforms. For those so inclined, trails lead to the dunes and beach.

About 6 miles south of Reedsport, a road leads west off U.S. 101 to **Umpqua Lighthouse State Park,** where there are hiking trails, picnic areas, a lake with a beach, abundant wildlife, superb views, unlimited photographic opportunities, and the Umpqua lighthouse, or **Umpqua River Light Station,** as it was commissioned.

The original Umpqua lighthouse, built in 1857 near the mouth of the river, was the first such structure erected in Oregon. But the flooding Umpqua undermined its foundation and toppled the building in February 1861.

The present light, which stands on a bluff high above the beach and dunes and has a focal plane 165 feet above the sea, has been operating since 1894. The red-and-white light beaming from its 65-foot tower is visible 19 miles out.

About 3 miles east of U.S. 101 on State Route 38 is the **Dean Creek Elk Viewing Area,** which is a *must see.* Magnificent Roosevelt elk have been using the bottomlands along the Umpqua River for many years. What was once a 923-acre ranch is now an elk refuge in public ownership. From 50 to 150 elk are often near enough for excellent viewing and photography, even without the aid of binoculars and telephoto lenses, although such optics are recommended.

Water Sports and Activities

On Winchester Bay, at the small community by the same name, Salmon Harbor provides more than 900 boat slips with full hookups, showers, restrooms, sewage pumpout station, fuel docks, bait docks, launch ramps, repair and service facilities, and more, making this the largest sport-boat basin on the Oregon coast. From here, powerboats and sailboats can steer west across the bar and into the Pacific, or up the bay and Umpqua River. A large charter fleet also works out of Salmon Harbor.

Despite all the sport-boat traffic here, this is no place for the inexperienced boater. Take heed: The Umpqua River bar is tricky and often treacherous. Winds, currents, and tide rips can churn the lower Umpqua River and Winchester Bay into dangerous waters for small boats. Exercise caution and use common sense.

The Umpqua is one of the coastal rivers that get runs of spring chinook. Anglers catch the big salmon from the bar all the way to the head of tidewater, but one of the most popular areas is just downstream from the Scottsburg bridge. Launch facilities are nearby, just off State Route 38.

Another spring visitor is the American shad, which arrives in

May in great schools that move up the Umpqua and provide action from tidewater up. Shad are present in the Umpqua most of the summer, but the best fishing is in May and June.

Sea-run cutthroat trout enter the system in August and are taken through September in both the Umpqua and Smith rivers. Fall chinook follow closely, and about the time their numbers dwindle, the first of the winter steelhead arrive and offer superb angling above tidewater through February.

Striped bass are present in both the Umpqua and Smith, and some consider the latter to be Oregon's best striper water. While these great fish are not present in the numbers they once were, most are big fish. Every year, anglers take stripers of twenty to forty pounds, with occasional fifty-pounders brought to gaff.

The lower Umpqua also offers some of the best sturgeon fishing in the state, with the first fish of the year taken by hardy anglers in January and February, even though this is a year-round fishery. The best sturgeon fishing is in the deep holes, particularly in the Big Bend area near Gardiner. This is a bait and big-tackle fishery for a quarry that might be as long as your boat.

A smallmouth-bass fishery has developed on the Umpqua in recent years, and anglers are making some fine catches of this worthy gamester. The bass are present in the system all year and as far downstream as Reedsport. The best angling, however, is from late April, when the rains begin to subside and the water drops and clears, through the summer and fall until the rainy season. Best catches are made above tidewater, particularly from Elkton upstream.

Surfperch and seaperch start moving into Winchester Bay in late winter and provide angling opportunities through spring from boats, shore, or from docks and piers. Flounder, sole, rockfish, and lingcod round out the usual catch of bottomfish in the bay and lower river.

Crabbing is good throughout the bay, either from a boat or from docks and piers. Mud flats offer excellent clam digging on minus tides for horseneck, hard-shell, littleneck, and soft-shell clams and cockles. For razor clams, try the beaches north and south of the bay.

Gee Gee Charters, 2092 Hawthorne; Reedsport; 271–3152 or (home) 271–4134. Located at Winchester Bay at the top of **B** Dock. Four-hour salmon trips departing three times a day. Five-hour bottomfishing trips. All gear furnished. Private charters available. Junior and senior discounts.

Hannah Fishing Lodges, Winter: RR Box 94983; Elk River Road; Port Orford 97465; 332–8585. Summer: General Delivery; Elkton 97436; 584–2611. Guided fishing, including lodging and meals, on the Umpqua River for striped bass, sturgeon, and small-mouth bass.

Terry Jarmain, Umpqua River Guide; 1026 Hawthorne; 271–5583. Tidewater guide for various species on the Umpqua and Smith rivers—striped bass, sturgeon, perch, shad, and more.

The Main Charters/Stockade Market & Tackle, Fourth and Beach Boulevard; Winchester Bay; 271–3800 (24-hour phone). West of U.S. 101, 3 miles south of Reedsport. Four-hour salmon trips leaving daily at 6:00 A.M., and 2:00 P.M. Five-hour bottomfishing trips. Groceries, ice, bait, tackle, rainwear, crab-ring sales and rentals at the Stockade.

Reedsport Outdoor Store, 2049 Winchester Avenue; 271–2311. West side of U.S. 101, downtown Reedsport. Weekdays, 9:00 A.M. to 6:00 P.M.; Saturdays, 10:00 A.M. to 3:00 P.M. Full-service outdoor store, offering outdoor clothing, rainwear, boots, bait, tackle, and crabbing gear, as well as outboard and boat sales and service. Fishing licenses and tags. Good source of fishing, crabbing, and clam-digging information.

Golf and Tennis

Forest Hills Country Club, 1 Country Club Drive; 271–2626. West 0.7 mile off U.S. 101 at the southernmost traffic light in Reedsport. Nine-hole golf course. Pro shop, resident pro, club sales and repair, club and cart rental. Tennis courts, restaurant, and lounge on premises.

Rentals

Dune Odyssey Rentals, U.S. 101; Winchester Bay; 271–4011. East side of the highway, 3 miles south of Reedsport. Rents ORVs by the hour. Also rents fishing tackle, crabbing gear, and clam-digging equipment.

Tahkenitch Fishing Village, 271–5222. West end of Tahkenitch Lake, east side of U.S. 101, 7.5 miles north of Reedsport. Rents

14-foot fiberglass boats with 7.5-horsepower Evinrude outboards by the day. Canoes rented by the day or half day.

Events

For information about events listed without phone numbers, phone the chamber of commerce (see Travel Information).

February Storm Festival
March Oregon Dune Mushers' Mail Run, 271–3495
April Blessing of the Fleet
May Spring Wine and Dine Festival
June Sailboard Regatta
July Fireworks Display
Presbyterian Women's Quilt Show, 271–4152
Ocean Festival
September Kleo the Crab Contest
December Christmas Bazaar

Weather and Tide Information

U. S. Coast Guard, Umpqua River; Winchester Bay; recorded message, 271–4244

Travel Information

Lower Umpqua Chamber of Commerce, P.O. Box 11-B; 271–3495; Oregon, 1–800–247–2155

Oregon Dunes National Recreation Area; Suislaw National Forest; 855 Highway Avenue; 271–3611

Carnivorous plants *Darlingtonia californica*

Florence, Oregon 97439
Population: 4,955

Location: *At the junction of U.S. 101 and State Route 126, 60 miles west of Eugene, 21 miles north of Reedsport, at the mouth of the Siuslaw (si-*oos-*law) River*

One story says the city of Florence was named after State Senator A. B. Florence, who represented Lane County in the mid-nineteenth century. A more romantic and interesting version, and one more fitting the character of a charming seaport, is that the French ship *Florence* went aground near the mouth of the Siuslaw River in February 1875 and broke up in the surf. A plank bearing her name washed ashore, and several local Indians hung it above the entrance of the town's first hotel. Since then, the community has been known as Florence.

Like many river communities, Florence, in its early days, was

60

dependent upon the Siuslaw (an Indian word meaning "faraway waters") for transportation and commerce. People traveled from home to town and back by boat. Mail, food, and supplies were delivered by boat. Children went to school by boat.

Highways have replaced waterways for such purposes, but Florence's river heritage is still evident. Even as the town grows and spreads northward, it seems to cling to its moorings along the river's north bank.

Florence was born of the river, and its first buildings were clustered along it. Several of them still stand in the riverfront area known as Old Town. After years of neglect and decay, much of Old Town has been renovated and is now the most interesting part of the city. With all its shops and waterfront restaurants, Bay Street is doing its best to bustle, but it can't quite resist the urge to amble.

Lodging

Driftwood Shores, 88416 First Avenue; 997–8263; Oregon, 1–800–422–5091; elsewhere, 1–800–824–8774. Located 2.5 miles west of U.S. 101, via Heceta Beach Road, just north of Florence. Has 136 units with queen beds, cable TV, and ocean view. Studio and kitchen units available. Each 3-bedroom suite has full kitchen, fireplace, dining room, oceanfront balcony, master bedroom with private bath, and 2 smaller bedrooms with adjoining bath. Rollaways and cribs available. Excellent restaurant on premises. Wheelchair access. Moderate.

Money Saver Motel, 170 U.S. 101; 997–7131. East side of U.S. 101, downtown. Has 40 units with queen beds and cable TV. Wheelchair access. Near shops and restaurants. Inexpensive to moderate.

River House, 1202 Bay Street; 997–3933. On the north shore of the river, near Old Town, west of the bridge. Has 40 units with queen and king beds, some with in-room whirlpools. Cable TV, whirlpool, bay view. Moderate.

Campgrounds and RV Parks

Carter Lake Campground, Oregon Dunes National Recreation Area; 271–3611. West off U.S. 101, 11 miles south of Florence. Has 22 sites with picnic tables, fireplace, and water. Hiking trails, fishing, boating, wildlife observation, and photography. Inexpensive.

Driftwood II ORV Campground, Oregon Dunes National Recreation Area; 271–3611. Located 1.25 miles west of U.S. 101 on Siltcoos Dune and Beach Access Road, 10 miles south of Florence. Has 70 sites, some with picnic tables and fire pits. Trailer sites, turnaround, and restrooms. Water in summer only. No hookups. Beach and dune access from campground. Hiking trails, fishing, wildlife watching, and photography. Inexpensive.

Jessie M. Honeyman Memorial State Park, 84505 U. S. 101; 997–3851 (office); 997–3641 (booth). West side of U.S. 101, 3 miles south of Florence. A beautiful campground with 382 sites: 66 full-hookup, 75 electric, 241 tent. Showers, firewood, hiking trails, fishing and swimming at two lakes, dunes access, concession area. Well-maintained grounds. Reservations accepted. Moderate.

Lagoon Campground, Oregon Dunes National Recreation Area; 271–3611. Located three quarters of a mile west of U.S. 101 on Siltcoos Dune and Beach Access Road, 10 miles south of Florence. Has 40 campsites with picnic tables and fire pits. Trailer sites, turnaround, restrooms, water, no hookups. Beach and dune access. Hiking and nature trails, fishing, wildlife observation, and photography. Inexpensive.

Sutton Campground, Oregon Dunes National Recreation Area; 271–3611. On Sutton Beach Road, 2.5 miles north of Florence, eight-tenths of a mile west of U.S. 101. Has 92 campsites, no hookups. Trailer sites, turnaround, restrooms, water, hiking trails, and trail access to dunes and beach. Fishing in estuary, creek, and lake. Wildlife observation and photography. Inexpensive.

Tyee Campground, Oregon Dunes National Recreation Area; 271–3611. Located a tenth of a mile east of U.S. 101 on Westlake Road, 6 miles south of Florence. Has 14 campsites with picnic tables and fireplaces. Trailer sites, no hookups. Restrooms, water, boat ramp. Fishing and boating with access to Siltcoos River and Siltcoos Lake. Inexpensive.

Waxmyrtle Campground, Oregon Dunes National Recreation Area; 271–3611. Located three quarters of a mile west of U.S. 101 on Siltcoos Dune and Beach Access Road, 10 miles south of Florence. Has 56 sites with picnic tables, fire pits, no hookups. Trailer sites, turnaround, and water. Hiking, fishing, dune and beach access, wildlife observation, and photography. Inexpensive.

Food

The Bridgewater Seafood Restaurant & Oyster Bar, 1297 Bay Street; 997–9405. In Old Town, situated in a historic building erected in 1901. Lunch and dinner daily. Sandwiches, burgers, and such specialties as fettuccine with clam sauce, shrimp Creole, clam fritters, teriyaki chicken. Shrimp, crab, and calamari appetizers, as well as oysters on the half shell. Dinners include steak, chicken, and seafood. Oyster bar and garden patio. Cocktails, beer, and wine. Moderate.

Mo's Restaurant, 1436 Bay Street; 997–2185. In Old Town. Lunch and dinner daily. Local chain chowder and fish house, serving burgers, salads, soups, chili, clam chowder, oyster stew, fish and chips, and seafood sandwiches. Large dinner menu with such seafood favorites as salmon, halibut, lingcod, clam fritters, oysters, prawns, scallops, calamari, and cioppino. Beer and wine. Moderate.

Surfside Restaurant, 88416 First Avenue; 997–8263. At Driftwood Shores, 2.5 miles west of U.S. 101, via Heceta Beach Road, north of Florence. Breakfast, lunch, and dinner daily. Two-egg and three-egg omelets, pancakes, waffles, and various egg dishes and specials, including the Fisherman—two eggs, hashbrowns, toast or English muffin, with fillet of salmon or halibut. For lunch, hot or cold sandwiches, including burgers and French dip, or bay shrimp or Dungeness crab on English muffin topped with melted cheddar. Louis-style salads topped with crab, shrimp, or both for lunch or dinner. Dinners include prime rib, chicken, leg of lamb, broiled steaks, salmon, oysters, scallops, shrimp, scampi, halibut, and lobster. Cocktails, beer, and wine. Moderate.

Windward Inn, 3757 U.S. 101 North; 997–8243. West side of U.S. 101 at the north end of town. Breakfast, lunch, and dinner daily. Closed Mondays in winter. Breakfast menu includes homemade breads and pastries. Lunches and dinners include a variety of beef, veal, lamb, and seafood dishes. Full bar, including a wine list featuring Oregon wines. Moderate.

Shopping and Browsing

The Bay Window, 1312 Bay Street; P.O. Box 930; 997–2002. In Old Town. Daily, 10:00 A.M. to 5:00 P.M.; Sunday, noon to 3:30 P.M. An Old Town fixture, established in 1975, full of artworks, antiques, old and rare books, photographs, pipes, tobacco, and more. Custom framing available.

Sealines Nautical Gifts, 1193 Bay Street; 997–6873. West side of the bridge, just west of Old Town, across from the Lotus Restaurant. Daily, 9:00 A.M. to 6:00 P.M. Ships' lights, portholes, shells, nautical cards and stationery (made by the shop owners), ship-model kits, old and new brass, and much more. A *must see* for anyone interested in nautical items.

The Toy Factory, 88878 U.S. 101; 997–8604. West side of U.S. 101, 2.8 miles north of Florence. Daily, 11:00 A.M. to 5:00 P.M. Children's puzzles and books, toys and games from Oregon and around the world. Folk toys. Mail-order catalog. A great shopping and browsing stop for kids and grown-ups.

Wind Drift Gallery, 125 Maple Street; P.O. Box 547; 997–9182. Maple at Bay Street, in Old Town. Popular shop where marine art and nautical gift items are mainstays. Good selection of prints, sculpture, carvings, and castings.

Museum

Siuslaw Pioneer Museum; 997–7884. One mile south of the river, west side of U.S. 101. May 1 to Labor Day: Tuesday through Sunday, noon to 4:00 P.M. Winter: weekends, noon to 4:00 P.M. Displays of Indian artifacts, farm and homestead items, early logging equipment, and more.

Beaches, Parks, Trails, and Waysides

Beaches extend north and south from the mouth of the Siuslaw. For access to the dunes and beach south of Florence, turn west on South Jetty Road, south of the U.S. 101 bridge. On the north side of the river, take Rhododendron Drive west of U.S. 101 to North Jetty Road, Harbor Vista, and Heceta (huh-*see*-tah) Beach. Or, approach Heceta Beach by turning west off U.S. 101 onto Heceta Beach Road, north of town.

Also north of town, about 6 miles and just east of U.S. 101, is the **Darlingtonia Botanical Wayside,** with interpretive signs and a short trail through a bog where the rare *Darlingtonia californica* grows. This unusual plant, also known as the cobra lily or pitcher plant and native to southwestern Oregon and northwestern California, is carnivorous. Nectar lures insects into the opening under the plant's hood, where they become entrapped and are eventually consumed. These unusual plants bloom in May and June but are worth viewing any time.

If awards were given for most beautiful and best-kept parks, **Honeyman State Park** would certainly take top honors. Situated off both sides of U.S. 101, 3 miles south of Florence, this lovely park offers camping, picnicking, fishing and swimming in two lakes, and hiking on well-maintained trails.

Water Sports and Activities

About 6 miles south of Florence, Westlake Road exits east off U.S. 101 and leads to a public boat ramp and fishing dock on **Siltcoos Lake.** This is the largest lake on the Oregon coast, and it offers some of the best freshwater fishing in the Florence area. Angling here is mainly for trout and warm-water species, namely good populations of rainbows and native cutthroat, largemouth bass, bluegill, crappie, yellow perch, and brown bullhead. The lake also gets a small run of coho salmon in late fall.

The Siuslaw River is important to local anglers. The river rises in the Coast Range and switchbacks some 100 miles through the mountains to empty into the Pacific near Florence. The lower 20 miles are navigable by sport boats and offer a good variety of angling that is sometimes outstanding.

The estuary is good for surfperch and seaperch from early spring through summer. Anglers take flounder and other bottom species here as well. Crabbing is good from boats or docks, and clam digging is good on minus tides for cockles and soft-shell clams.

Although the river gives up the occasional striped bass or sturgeon, the main effort is for the migrating salmonids. Action picks up in later summer when schools of sea-run cutthroat enter the river and provide sport for trollers and spinfishermen from the estuary upstream to the head of tidewater near Mapleton.

Both coho and chinook salmon use the Siuslaw system, and angling for them can be quite good from September through November. Jack salmon move in with the cutthroat and are present through the fall months. Steelhead follow in December and are present upriver through the winter.

Florence

There are good launching facilities, moorage, and camp-grounds along the river from Florence to Mapleton, where State Route 126 parallels the river.

Golf

Florence Golf Course, 3315 Munsel Lake Road; 997–3232. Located 1.6 miles east of U.S. 101, just north of Florence. Attractive 9-hole, 2,700-yard public course with driving range, snack bar, pro shop, and cart and club rental.

Other Attractions

C & M Stables, 90241 U.S. 101 North; 997–7540 or 997–3021. East side of U.S. 101, 8 miles north of Florence. From Memorial Day to November 1: daily, 9:00 A.M. to dusk. From November 1 to Memorial Day: Wednesday through Sunday, 11:00 A.M. to 4:00 P.M. Half-hour and one-hour mountain horseback rides through stands of alder and mountain meadows. Beach rides up to three hours, and two-hour sunset rides. Daily, weekly, and monthly horse boarding.

Sea Lion Caves, 91560 U.S. 101; 547–3111. West side of U.S. 101 (parking on east side), 11 miles north of Florence, 38 miles south of Newport. Daily, 9:00 A.M. to 6:30 P.M. One of the most popular attractions on the Oregon coast. Huge natural sea cave is home to hundreds of sea lions. Walkways and stairways to elevator that descends 208 feet into the caves. Spectacular views of ocean, Heceta Head, and lighthouse. Good spot for watching birds and whales. Gift shop on premises.

Events

March   Rhododendron and Azalea Show, 997–8697
May   Rhododendron Festival, 997–3128
July   Independence Day Celebration, 997–3128
August   Salmon Barbecue, 997–3128
October   Fall Festival, 997–3128
December Christmas Parade and Party, 997–3128

Travel Information

Florence Chamber of Commerce, 270 U.S. 101; 997–3128

Mouth of the Yachats River

Yachats/Waldport, Oregon 97498/97394
Population: 560/1,590

Location: *Yachats is on U.S. 101, 8 miles south of Waldport, 24 miles north of Florence; Waldport is at the junction of U.S. 101 and State Route 34, on the south shore of Alsea Bay, 15 miles south of Newport, 65 miles west of Corvallis*

Yachats (*yah*-hots) is a corruption of the Chinook word *yahuts,* meaning "dark waters at the foot of the mountain," which is certainly descriptive of this area where the Coast Range abuts the ocean in an unyielding tumult of relentless surf against basalt bastions. On a calm day it can be an exciting contest to witness; in stormy weather it is awesome. Consequently, this is a favorite stretch of coastline for watching winter storms. It is equally popular for hiking, biking, and auto-touring in the summer.

That more than fifteen motels serve such a small community

67

should attest to the area's importance as a resort destination. Several motels are so near the sea that visitors not only can hear the pounding waves but also can feel them. The cocktail lounge at the Adobe has heavy plate-glass windowpanes to keep stormy seas from crashing right through.

South of town, **Cape Perpetua** offers one of the best views on the coast. Just south of the Devil's Churn, Klickitat Ridge Road (USFS Road No. 55) exits east off U.S. 101. About eight tenths of a mile beyond, turn north on USFS Road No. 5553, which leads to the **Cape Perpetua Overlook,** where, on a clear day, the view is as far south as Cape Blanco and north to Cape Foulweather.

Klickitat Ridge Road is also the starting point for a self-guided auto tour that leads into the forested Coast Range then back to Yachats, via Yachats River Road. The 22-mile trip with sixteen planned stops takes at least one hour, but you could easily devote a half day or more.

Waldport, settled in the 1870s and 1880s, is said to have derived its name from the German *Wald,* meaning "forest," and the English "port," making "forested port" a descriptive name. In the past, the wood-products industry was important here, but while logging remains a viable business, the sawmills are gone. Gone, too, are the canneries along the bay and river and all vestiges of once-thriving dairy farms.

Alsea (*al*-see) Bay and River were named after the Alsi tribe that lived here when the white settlers arrived. The word *alsi* means "peace." Peace has come to the Alsea River, which is now used primarily for recreation. And peaceful is an appropriate word to describe the tiny town of Waldport.

Lodging

The Adobe, 1555 U.S. 101; P.O. Box 219; Yachats; 547–3141. West side of U.S. 101. Queen beds, cable TV, and HBO in 56 units, most with an ocean view, some with fireplaces and balconies. Honeymoon suite and several apartment units available. Sauna and whirlpool. Comfortable cocktail lounge and superb restaurant and lounge on premises—both with ocean view. Moderate.

Cape Cod Cottages, 4150 Southwest Pacific Coast Highway; Waldport; 563–2106. West side of U.S. 101, 2 miles south of Waldport. Cable TV in 10 1-bedroom and 2-bedroom cottages with kitchens, fireplaces, decks, and garages. Cottages accommodate two to ten persons. Gift and lapidary shop on premises. Moderate.

Oceanaire Rest Bed & Breakfast, 95354 U.S. 101; Yachats; 547–3782. Six miles south of Yachats, 19 miles north of Florence. Two guest rooms with queen beds and ocean view—first floor with shared bath, second floor with private bath. Two decks, lounge with fireplace. Short hike through a meadow to the beach. Moderate.

The Oregon House, 94288 U.S. 101; Yachats; 547–3329. Nine miles south of Yachats, on three and a half acres with trees, creek, and ocean beach. Attractive and unusual lodging facilities offering 7 suites and studios accommodating two to eight persons—all units with kitchens, some with fireplaces—and 3 bed-and-breakfast rooms with private baths. Great ocean view, privacy, trail to driftwood-strewn beach. No phones, radios, or TV. Inexpensive to moderate.

Shamrock Lodgettes, P.O. Box 346; Yachats; 547–3312. West side of U.S. 101 in Yachats, on the south bank of the river. Cable TV and HBO in 19 units. Rooms with king beds, fireplaces, and whirlpool tubs. Some kitchen units. Individual log cabins with fireplaces and kitchens. Coffee and tea in rooms. Beach and river access. Moderate.

Ziggurat Bed & Breakfast, 95330 U.S. 101; Yachats; 547–3925. West side of U. S. 101, 6.5 miles south of Yachats, 18 miles north of Florence. Queen beds in 2 rooms with shared bath and 1 suite with private bath in an architecturally unusual and attractive building resembling a split-level pyramid. Decks, library, ocean view, easy beach access. Moderate to expensive.

Campgrounds and RV Parks

Beachside State Park, P.O. Box 1350; Newport 97365; 563–3220. West side of U.S. 101, 4 miles south of Waldport. Has 20 RV sites with electric and water hookups, picnic tables, and fireplaces; 61 tent sites with fireplaces, picnic tables, and nearby water. Showers, firewood, trails, and beach access. Reservations accepted. Moderate.

Cape Perpetua Campground, Siuslaw National Forest; 547–3289 (visitor center) or 563–3211 (Waldport Ranger Station). East of U.S. 101, 2.5 miles south of Yachats. Has 37 tent and trailer sites for RVs to 22 feet. Picnic tables, fireplaces, restrooms, tank dump, water, handicapped access. Hiking trails and beaches nearby. Inexpensive.

Sea Perch Campground, 95480 U.S. 101; Yachats; 547–3505. West side of U.S. 101, 5.8 miles south of Yachats. Has 20 RV sites with full hookups, picnic tables, and fire pits. Showers, laundry, cable TV, and beach access. Store with groceries, ice, deli foods, snacks, beer, and wine. Gift shop adjacent. Moderate.

Tillicum Beach Campground, Siuslaw National Forest; 563–3211. West side of U.S. 101, 4.5 miles south of Waldport. Has 57 sites for tents and RVs to 32 feet. Picnic tables, fireplaces, restrooms, and water. A beautiful campground set in the shore pines along the ocean. Summer naturalist programs. Inexpensive.

Carl W. Washburne Memorial State Park, 547–3416. West side of U.S. 101, 14 miles south of Yachats. Has 58 full-hookup RV sites and 8 tent sites. Showers and firewood. Fishing, hiking, beachcombing, kite flying, and clam digging. Good area for exploring tide pools. Moderate.

Food

The Adobe, 1555 U.S. 101; Yachats; 547–3141. West side of U.S. 101, in Yachats. Breakfast and dinner Monday through Saturday, brunch and dinner, Sunday. Unusual pancake and French toast dishes, sumptuous rolled omelets, Hangtown fry, and French-style and Spanish-style egg dishes. Soups, chowder, and oyster stew. Large appetizer menu, steaks, and chicken, but seafood is a specialty, with shrimp, scallops, crab, razor clams, combo plates, and wonderful Yaquina Bay oysters. Moderate.

La Serre Restaurant, Second and Beach; Yachats; 547–3420. West side of U.S. 101, downtown. Lunch and dinner daily, weekend breakfast. Poppy-seed griddle cakes, egg dishes, and omelets, including smoked salmon, shrimp, and fresh spinach and mushroom. Large, deli-style sandwiches, soups, and salads. Dinners include steaks, roasted chicken, chicken pot pie, and seafoods, such as razor clams, Dover sole with shrimp, bouillabaisse, and cioppino. Moderate.

Shopping and Browsing

Galerie De Chevrier, 430 U.S. 101 North; P.O. Box 189; Yachats; 547–3988. East side of U.S. 101, downtown. Daily, 11:00 A.M. to 5:00 P.M. Several artists represented here, with works in various media. Sculptures, photographs, oil paintings, acrylics, pastels, watercolors. Pen-and-ink, pencil, and charcoal drawings. Landscapes, fishing boats, and coastal scenes. Small but pleasing gallery.

Ragan Gallery, 95020 U.S. 101; Yachats; 547–3596. West side of U.S. 101, 6.7 miles south of Yachats. Daily, summer only. Interesting little gallery on the ocean, featuring the works of artists from California, Washington, and Oregon. Some excellent marine and wildlife art. Paintings, pottery, carvings, photographs, scratchboard, and prints.

The Raindrop Factory, Waldport; 563–3242. In the lighthouse on the east side of U.S. 101, south end of downtown. Daily, 10:00 A.M. to 5:00 P.M. Delicate crystal hummingbird and raindrop ornaments and jewelry made on the premises. Other Oregon-made items on sale, too.

Sea Rose, 95478 U.S. 101; Yachats; 547–3005. West side of U.S. 101, 5.8 miles south of Yachats. Daily, 10:00 A.M. to 5:00 P.M. Large, well-stocked shell and gift shop. Large selection of collector's shells. Glass floats, carvings, wind chimes, and more. Shell museum on premises. A *must see* for anyone interested in shells.

Beaches, Parks, Trails, and Waysides

The **Devil's Churn Wayside,** about 2 miles south of Yachats, is one of the most interesting diversions along the Oregon coast, especially on an incoming tide when the ocean is in a foul mood. Incoming waves rush landward up a narrow trench in the basalt rock. When they reach the end of the slit, they burst skyward with an explosive boom and shower of spray. Trails lead from the parking lot to the water's edge, where there are many tide pools to explore.

The **Cape Perpetua Visitor Center** is 2.5 miles south of Yachats, off the east side of U.S. 101. Stop here for information on and for maps of the cape and Siuslaw National Forest. The center is open daily in the summer from 9:00 A.M. to 6:00 P.M. and is closed

Wednesday and Thursday in the off-season. The visitor center offers interpretive displays, films, slide shows, an information desk, restrooms, and books and booklets for sale.

Water Sports and Activities

The main attraction in the Yachats area for fishermen are the silver smelt, which gather by the tens of thousands along the ocean beaches and rocky coves from mid-April to mid-October. Fishermen take them with long-handled, fine-mesh dipnets and seines. The fish are excellent fare, pan-fried or smoked. They're also good bait for a variety of game-fish species.

Lower Alsea Bay is a popular crabbing and clam-digging area. Crabbing requires a boat, but gathering cockles is easy with a shovel or rake and hip boots or waders. Farther upbay, along State Route 34, minus tides expose mud flats where you can dig soft-shell and horseneck clams.

Later summer offers excellent fishing for sea-run cutthroat trout and jack salmon on the lower bay and river. But the fall is prime time on the Alsea with good runs of coho and chinook salmon. The river is known for its strain of big chinook, and every year fish of forty to fifty pounds or more are caught. The best fishing is upriver, above the delta area, where the river narrows and deepens. For about 10 miles east of Waldport, there are campgrounds, RV parks, and marinas along State Route 34.

Golf

Crestview Hills Golf Course, 1680 Crestline Drive; 563–3020. Located 0.8 mile east of U.S. 101 on Range Drive, 1 mile south of Waldport (turn at the Burger Bar). Summer: daily, 7:00 A.M. to dusk. Off-season: daily, 8:00 A.M. to dusk. Nine-hole course, pro shop, club and cart rental. Restaurant on premises, open for breakfast and lunch.

Events

March	Yachats Arts & Crafts Festival, 547–3530
June	Beachcomber Days, Waldport, 563–4859

July   Fireworks, Waldport, 563–3752
               Community Smelt Fry, Yachats, 547–3530
September Salmon Derby and Bake, Waldport, 528–3251
               St. Jude's Bike-A-Thon, Waldport, 528-7741
               Port of Alsea Crab Derby, Waldport, 563–3872
October   Yachats Kite Festival, 547–3530
November   AARP Bazaar, Waldport, 563–4934
December   Community Christmas, Waldport, 563–3231

Travel Information

Siuslaw National Forest, Waldport Ranger Station; 563–3211
Waldport Chamber of Commerce, P.O. Box 669; 563–2133
Yachats Area Chamber of Commerce, P.O. Box 174; 547–3530

Yaquina Bay and Newport's Old Town waterfront

Newport, Oregon 97365
Population: 8,350

Location: *At the junction of U.S. 101 and U.S. 20, along the north shore of Yaquina Bay, 25 miles south of Lincoln City, 8 miles north of Waldport, and 57 miles west of Corvallis*

No doubt, Newport is coastal Oregon's premier resort destination. It is centrally located and situated on beautiful Yaquina Bay, with broad beaches extending north and south. It's an easy and pleasant drive from the population centers of the Willamette Valley, and it is only two hours from Portland. Moreover, it offers visitors a wide assortment and diversity of activities and accommodations, from crabbing and clam digging to a spirited nightlife, from windsurfing and scuba diving to shopping and art-gallery hopping, from golf courses and tennis courts to museums and theaters, from burger joints and pizza parlors to fine restaurants, from RV parks and budget motels to plush condominiums and luxurious resort hotels.

Newport has grown considerably in recent years, and not without suffering the consequences. Escape the urban sprawl and congestion, however, by getting off U.S. 101 and visiting the more charming parts of the city.

East of U.S. 101, along the north shore of Yaquina Bay, is the Old Town bayfront, with restaurants, shops, and galleries galore, mingled with the working waterfront businesses. With trucks and vans being loaded with fresh seafoods, and visitors and residents coming and going on narrow, crowded streets, gridlock is inevitable and parking impossible. But by planning the day and getting there early—say for breakfast—there should be no problem finding a parking spot.

Opposite Old Town, on the south shore of the bay, is the South Beach area, a *must see,* if for no other reason than a visit to the famed **Marine Science Center.** Also in this area are a huge marina, an RV park, a public fishing pier, access to the south jetty area, and more to come as plans for the future are fulfilled.

Something Newport doesn't have much of these days is an off-season. With the increasing popularity of watching whales and winter storms and the various winter festivals and activities, Newport is becoming a year-round resort town.

Lodging

Sylvia Beach Hotel, 267 Northwest Cliff; 265–5428. West of U.S. 101, on Nye Beach. Billed as an "oceanfront bed & breakfast for book lovers." Built between 1910 and 1913. Named after Sylvia Beach, a patron of literature and a Paris bookstore owner in the 1920s and 1930s. Has 20 rooms named after authors, each distinctly decorated: Agatha Christie, Mark Twain, E. B. White, Hemingway, Tennessee Williams, Willa Cather, Oscar Wilde. Rates include breakfast. Excellent restaurant on premises. Beer and wine list. Hot wine served in the library at 10:00 P.M. Moderate to expensive.

Embarkadero Resort Hotel & Marina, 1000 Southeast Bay Boulevard; 265–8521. East of U.S. 101 on the north shore of the bay. One- and 2-bedroom condo units with kitchens, cable TV, fireplaces, queen beds, and decks overlooking the marina and bay.

Restaurant and lounge on the premises. Moorage, bait-and-tackle shop, boat and moped rentals. Fishing and crabbing from private docks. Fish-cleaning station, crab cooker, and barbecue pit. Heated indoor pool, sauna, and whirlpool. Moderate to expensive.

Moolack Shores Motel, Star Route, Box 420; 265–2326. West side of U.S. 101, 3 miles north of Newport. A dozen thematically decorated rooms, plus a guesthouse, beach house, and condominium—all with cable TV. Antique, nautical, whaling, western, and Hawaiian motifs, as well as Racer's Room, Camelot Room, Art Gallery Room, Hunting Lodge, and Oregon Room. Most rooms with ocean view, fireplaces, vaulted and beamed ceilings, and queen beds. Some have decks and kitchens. All have binoculars for whale and wildlife watching. Moderate to expensive.

Oar House Bed & Breakfast, 520 Southwest Second; 265–9571. Two blocks west of U.S. 101, between Hurbert and Brook streets. Two rooms with king and queen beds and private baths. Indoor whirlpool and sauna. The attractive three-story structure has a lookout tower with widow's walk to command a 360-degree view of ocean, beach, and community. Full breakfast. Moderate.

Shilo Inn, 536 Southwest Elizabeth; 265–7701 or 1–800–222–2244. West of U.S. 101, in the Nye Beach area. Watch for signs. Queen and king beds, cable TV, and Showtime in a variety of accommodations at this full-service resort. Main complex with 112 rooms, 2 family units, 1 master suite, heated indoor pool, and 4J's Restaurant. Also, 60 rooms, 3 parlor suites, 1 luxury suite, heated indoor pool, and Flagship Restaurant in the new addition. Suites and rooms available with in-room whirlpool tubs and kitchenettes. All rooms have remote-control TV, refrigerator, and king or queen beds. Ocean view. Moderate to expensive.

Campgrounds and RV Parks

Beverly Beach State Park, Star Route North; Box 684; 265–9278. East side of U.S. 101, 6.3 miles north of Newport, 6.5 miles south of Depoe Bay. Has 279 campsites: 52 full-hookup, 75 electric-hookup, 152 tent. Showers, tank dump, and firewood. Hiking trails and easy access to several miles of broad beach. Situated along Spencer Creek in a beautiful park setting, with protected sites in wooded area. Reservations accepted. Moderate.

Newport Marine & RV Park, 600 Southeast Bay Boulevard;

867–3321. East of U.S. 101, on south shore of bay, at South Beach. Has 38 RV sites near store and tackle shop, charter service, restaurant, public fishing pier, launch ramp, and full-service marina. Showers, full hookups, cable TV. Moderate.

Pacific Shores RV Resort, 6225 North Coast Highway; 265–3750 or 1–800–666–6313. About 3 miles north of Newport, on west side of U.S. 101. Has 287 sites, 100 pull-throughs, full hookups, cable TV, fire pits, picnic tables, showers, laundry, heated indoor pool, sauna, whirlpool, exercise room, and ocean view. Two adult lounges with TVs, fireplaces, and game tables. Billiard room, game room, children's lounge, and playground. Convenience store and gift shop on premises. Ice and propane available. Nature trails. Moderate to expensive.

South Beach State Park, P.O. Box 1350; 867–3011. West off U.S. 101, 2 miles south of Newport. Has 265 sites, each with water, electricity, picnic table, and fireplace. Showers, tank dump, and firewood. Easy beach access. Reservations accepted. Moderate.

Food

Flagship Restaurant, 358 Elizabeth Street; 265–2449. At the Shilo Inn, on Nye Beach. Lunch and dinner daily. Great luncheon specialties, such as shrimp-stuffed tomatoes, Louisiana-style shrimp, grilled Pacific oysters, taco salad, lox and bagels, burgers, and other sandwiches, as well as soups, chowder, and oyster stew. For dinner, such tempting appetizers as bagel chips and lox mousse, stuffed mushrooms, and a half-dozen others; special salads; and entrees of halibut, oysters, razor clams, stuffed sole, prawns, scallops, lobster, various steaks, chicken, and pasta. Full bar, including fifty-five imported beers. Moderate.

Mo's and Mo's Annex, 622 and 657 Southwest Bay Boulevard; (Mo's) 265–2979; (Annex) 265–7512. In Old Town bayfront district. Lunch and dinner daily. Local chain chowder and fish house, serving burgers, salads, soups, chili, clam chowder, oyster stew, fish and chips, and seafood sandwiches. Large dinner menu with such seafood favorites as salmon, halibut, lingcod, clam fritters, oysters, prawns, scallops, calamari, and cioppino. Beer and wine. Moderate.

Tables of Content, 267 Northwest Cliff; 265–5428. At Sylvia Beach Hotel, west of U.S. 101, on Nye Beach. Dinner daily, by reservation. Most meals are based around the freshest seafoods available in season. Menu changes each night, and dinners served family style. Sample menu includes smoky currant soup, tossed salad, honey whole wheat bread, lingcod Dijonaise, asparagus with walnut butter, oven-roasted potatoes, chocolate Grand Marnier cheesecake, and coffee or tea. Reasonable price includes everything from appetizer to dessert. Beer and wine available. Phone for day's menu. Moderate.

Welton's Towne House, 5251 North Coast Highway; 265–7263. Just south of Pacific Shores RV Resort, about 2 miles north of Newport, on west side of U.S. 101. Dinner daily. Menu includes appetizers, shrimp or crab Louis, steaks and prime rib, light dinners, and a large selection of seafoods. Seafood specialties are Dungeness crab legs, sea scallops, curried prawns, Cajun barbecued prawns, Eastern-style crab cakes, and seafood fettuccine. Great homemade desserts. Cocktails, beer, and wine. Excellent view from one of the area's finest supper clubs. Complimentary limousine service from Lincoln City to Newport and points between, in either black or white Cadillac limo. Expensive.

The Whale's Tale, 452 Southwest Bay Boulevard; 265–8660. In Old Town bayfront district. Breakfast, lunch, and dinner daily. Delicious egg dishes include huevos rancheros, eggs Benedict, and eight great omelets. Poppy-seed pancakes made with stone-ground wheat flour are a breakfast favorite. Burgers, deli-style sandwiches, soups, chowder, stews, and salads round out lunch menu. Popular dinners include a seafood sauté, grilled Yaquina oysters, mussels marinara, lasagna, cioppino, and German plate: a selection of sausage and meat, German potato salad, sauerkraut, and wonderful homemade black bread. Also, some excellent dinner specials. Beer and wine. Moderate.

Shopping and Browsing

Facets Gem & Mineral Gallery, 1125 Southwest Coast Highway; 265–6330. East side of U.S. 101, just north of the bridge. Large selection of shells, gemstones, mineral specimens, jewelry, and various gift items, tastefully displayed. Many rare and hard-to-find collector's items, including fine, museum-quality fossils. An interesting shop for nearly everyone. A *must see* for those interested in minerals, gemstones, fossils, and the like.

Oceanic Arts, 444 Southwest Bay Boulevard; 265–5963. In Old Town bayfront district. Daily, 10:00 A.M. to 6:00 P.M. Large gallery featuring a great variety of works in different media. Originals, prints, and contemporary crafts. Excellent custom-matting and framing services as well.

Rickert Gallery, 754 Southwest Bay Boulevard; 265–5430. In Old Town bayfront district. Daily, 10:00 A.M. to 5:30 P.M. A small, but pleasing, gallery featuring fine marine and wildlife art, limited-edition prints, oils, acrylics, and watercolors. More than thirty artists represented.

Rocky Joe's, 4424 North Coast Highway; 265–7368. East side of U.S. 101, north of Newport. Well-stocked rock shop offering gemstones, crystals, craft supplies, jewelry, and lapidary equipment. Information on local rock hounding.

The Wood Gallery, 818 Southwest Bay Boulevard; 265–6843. In Old Town bayfront district. Daily, 10:00 A.M. to 6:00 P.M. One of the finest and most interesting galleries on the coast. Many artworks and gift items. Best wood products and carvings to be found. Wildlife, marine art, whimsical objects—even an entire Porsche engine duplicated in wood at full scale. Mark this one *must see.*

Museums

Burrows House Museum, 545 Southwest Ninth; 265–7509. One block east of U.S. 101, just beyond the visitor information center. June through September, 10:00 A.M. to 5:00 P.M.; October through May, 11:00 A.M. to 4:00 P.M. Closed Monday. Built in 1895. Displays depicting Lincoln County history, as well as period clothing and household antiques. Headquarters for Lincoln County Historical Society.

Mark O. Hatfield Marine Science Center, Marine Science Drive; 867–3011. East of U.S. 101, on the south shore of the bay, at South Beach. Daily, 10:00 A.M. to 4:00 P.M. Outstanding museum and aquarium operated by Oregon State University. Many fine marine wildlife exhibits, ship models, aquaria, a hands-on tide pool, and book shop. Summer Seataqua program offers lectures, walks, tours, trips, workshops, and films. No admission fee. Classified a *must see.*

Log Cabin Museum, 579 Southwest Ninth; 265–2013. One block east of U.S. 101, next to Burrows House. June through September: daily, 10:00 A.M. to 5:00 P.M. Good collection of Indian artifacts, logging apparatus, farm implements and tools, maritime exhibits, and old photographs of the area.

Beaches, Parks, Trails, and Waysides

The Newport area is blessed with an abundance of beaches with excellent access north and south off U.S. 101, in town off Elizabeth Street and Coast Street, and between Agate Beach and Newport off Ocean View Drive.

South Beach State Park lies west of the highway about 2 miles south of town. Here are several miles of broad beach for hiking and beachcombing and two picnic areas—one near the beach and the other in a spot sheltered by trees and dunes.

Agate Beach is in a small community by the same name, north of Newport and west of U.S. 101. The beach is a favorite of rock hounds who search the sands for agates, jasper, and petrified wood.

Farther north is **Beverly Beach,** with ample parking along the west side of U.S. 101. The beach is wide and windswept and is a favorite spot for flying kites. There's even a kite shop nearby. Also close by is a state park for picnics out of the wind.

Nye Beach is right in town, flanked on the west by the tumbling Pacific surf and on the east by one of Newport's older neighborhoods. This is also where most of the town's resort hotels stand.

Also in town, just north and west of the U.S. 101 bridge, is **Yaquina Bay State Park,** situated atop a bluff overlooking the north jetty and commanding a view of the bridge, bay, and ocean. In the park are many beautiful picnic sites and an old lighthouse.

The **Yaquina Bay Lighthouse,** which combines the keeper's quarters and light tower, is the oldest building in Newport. It was erected to serve as a harbor-entrance light, which first shone on November 3, 1871. Its life as a working lighthouse was short, because, as any Kansas landlubber could tell at first glance, the light was invisible to ships approaching from the north.

In 1974, the state restored the old lighthouse and furnished it with antiques on loan from the Oregon Historical Society. It is now on the National Register of Historic Places.

As any self-respecting deserted lighthouse ought to be, the

Yaquina Bay Lighthouse has been haunted for most of its years, and yarns about its netherworld inhabitants abound. It is said to have guided ships through fog and unfriendly seas long after its lamp was snuffed.

Newport has another lighthouse that has been serving this stretch of coast since August of 1873, but even this stalwart sentinel, which seems to have been placed ideally on a westward promontory to serve as both a harbor and seacoast light, was built in the wrong place. It was to have been erected at Otter Crest, several miles north, but the building materials were mistakenly landed on Yaquina Head, with no small amount of effort and danger to men and their vessels. When the mistake was discovered, nobody had any interest in reloading the materials, via the angry surf, and taking them north to their proper destination. Instead, the new structure became the **Yaquina Head Light,** rather than the Otter Crest Light.

Water Sports and Activities

Yaquina Bay is an active center for waterborne recreation of every kind. Bay anglers catch perch and bottom fish from the jetties, shore, docks, and the public fishing pier. Crabbers, working from docks, piers, and boats, take tasty Dungeness crabs. Minus tides expose mud flats and bring out the clam diggers.

Offshore, salmon are popular but are often overshadowed by the plentiful and more reliable bottom species. Reefs and other offshore structures here are among the most productive fishing grounds along the coast. A large charter fleet, headquartered at Yaquina Bay, plies these waters, with several trips a day when the weather is good.

Additionally, charter operations offer long trips to tuna grounds and halibut habitats well offshore, as well as shorter bay cruises and sightseeing trips. Bay crabbing trips and whale-watching excursions are also popular.

Newport Marina, 600 Southeast Bay Boulevard; 867–3321. East of U.S. 101, on the south shore of the bay, at South Beach. Has 600 rental slips for vessels up to 58 feet. RV spaces, cable TV, launch ramp, sling hoist, and boat-trailer parking.

Newport Sportfishing, Embarcadero Marina, 1000 Southeast Bay Boulevard; 265–7558 (24-hour phone). East of U.S. 101, on the north side of the bay. Four- and five-hour salmon trips, seven- and nine-hour combination trips, five-hour trips to inner reefs, eight-hour trips to "the rockpile," and twelve-hour trips to Heceta Banks for halibut. Bay crabbing and diving trips. Whale-watching and sightseeing excursions. Sailboat excursions.

Newport Tradewinds, 653 Southwest Bay Boulevard; 265–2101 (24-hour phone). In the Old Town bayfront district. Five-hour salmon and bottomfishing trips, ten-hour combination trips. Eight-hour trips to "the rockpile," and twelve-hour trips to Heceta Banks for halibut and reef species. August to October, twelve-hour and thirty-three-hour trips for albacore tuna from 50 to 100 miles off-shore. Bay crabbing. Whale-watching and scenic cruises.

Newport Water Sports, South Jetty Road; 867–3742. West of U.S. 101, south side of the bay. Weekdays, 9:00 A.M. to 5:00 P.M.; Saturday, until 6:00 P.M.; Sunday, until 4:00 P.M. Complete scuba shop. Equipment sales and rental. Sailboards, surfboards, boogie boards. Fishing tackle and bait. Ice, beer, and pop.

South Beach Charters, P.O. Box 1446; 867–7200. East side of U.S. 101, on south shore of the bay, at South Beach. Five-hour salmon and bottomfish trips. Eight-hour bottomfish, nine-hour combination, and twelve-hour halibut trips. Light-tackle fishing. Ocean and river excursions.

Golf

Agate Beach Golf Course, 4100 Northeast Golf Course Drive; 265–7331. About 2.5 miles north of Newport city center, east side of U.S. 101. Nine-hole course with ocean view, pro shop, resident pro, driving range, and rental carts. Cafe on premises.

Events

February	Seafood & Wine Festival, 265–8801
May	Loyalty Days & Seafair Festival, 265–8801
June	Oregon Coast Gem & Mineral Show, 265–6330
	Red, White, and Blue Kite Festival, 994–9500
July	Lincoln County Fair & Rodeo, 265–6237
November	Santa Claus Comes to Town, 265–8801
December	Whale Watch Week, 867–3011

Weather and Tide Information

U.S. Coast Guard, Newport; recorded message, 265–5511

Travel Information

Greater Newport Chamber of Commerce, 555 Southwest Coast Highway; 265–8801 or 1–800–262–7844

Otter Crest, south of Depoe Bay

Depoe Bay, Oregon 97341
Population: 800

Location: *On U.S. 101, 12 miles north of Newport, 12 miles south of Lincoln City*

Depoe Bay is a tiny town with a tiny harbor. A 50-foot-wide channel cuts 300 feet through rocky shoreline to connect the Pacific with a harbor that's only 750 feet long, 390 feet wide, and 8 feet deep at mean low tide. Nevertheless, more than 100 commercial and sport boats are moored here all year, and another 150 crowd in during the summer. The attraction, of course, is the proximity of the ocean—from dock to sea in two minutes.

Sharp-eyed film buffs will recognize the harbor, which was featured in the movie *One Flew Over the Cuckoo's Nest*, based on the novel by Oregon author Ken Kesey. This is where Randle Mc-Murphy (Jack Nicholson) took his fellow escapees aboard a charter boat and headed out for a day of salmon fishing.

84

U.S. 101 is close to the ocean at Depoe Bay, where storm-tossed breakers wet the pavement and promenade and shoot misty geysers 60 feet into the air through spouting horns. Two such natural fountains exist in the volcanic rubble next to the seawall in downtown Depoe Bay.

Lodging

Channel House Bed & Breakfast Inn, P.O. Box 56; 765–2140. West side of U.S. 101, along the south bank of the harbor channel, next to the bridge. Double, queen, and king beds in 11 units, cable TV and Showtime. Kitchen units available. Spectacular ocean and channel view. Walk to harbor and shops. Rates include full breakfast for two. Moderate to expensive.

Surfrider Motel & Restaurant, P.O. Box 219; 764–2311. West side of U.S. 101, just north of Depoe Bay, at the mouth of Fogarty Creek. Queen and king beds in 40 units, cable TV, Showtime, and refrigerators. Kitchen units available. Some rooms have in-room whirlpools. Some have fireplaces. Also 3-bedroom house available, 1 1/2 baths, sleeps twelve. Beach access. Oceanfront balconies and patios. Excellent restaurant on premises is a local favorite. Moderate.

Campgrounds and RV Parks

Holiday RV Park, P.O. Box 433; 765–2302; Oregon, 1–800–452–2104. West side of U.S. 101, at north end of town. Has 110 ocean-view and oceanfront sites with full hookups and cable TV. Pull-throughs, showers, heated indoor pool, sauna, whirlpool, game room, playground, and laundry. Store on premises. Propane available. Moderate to expensive.

Food

Sea Hag Food & Grog, P.O. Box 278; 765–2734. East side of U.S. 101, north of the bridge, downtown. Breakfast, lunch, and dinner daily. Breakfast fare includes omelets, egg dishes, and homemade biscuits and gravy. Sandwiches, chowder, and salad bar are luncheon specialties. Fresh seafood dominates the dinner menu. Friday seafood buffet includes salmon, halibut, lingcod, steamer clams, crab, shrimp—all you can eat. Cocktails, beer, and wine. Moderate.

Surfrider Restaurant, P.O. Box 219; 764–2311. West side of U.S. 101, just north of Depoe Bay, at Surfrider Motel. Breakfast, lunch, and dinner daily. Excellent breakfast menu includes various egg dishes, omelets, hotcakes, fruit waffles, and rollups. Large selection of traditional sandwiches, soups, seafoods, and salads fill out the lunch menu. Dinners include a variety of fish and shellfish, beef, chicken, ham, and liver. Wednesday buffet from 5:00 to 10:00 P.M. features prime rib or seafood plate at a bargain price. Cocktails, beer, and wine. Moderate.

Shopping and Browsing

Richard Hazelton Art Gallery, 479 Northwest U.S. 101; P.O. Box 171; 765–2720. West side of highway, a quarter mile north of the bridge. March through October: daily, 10:00 A.M. to 5:00 P.M. November through February: Friday through Sunday, 10:00 A.M. to 4:00 P.M. A deceptively large and pleasing gallery, displaying paintings and limited-edition prints as well as pottery, wood carvings, and stained glass. Superb marine and wildlife art.

The Lookout Observatory and Gift Shop, P.O. Box 248; 765–2270. West of U.S. 101, on Otter Crest Loop, between Depoe Bay and Newport. Weekdays, 9:00 A.M. to 5:30 P.M.; weekends, until 6:00 P.M. Many products made of Oregon myrtlewood and cedar, nautical items, shells, coral, prints, and jewelry. Situated atop Cape Foulweather, 500 feet above the ocean. Ample parking provided by the state. Excellent lookout area.

Recollections Antiques, P.O. Box 652; 765–2221. East side of U.S. 101, just north of downtown. Summer: daily, 10:00 A.M. to 7:00 P.M. Winter: daily, 11:00 A.M. to 4:00 P.M. A small but tastefully arranged shop, featuring antiques as well as old and new collectibles.

Something Blue, 104 Southeast U.S. 101; P.O. Box 447; 765–4323. East side of the highway, next to Fuddy Duddy Fudge. Daily, 10:00 A.M. to 5:00 P.M. A country-style variety shop, featuring clothing, stuffed animals, cookware, baskets, wood products, art prints, candy, cookbooks, and more.

Beaches, Parks, Trails, and Waysides

Boiler Bay State Park, 1 mile north of Depoe Bay, overlooks a picturesque cove where a small disabled freighter drifted ashore on May 18, 1910. The steam schooner *J. Marhoffer* caught fire while steaming northward above Yaquina Head. Officers and crew were forced to abandon ship, and the burning vessel eventually went aground. Her boiler and shaft broke loose, and the rest of the ship eventually succumbed to the fire and ravages of nature. But the boiler remains, even today, visible at low tide. Hence the name, Boiler Bay.

Two miles north of town is **Fogarty Creek State Park,** which is the site of an annual Indian-style salmon bake. This is a beautiful picnic spot with a creek to wade and explore, hiking trails, and a small but attractive beach.

South of Depoe Bay, **Otter Crest Loop** takes travelers along a stretch of forested coastline with dizzying cliffs and promontories offering great ocean views. **Otter Crest State Park** is situated atop cape Foulweather, 500 feet above the surf. Here, clear weather offers views north, south, and seaward for miles. This is a good spot for watching whales.

Water Sports and Activities

Water recreation in the Depoe Bay area amounts mainly to ocean fishing and sightseeing, both of which are year-round activities, weather permitting. Those who tow boats to the coast will find a launch ramp at the harbor, east of U.S. 101. For others, there's a fleet of charter boats specializing in salmon angling and fishing the nearby reefs for bottom species. They also offer whale-watching and sightseeing excursions.

Dockside Charters, P.O. Box 1308; 765–2545. East side of the bay, next to the Coast Guard Station. Daily five-hour trips for salmon and bottomfish. Whale-watching and sightseeing trips from under an hour to four hours.

Tradewinds, P.O. Box 123; 765–2345. Depoe Bay harbor, east side of U.S. 101, north end of the bridge. Charter service with twelve-vessel fleet. Five-hour salmon trips leave three times a day, bottomfish trips twice daily. Long-distance trips and all-day tuna trips in season. One-hour and two-hour whale-watching trips. Sightseeing trips of up to an hour leave every hour.

Depoe Bay

Events

January	Celebration of the Whales, 765–2889
May	Fleet of Flowers Memorial Service, 765–2345
September	Indian-style Salmon Bake, 765–2889

Travel Information

Depoe Bay Chamber of Commerce, P.O. Box 21; 765–2889

Winter Storm near Roads End Wayside

Lincoln City, Oregon 97365
Population: 6,035

Location: *On U.S. 101, 42 miles south of Tillamook, 24 miles north of Newport, and 88 miles southwest of Portland*

On December 8, 1964, the cities of Oceanlake, Delake, and Taft and the unincorporated communities of Cutler City and Nelscott combined to form Lincoln City. Evidence of the five districts still exists in the names of businesses, in listings on maps, and in the diversity of architectural and urban planning, or the lack of planning—business, industrial, and residential areas are strung together along U.S. 101, interspersed with wooded areas and vacant land. An art gallery might be neighbors with a construction company; a nice restaurant might be adjacent to a lumber yard. Overlook these minor shortcomings and enjoy a visit to Lincoln City.

The townspeople boast of having more oceanfront rooms

available than any other city on the Oregon coast. The city also has several fine restaurants, a variety of interesting shops, and some topnotch galleries, not to mention the beaches, parks, opportunities for indoor and outdoor recreation, and a couple of interesting oddities.

For example, the golf course just north of town straddles the forty-fifth parallel, the midway point between the equator and the North Pole.

Lodging

The Brey House Bed & Breakfast, 3725 Northwest Keel; 994–7123. West of U.S. 101 in the Roads End area, off Northwest Logan Road. Two guest rooms with fireplaces and shared bath. Cable TV, pool table, dart board, horseshoe pit, barbecue grill, picnic table, exercise room, and hot tub. Kitchen privileges by arrangement. Short walk to the beach. Near shops and restaurants. Full breakfast. Moderate.

'D' Sands Motel, 171 Southwest U.S. 101; 994–5244. West side of U.S. 101 in the Delake district, next to D River Wayside. Has 63 condominium units with full kitchens, balconies, and cable TV, some with fireplaces. Heated indoor pool and whirlpool. On the beach. Walk to galleries, shops, and restaurants. Moderate.

Ocean Terrace Condominium Motel, 4229 Southwest Beach; 996–3623 or 1–800–648–2119. West of U.S. 101 in the Taft district. Has 36 rentable units with kitchens, queen and king beds, cable TV, and Showtime. Some with electric fireplaces. Beach access—forty steps to the sand. Heated indoor pool, sauna, ocean view. Moderate to expensive.

Salishan Lodge, Gleneden Beach, Oregon 97388; 764–3600; Oregon, 1–800–452–2300; elsewhere, 1–800–547–6500. East side of U.S. 101, 3 miles south of Lincoln City. Award-winning resort features 150 luxurious rooms with king beds, cable TV, balconies, fireplaces, and view of golf course, forest, or Siletz Bay. Heated indoor pool, sauna, whirlpool, golf course, indoor and outdoor tennis courts, miles of hiking trails, secluded beach, restaurants, gift shop, art gallery, library, beauty salon, fitness center, children's game room and playground, and covered bridges and walkways to main lodge. Expensive.

Sea Gypsy, 145 Northwest Inlet; 994–5266; Oregon, 1–800–

452–6929; elsewhere, 1–800–341–2142. West one block off U.S. 101, north bank of D River, Delake district. Queen and king beds in 159 studio, 1-bedroom, and 2-bedroom condo units with fully equipped kitchens, cable TV, and Showtime. Heated indoor pool and sauna. Ocean view. On the beach. Moderate.

Shilo Inn, 1501 Northwest 40th Street; 994–3655 or 1–800–222–2244. West off U.S. 101 at the north end of town, just before Lighthouse Square shopping center. Queen and king beds in 197 comfortably appointed rooms with satellite TV, Showtime, and refrigerators. Heated indoor pool, sauna, whirlpool, gift shop, game room, laundry, cocktail lounge with evening entertainment, restaurant, and room service. On the ocean with easy beach access. Moderate to expensive.

Surftides Beach Resort, 2945 Northwest Jetty Avenue; P.O. Box 406A; 994–2191; Oregon, 1–800–452–2159. West of U.S. 101 in the Oceanlake district. Has 91 rooms and suites with queen and king beds, cable TV, and balconies, most with ocean view. Heated indoor pool, sauna, whirlpool, tennis courts, gift shop, and gallery. Moderate.

Campgrounds and RV Parks

West Devils Lake State Park, 1450 Northeast Sixth Drive; 994–2002. One mile east of U.S. 101. Has 32 full-hookup and 68 tent sites. Showers, tank dump, and firewood. On Devils Lake with boat-launch facilities. Short drive or walk to ocean beach, shop, and restaurants. Reservations accepted. Moderate.

KOA Kampground, Route 2; Box 255; Otis 97368; 994–2961. On East Devils Lake Road, 1.3 miles east of U.S. 101, north of Devils Lake and Lincoln City. Full hookups, cable TV, showers, firewood, game and recreation room, horseshoes. Propane available. Near lake, ocean, and beaches. Moderate.

Food

Bay House Restaurant, 5911 Southwest U.S. 101; P.O. Box 1010; 996–3222. West side of U.S. 101, south end of town, in the Cutler City district. Dinner daily. Carefully prepared dinners include rack of lamb, Tuscan brochettes, steak and seafood combo, steamed shellfish, Australian rock lobster tail, and prawns. Cocktails, beer, and wine. Large wine list. Good view of Siletz Bay. Expensive.

Dory Cove, 5819 Logan Road; 994–5180. West 0.7 mile off U.S. 101 at the north end of town. Turn at Lighthouse Square. Lunch and dinner daily. Great fish and chips, chowder, burgers, grilled fillets, and steaks. Homemade pies. Beer and wine. Casual dining in a beautiful oceanfront setting. Moderate.

The Gourmet Room, Salishan Lodge; Gleneden Beach 97388; 764–3635. East side of U.S. 101, 3 miles south of Lincoln City. Dinner daily. Appetizers such as lobster bisque with cognac, scallops Normandy, Oregon shrimp cocktail, and French mushroom salad. Dinners include fresh local seafoods, beef, pork, and rack of Oregon lamb—a Salishan specialty. Largest wine list on the West Coast, with more than 1,500 offerings, including foreign, domestic, and Oregon wines. The cellar is stocked with more than 21,000 bottles. Expensive.

Kip's Restaurant, 4095-B Northwest Logan Road; 994–3736. At Lincoln City Plaza, west side of U.S. 101, north end of town. Lunch and dinner daily. Italian menu with deli-style sandwiches, soups, salads. Spaghetti, ravioli, tortellini, manicotti, lasagna, cannelloni, and clam linguine, served with salad and garlic bread. One of the best dining bargains on the coast. Beer and wine. Inexpensive.

Lighthouse Brew Pub, 4157 North U.S. 101; Suite 117; 994–7238. At Lighthouse Square, west side of U.S. 101, north end of town. Daily, 11:00 A.M. to 11:00 P.M. Brewery and pub—a great spot for anyone who enjoys beers, ales, and stouts. Has 25 brews on tap, including a half-dozen made on the premises. Hot deli-style sandwiches, pizza bread, burgers, soups, or salads. Food and brews to go. Moderate.

Shilo Restaurant & Lounge, 1501 Northwest 40th Street; 994–5255. West off U.S. 101 at the north end of town. Breakfast, lunch, and dinner daily. Extensive menu includes hearty breakfasts of hotcakes, waffles, crepes, omelets, croissant Benedict, New York steak and eggs, and various combinations. Lunch features deli-style and grilled sandwiches, large salads, pastas, seafood, and chicken. Appetizer and snack list includes smoked seafood platter, seafood sampler cocktail, oyster shooters, and more. Dinner features a large selection of salads and pasta dishes, beef, lamb, chicken, and fresh seafood: veal au lemon with pinenuts, scallops with chicken and tarragon, blackened sturgeon, Szechuan bay shrimp sauté, or orange roughy hazelnut. Full bar and wine list. Superb ocean view in lounge and dining restaurant. Moderate.

Welton's Sip & Sand, 317 Southwest U.S. 101; 994–3550. West side of U.S. 101 in the Delake district. Breakfast, lunch, and dinner daily. Breakfast is hearty helpings of traditional and unusual, including eleven omelets. For the biggest appetites, the Deli Gut Buster is three eggs, ham, bacon, sausage, spuds, a pancake or two, toast, and muffins. Lunch features deli-style sandwiches and a dozen different burgers, soups, chowder, chili, and salads. Dinners include veal cutlet, ham steak, New York steak, fish and chips, crab cakes, oysters, and steamer clams. Everything is homemade here and made from scratch, including sauces, dressings, jams, breads, biscuits, desserts, and ice cream. Cocktails, beer, and wine. Moderate.

Shopping and Browsing

Honeywood Winery & Tasting Room, 30 Southeast U.S. 101; 994–2755. East side of the highway at D River Village. Weekdays; 9:00 A.M. to 5:00 P.M.; Saturday, 10:00 A.M. to 5:00 P.M.; Sunday, 1:00 to 5:00 P.M. Fruit wines, including blackberry, apricot, spiced apple, rhubarb. Eight varietal wines, including chardonnay, pinot noir, and white riesling. Available by the bottle, three-pack, half-case, and case. Complimentary wine tasting.

Judith Anne's Antiques, 412 Southeast U.S. 101; 994–9912. East side of U.S. 101, across from Pier 101 in the Delake district. Wednesday through Sunday, 10:00 A.M. to 5:00 P.M. An uncluttered, tastefully arranged shop featuring a wide variety of antiques, furniture, artworks, and collectibles. Good selection of china, crystal, glassware, jewelry, and more.

Lincoln Art & Gift Gallery, 620 Northeast U.S. 101; 994–5839. East side of U.S. 101, in the Delake district. Summer: daily, 9:00 A.M. to 9:00 P.M. Off-season: daily, 10:00 A.M. to 6:00 P.M. A large selection of gift items and exquisite wildlife and marine art.

Mossy Creek Pottery, P.O. Box 368; Gleneden Beach 97388; 996–2415. A half-mile east of U.S. 101 on Immonen Road, 3 miles south of Lincoln City, just north of the traffic light in Gleneden Beach. Daily, 9:00 A.M. to 5:00 P.M.; Sunday open at 10:00 A.M. Charming gallery and studio in idyllic setting. The fine works of nearly

Lincoln City

twenty Oregon potters tastefully displayed and available in all price ranges.

Nelscott Leatherworks, 3259 Southwest U.S. 101; 996–3316. West side of the highway on the Nelscott Strip, with several nice shops. Daily, 10:00 A.M. to 5:00 P.M. Fine handmade leather products: jackets, hats, purses, belts, luggage, briefcases. Beautifully made items at reasonable prices.

Oceanlake Studio Gallery, 20 Southeast U.S. 101; 994–5335. East side of the highway, across from D River Wayside. Daily, 10:00 A.M. to 5:00 P.M. Fine watercolors, oils, acrylics, limited-edition prints, sculptures, and gift items. The Hall of Living Light exhibit—a remarkable display of John Plumer Ludlum's unique paintings that change character according to ambient light levels—is stunning. The museum-quality exhibit is valued at more than $6 million.

Ocean Memories, 565 Northwest U.S. 101; 994–9447 or 994–8429. West side of the highway at Seven Gables Shops, in the Delake district. Summer: daily, 10:00 A.M. to 5:00 P.M. Closed Tuesday and Wednesday in off-season. Chock-full of shells, clocks, T-shirts, windsocks, cards, nautical items, and many other gifts and souvenirs. A good browse.

Pickering Studio, 3200 Southeast U.S. 101; 996–4111 or 996–2321. East side of the highway, in the Nelscott district. Monday through Saturday, 10:00 A.M. to 5:00 P.M.; Sunday, noon to 5:00 P.M. A fine gallery, offering paintings, sculptures, carvings, and many unusual or unique works. Good selection of wildlife and marine art. Antiques and collectibles.

Ryan's Oceanside Gallery, 4270 North U.S. 101; 994–5391. East side of the highway, north end of town. Daily, 10:00 A.M. to 5:00 P.M. Spacious and pleasant gallery with 3,000 square feet of exhibit area on two levels. Carvings, metal sculptures, batiks, oils, and watercolors. Good selection of wildlife, marine, and Western art.

Snug Harbor Antiques, 5030 Southeast U.S. 101; 996–4021. East side of the highway, in the Taft district. Summer: Tuesday through Thursday, 10:00 A.M. to 4:00 P.M. Winter: Thursday through Sunday, 10:00 A.M. to 4:00 P.M. Top-quality antique furniture, appliances, cookware, and collectibles. An interesting shop.

Beaches, Parks, Trails, and Waysides

More than 7 miles of beaches extend northward from Siletz (suh-*lets*) Bay to Roads End, north of Lincoln City. This great expanse of beach is popular for hiking, kite flying, and other ocean-front activities and is easily accessible for the entire length of the city. Improved public access areas are at the west end of Southwest 11th, 33rd, and 51st streets; and Northwest 15th, 21st, 26th, 35th, and 39th streets.

The **D River State Wayside** is a popular spot in downtown Lincoln City. It's located on the west side of U.S. 101, on the south bank of the river. The wayside has ample parking, restrooms, and easy beach access.

Roads End State Wayside is 1 mile north of Lincoln City and offers access to several miles of beach. Turn west off U.S. 101 on Northwest Logan Road at Lighthouse Square.

East Devils Lake State Park lies 2 miles east of U.S. 101 on East Devils Lake Road. It offers picnic sites, restrooms, a boat ramp, fishing, and swimming.

Water Sports and Activities

Water recreation in the Lincoln City area focuses on Siletz Bay and Siletz River in the south, Salmon River and its estuary in the north, and Devils Lake in and east of town.

Siletz Bay offers good crabbing from boats or docks at high tides and clam digging on the mud flats on minus tides. A variety of fishing opportunities exist all year on the 5-mile-long bay. Shore access is good in the Taft area, and boat fishermen work the entire bay. The bar is dangerous, however, so don't attempt to cross it.

For access to the river, drive south on U.S. 101 to Kernville, and turn east on State Route 229, which follows the river's course for some miles. The lower portion of the river is navigable by motorboats, the upper reaches by drift boat.

From early spring through summer, bay angling is fair to good for seaperch and surfperch and several species of bottomfish. A few early chinook and coho venture into the bay in July and are taken near the Siletz Jaws, where Salishan Spit nearly touches the north shore at Taft.

In August, sea-run cutthroat along with jack salmon move into

95

the bay; they are taken well into September in the bay and river. September is also the month when the big chinook, sometimes reaching forty pounds or more, arrive and move upriver. Coho numbers increase then, too.

Salmon fishing holds up on the river well into the fall. As their numbers begin to dwindle, the first runs of winter steelhead begin showing.

North of Lincoln City, the diminutive Salmon River draws crowds of anglers to its banks for what is sometimes outstanding salmon and steelhead fishing. The river, which heads in the Coast Range, is only about 24 miles long, and where U.S. 101 crosses it, it's only about a half-cast wide.

Bank access on the river is good, and boat anglers use the lower river and estuary. The first sea-run cutthroat show up in July and, with the jack salmon, are present through September. Both coho and chinook salmon provide action from September well into October, and the steelhead follow in December and offer good sport until March.

The U.S. 101 bridge crosses the Salmon River north of Lincoln City just past the State Route 18 junction. About 0.6 mile beyond, Three Rocks Road exits to the west and leads about 3 miles to Knight Park on the north shore of the estuary, where there are picnic facilities and a public boat ramp.

Devils Lake is more than 2 miles long and covers about 640 surface acres. It's a shallow lake providing habitat mainly for warm-water species, although stocked trout provide a fair fishery. Bullhead fishing is good during the summer, especially at night. Crappie and bluegill are also present in good numbers. Largemouth-bass fishing is sometimes good.

Boating, canoeing, water-skiing, and sailing are popular pastimes on the lake. And the shallow waters warm up enough in the summer for comfortable swimming.

Blue Heron Landing, 4006 West Devils Lake Road; 994–4708. East just off U.S. 101, north of town. Full-service marina with moorage space for rent, fuel, ice, soft drinks, snacks, bait, tackle, fishing licenses, launch ramp, and rentals.

Golf and Tennis

Devils Lake Golf and Racquet Club, 3245 Club House Drive; P.O. Box 30; 994–8442. West of U.S. 101, north of town. Plans are for an 18-hole golf course. Currently thirteen holes completed. Open all year. Resident pro. Rental clubs and carts. Well-lighted indoor tennis courts, racquetball courts, exercise and weight room, whirlpool, sauna, and tanning beds.

Salishan Lodge Golf Links & Pro Shop, Gleneden Beach 97388; 764–3632. West side of U.S. 101, just south of the traffic light, 3 miles south of Lincoln City. Par-72, 18-hole links, driving range, putting green, full-service pro shop, and resident pro.

Salishan Lodge Tennis Courts, Gleneden Beach 97388; 764–3633. East side of U.S. 101, at the traffic light, 3 miles south of Lincoln City. Outdoor courts and indoor courts with indirect lighting, spectator lounge, pro shop, and resident teaching pro.

Surftides Beach Tennis Club, 2945 Northwest Jetty Avenue; 994–9667. West off U.S. 101 at the north end of town. Two public indoor courts. Pro shop.

Rentals

Blue Heron Landing, 4006 West Devils Lake Road; 994–4708. East just off U.S. 101, north of town. For fun on land or water, rent mountain bikes, canoes, aquabikes, paddle boats, 12- to 15-foot aluminum boats with 6- or 8-horsepower outboards. Also, pontoon boat available for parties on the water.

Events

February	Firemen's Ham Dinner, 994–3100
April	Oregon Wines Festival, 994–8293
	Senior Craft and Art Show, 994–2722
May	Spring Fling, 994–3316
	Spring Kite Festival, 994–3070
June	Nelscott Arts & Crafts Faire, 994—2456
July	Parade & Fireworks, 994–3070
	Sandcastle Building Contest, 994–2131
	Ocean's Edge 10K Run, 994–2131
August	Flower & Garden Show, 994–2131
	Children's Festival and Kids' Art Show, 994–2131
	Dollhouse & Miniature Show, 994–5726
September	Grass Carp Festival, 994–3601
	International Kite Festival, 994–3070

Lincoln City

October   Oktoberfest Dinner, 994–8793
Horse Races on the Beach: Driftwood Derby, 994–3070
Artists' & Artisans' Fair, Gleneden Beach, 764–2305
November Christmas Bazaar & Lunch, 994–8793
North Lincoln Hospital Auxiliary Christmas Bazaar, 994–3661
December Christmas Festival, Parade, and Auction, 994–3070

Travel Information

Lincoln City Chamber of Commerce, 3939 Northwest U.S. 101; 994–8378; Oregon, 1–800–452–2151

Surf fishing is popular along the beach near Neskowin.

Neskowin, Oregon 97149
Population: 180

Location: *On U.S. 101, 12 miles north of Lincoln City, 30 miles south of Tillamook*

If it weren't for the modern highway leading to Neskowin (ness-*cow*-in), the traveler might believe he had taken a trip in a time machine. In many ways, the tiny community exists in a time warp. It's a pastoral place, reminiscent of simpler days when folks weren't in such a rush.

There's not much to this little village: a state wayside, a grocery store, small galleries, a couple of restaurants, and adequate accommodations—even for conventions. A few creeks tumble down from nearby hills to keep things green in summer, wet in winter. Narrow streets, better suited to foot traffic and horses than to automobiles and recreational vehicles, wind through a tree-shaded residential area.

Neskowin

With two golf courses, Neskowin has more space given to fairways, roughs, and greens than to anything else. It's possible to play the first nine holes in the rolling hills east of the highway, then the next nine in the flat, but deceptively challenging, creek bottoms west of the highway. Golf makes Neskowin a good place to visit, and it's equally accommodating as a peaceful, quiet place to relax.

Lodging

Neskowin Resort, 58990 U.S. 101 South; P.O. Box 728; 392–3191. West side of the highway, in Neskowin. Queen and king beds in 55 units with cable TV. Rooms, studios, and suites. Kitchens, private decks, ocean view, recreation room, and play area. Cribs and rollaways available. Restaurant and lounge on premises. Short walk to the beach. Moderate.

Proposal Rock Inn, P.O. Box 790; 392–3115. West side of U.S. 101, next to Neskowin Resort. Twin and queen beds, rollaways and sleeper couches in 40 units with cable TV. Rooms and studios sleep two to four. Suites sleep up to eight. Studios and suites have full kitchens and fireplaces. Some units with ocean view. Beach access. Inexpensive to moderate.

Campgrounds and RV Parks

Neskowin Creek RV Resort, 50500 U.S. 101 South; 392–3120. Has 49 full-hookup sites. Pull-throughs and showers. Log lodge with kitchen facilities and card and game tables. Shuffleboard, tennis courts, heated and covered swimming pool, gazebo, and creek—all in a beautiful setting. Expensive.

Golf

Hawk Creek Golf Course, 48480 South U.S. 101; 392–4120. East side of the highway, in a beautiful valley with trees and a creek. Nine holes, 2,623 yards. Rental carts and clubs. Open all year.

Neskowin Beach Golf Course, 1 Hawk Avenue; P.O. Box 839; 392–3377. West of U.S. 101. Nine holes, 3,012 yards. Flat, easy walking. Trees and two creeks. Excellent greens. Rental carts and clubs, full pro shop, resident pro, snacks, beer, and wine. Open April 15 to November 1.

Events

July Independence Day Celebration
October Neskowin Valley School Harvest Festival, 392–3124

Dories in the surf near Haystack Rock

Pacific City, Oregon 97135
Population: 1,500

Location: *2.5 miles west of U.S. 101 on Three Capes Loop, just south of Cape Kiwanda, 15 miles north of Lincoln City*

A small retirement and vacation community at the south end of scenic Three Capes Loop, Pacific City is scattered about a coastal plain that lies beneath Cape Kiwanda along a photogenic bit of beach extending south to Nestucca (ness-*tuck*-uh) Bay. Just offshore stands the larger of two Oregon coast formations called Haystack Rock; this one is 327 feet tall.

This is an area popular with hang-glider and dune-buggy enthusiasts. The town's main claim to fame, however, is the Pacific dory fleet. Commercial fishermen and sport anglers launch their craft from the beach into the surf, as fishermen have for more than sixty years.

Dory fishing developed here as a response to the closure of the Nestucca River system to gillnetting in the 1920s. Good fishing grounds lie offshore, but because of the treacherous bar conditions on the bay, the only way to reach them is by flat-bottom dories that can be launched in the surf.

The fleet is said to be about 300 strong, though far fewer boats are launched on any given day. Nevertheless, during the summer, dozens of four-wheel-drive boat-hauling rigs cross the soft sands to the firm beach each morning and are parked along the beach until the dories return. It's quite a show to watch and photograph. It is possible to find a charter operator willing to take individuals out for the ride and the fishing.

Lodging

Sandlake Country Inn, 8505 Galloway Road; Cloverdale 97112; 965–6745. A half-mile west of the Loop Highway at Sandlake Grocery, 8.5 miles north of Pacific City. Queen beds in 2 guest rooms with shared bath. Breakfast of fresh fruit granola parfait, coddled eggs, and homemade breads delivered to the room. Extras include a well-stocked picnic basket for lunch at the inn or on the beach. Barbecued-chicken supper served in the room or a five-course dinner featuring fresh local fish, garden salad, berries, and dairy products served by the innkeepers in period clothing. The inn is situated on well-kept grounds in a quiet, rural area. Peace and quiet are top priorities here. The house was built in 1894 and is handsomely decorated. Inexpensive to moderate.

Campgrounds and RV Parks

Cape Kiwanda RV Park, P.O. Box 129; 965–6230. On the east side of the highway, across from the dory-launch area. Has 130 sites with pull-throughs available. Full hookups, showers, laundry, and firewood. Seventh day and fourth week free. Moderate.

Sandlake Campground, 7000 Galloway Road; Cloverdale 97112; 965–6097. About 2.25 miles west of Three Capes Loop at Sandlake Grocery, 8.5 miles north of Pacific City. A U.S. Forest Service campground with 215 campsites. Hiking trails, beach access, dunes access, restrooms, and water. Popular with ORV enthusiasts. Inexpensive.

Pacific City

Whalen Island County Park. Located about 2.5 miles south of Sandlake Grocery and 6 miles north of Pacific City, just west of Three Capes Loop. Situated on a tiny island with 26 sites, picnic tables, fire rings, water, and restrooms. Inexpensive.

Food

Riverhouse Restaurant, 34450 Brooten Road; 965–6722. A quarter mile north of the stoplight on the west side of the road. Lunch and dinner daily; brunch Sunday; closed Monday and Tuesday in winter. On the Nestucca River. A local favorite. Small—only eleven tables—but an ambitious menu. Brunch: quiche, huevos rancheros, omelets, pancakes, and crepes filled with ham and asparagus or shrimp and eggs and topped with creamy cheese sauce. Homemade soup and chowder daily; large open-face sandwiches served with choice of three salads. Also lunch-size salads and burgers. Dinners include Coquille St. Jacques, fillet of fish amandine, steamer clams, and salmon. Cocktails, beer, and wine. Live entertainment on Saturday nights. Moderate.

Water Sports and Activities

This is one of the most productive fishing areas on the coast. In addition to the superb salmon and bottomfish angling offshore, out to 7 miles and reached by surf dory, Nestucca Bay, the Nestucca River, and Little Nestucca River also are top producers.

On the bay, spring chinook angling begins in May and lasts into July. Fall chinook and coho angling is in September and October, and summer steelhead from spring to early fall. Sea-run cutthroat move into the bay in late summer and are available until early fall. And spring through summer is the time for surfperch, seaperch, flounder, and other saltwater species. Crabbing is good in the deeper parts of the bay. Clam digging on the flats and in the upper reaches of the bay is good on minus tides.

The Nestucca River is among the best spring-chinook streams on the coast, with good action from May through July. Fall chinook run from late August through September, and some big fish are caught each year in good numbers. Summer steelhead are in the river from mid-spring through the summer, and winter steelhead from mid-November to mid-February. Sea-run cutthroat and jack salmon are available in good numbers in September and October. The Little Nestucca is a top cutthroat stream in late summer. Fall-chinook and coho fishing starts in October. And there's excellent steelhead fishing through the winter. Bank access is good along the lower river.

Tommy Brennan, River Outfitter, 32910 State Route 22; Hebo 97122; 392–3019. Guided fishing trips on the Nestucca River for spring and fall chinook and summer and winter steelhead.

Nestucca Country, 34650 Brooten Road; P.O. Box 729; 965–6410. Located 0.3 mile north of the stoplight, on the Nestucca River. A full-service tackle shop and marina. Bait, licenses, and tags. Good source of information on local fishing, crabbing, and clam digging. Check here for information on sport dory trips on the ocean. Weigh station for trophy catches. Rents 12-foot aluminum boats (no motors).

Events

May Memorial Day Fish Fry, 965–6161
July Fireworks at Cape Kiwanda, 965–6161
Dory Derby Festival, 965–6161

Travel Information

Pacific City Chamber of Commerce, P.O. Box 313; 965–6161

Oceanside and Three Arch Rocks National Wildlife Refuge

Oceanside/Netarts, Oregon 97134/97143
Population: 250/200

Location: *Oceanside is about 10 miles west of Tillamook and U.S. 101 on the Three Capes Loop; Netarts is about 2 miles south of Oceanside and 18 miles north of Pacific City*

The town buildings of Oceanside cling like lichens to the steep slope of a rocky headland overlooking a beach as broad as a boulevard. **Three Arch Rocks National Wildlife Refuge** stands offshore as a haven for sea lions, seals, and birds by the thousands.

South of Oceanside is the tiny community of Netarts and a bay by the same name. Netarts Bay is an elongate, shallow body of water, extending about 7 miles south to north. It is bounded on the east by Three Capes Loop and on the west by a long, club-shaped stretch of sand known as Netarts Spit.

106

Lodging

House on the Hill, Maxwell Point; Oceanside; 842–6030 or 1–800–235–6030. On a promontory overlooking the Pacific and Three Arch Rocks. Queen beds in 24 units with cable TV. Some kitchen units available. Moderate.

Sea Haven Inn, 5450 South Avenue Northwest; P.O. Box 203; Tillamook 97141; 842–3151. West off Three Capes Loop, between Oceanside and Netarts. A beautiful new bed-and-breakfast inn with 7 guest rooms, queen and king beds, ocean view, and cable TV. On the ocean with a steep trail to the beach. Handsomely appointed rooms and suites. Full breakfast served. Moderate to expensive.

Terimore Motel, 5105 Crab Avenue; P.O. Box 102; Netarts; 842–4623. In town, on the bay. Queen beds in 26 units with cable TV, HBO, kitchens, and some fireplaces. Laundry facilities. Cottages also available—1 or 2 bedrooms with kitchens. Near all beach and bay activities. Inexpensive to moderate.

Campgrounds and RV Parks

Bay Shore Trailer Park, P.O. Box 218; Netarts; 842–7774. On the east side of Three Capes Loop, overlooking Netarts Bay. A clean, well-maintained park with 58 sites: 55 full-hookup, 3 water and electric. Showers, laundry, boat rentals, launch ramp. Moderate.

Cape Lookout State Park, 13000 Whiskey Creek Road West; Tillamook 97141; 842–4981. West of Three Capes Loop, 12 miles southwest of Tillamook. Has 53 full-hookup RV sites and 197 tent sites. Showers, tank dump, laundry, firewood. Some facilities for handicapped. Reservations accepted. Moderate.

Happy Camp Resort, Netarts; 842–4012. In Netarts, on the bay and beach. has 71 sites, full hookups, showers, and rental boats. Open all year. Near crabbing, clam digging, and beach activities. Moderate.

Food

Roseanna's Oceanside Cafe, 1490 Pacific Northwest; Oceanside; 842–7351. On the west side of the highway, in town. Breakfast, lunch, and dinner daily. A small cafe with a large menu, good food, and a great view. Specialties are fresh seafoods, home-made chowder, and homemade desserts and pastries. Tillamook dairy products. Weekend entertainment. An area favorite. Moder-ate.

Wee Willie Restaurant, 6060 Whiskey Creek Road; Netarts; 842–6869. Just south of Netarts on the west side of Three Capes Loop. Lunch and dinner daily. Traditional diner fare, including burgers, hot dogs, chili burgers and dogs, sandwiches. Soups, chowder, oyster stew, chili, salads, and a good selection of sea-foods: oysters, shrimp, clam strips, crab, and such. Homemade desserts and fountain selections including malts, shakes, and sun-daes. Inexpensive.

Beaches, Parks, Trails, and Waysides

Cape Meares State Park lies 3 miles north of Oceanside and has hiking trails, beaches, and superb viewpoints. Here, too, is the famous Octopus Tree, so named because of its unusual shape. Its splayed branches, creating a 10-foot-wide cradle at the base, are said to have been shaped by Indians when the tree was young, perhaps 2,000 years ago. The purpose, according to legend, was to create a burial tree for a tribal chief and his canoe.

Cape Meares Light, also in the park, was completed in 1890 and operated until 1963. Its tower stands 40 feet high and is built of iron. With a focal plane 217 feet above the sea, the fixed white light with red flashing beacon was visible 21 miles out to sea.

A mile north of Cape Meares is **Bayocean Spit,** where once stood a resort complex called Bayocean that was eventually swal-lowed by the encroaching seas. This is now a marsh, supporting abundant wildlife, especially seabirds, shorebirds, and waterfowl.

Netarts Spit and nearby beaches are popular beachcombing areas. The best beachcombing is in the winter and spring or any other time after storms. Winter storms often uncover rocky areas and gravel beds, exposing agates, jasper, and petrified wood. Strong westerlies blow glass floats and driftwood ashore.

There are good trails at both **Cape Meares** and **Cape Look-out State parks.** Beaches there are also popular with beachcomb-ers and hikers.

Water Sports and Activities

Although anglers take a few bottomfish and the occasional chum salmon from Netarts Bay, the fishing here is only fair at best. Crabbing, however, can be outstanding, particularly from September to December. Rental equipment is available.

A boat will get you to the best clam-digging areas, too. Most flats give up horseneck, hard-shell, and littleneck clams, as well as cockles. Upbay, there are soft-shell beds, downbay a few razor clams.

Salmon Anglers on Tillamook Bay

Tillamook, Oregon 97141
Population: 3,830

Location: *On U.S. 101, 42 miles north of Lincoln City, 66 miles south of Astoria, and 74 miles southwest of Portland*

Situated on the rolling hills and tucked into the verdant valleys of Tillamook County's 1,115 square miles are 565 dairy farms that supply the raw material for Tillamook's booming cheese business. The county is home to approximately 21,300 persons and 22,000 cows.

Cheese is big business here. It takes five pounds of milk to make one pound of cheese, and at the Tillamook County Creamery Association (a.k.a. The Cheese Factory), cheesemakers produce forty-five million pounds of cheese a year and are planning to increase their capacity to sixty million pounds. One might expect the rivers here to be running white.

110

Approaching Tillamook from the east, on State Route 6, along the Wilson River and through the Tillamook State Forest, travelers might never know that the area was consumed by the worst forest fires of the twentieth century between 1932 and 1945.

The fiercest of those fires, started by a logging operation in the tinder-dry Coast Range during drought conditions, broke out on August 14, 1933. By the time the 3,000 firefighters brought the blaze under control, it had destroyed 270,000 acres of old-growth timber.

So great was the conflagration that it sent dense clouds of smoke and ash 40,000 feet in the air, blocking the sun's rays and sending chickens to roost in midday. The fire's ashes fell on ships 500 miles out to sea and accumulated along Tillamook County's beaches to a depth of 2 feet.

Two miles south of town and east of U.S. 101 stand two imposing buildings that have dominated the landscape since 1943. Built by the U.S. Navy as hangars for a fleet of eight K-type blimps, they are, according to the *Guinness Book of World Records,* the largest all-wood buildings in the world, measuring 1,000 feet long, 296 feet wide, and 170 feet tall. Ten million board feet of lumber went into their construction.

During World War II, blimps of the U.S. Naval Air Station at Tillamook patrolled the Pacific coast from Eureka, California, to the San Juan Islands in Puget Sound. Although the blimps have been gone since 1945, the hangars remain intact. As property of the Port of Tillamook, they serve in various capacities, housing several businesses.

Northwest of Tillamook and north of Cape Meares, a narrow finger of sand—known variously as Tillamook Spit, Bayocean Spit, and Bayocean Peninsula—pokes between Tillamook Bay and the ocean. It's hard to believe that this was once a booming resort town, begun in 1906 by developer T. B. Potter. Among the 100 buildings that once stood at Bayocean were a forty-room hotel and a huge natatorium containing a 50-by-160-foot heated saltwater pool with a wave-making machine and waterfall, as well as a gallery that seated 1,000 spectators.

When the north jetty was built at the entrance to Tillamook Bay in 1917, the sea began to erode the peninsula on which Bayocean stood. Enlargement and extension of the jetty in 1932 caused erosion to increase dramatically. Powerful currents and incessant breakers devoured the broad beach and eventually reduced beach-front buildings, including the natatorium, to rubble and driftwood.

In 1952 the spit was breached at its southern end by a mile-wide opening to the sea, turning the hapless community into an island. The following year the Bayocean post office was closed, and the last residents left.

After the south jetty was built in 1965, currents changed, and the spit began rebuilding itself. Today, it's a popular spot for beachcombing, picnicking, and observing abundant wildlife, with scarcely a clue that there was ever a dwelling there, let alone a busy resort town.

Lodging

El-Rey Sands Motel, 815 Main Avenue; 842–6511. On U.S. 101, in town. Queen beds in 23 units with cable TV, HBO, Showtime, Cinemax, and Disney Channel. Small but comfortable rooms. Adjacent to restaurant, open for breakfast, lunch, and dinner. Moderate.

Shilo Inn, 2515 North Main; 842–7971 or 1–800–222–2244. East side of U.S. 101, north end of town. Queen and king beds in 68 comfortable and tastefully appointed units, each with remote-control cable TV, Showtime, wet bar, microwave oven, refrigerator and sofa bed. Heated indoor pool, sauna, whirlpool, steam room, and exercise room with weight machines. Minimart—open 24 hours—sells deli foods, groceries, magazines, beer, wine, bait, tackle, ice, Shell gas and oil. Superb restaurant and lounge on the premises. A full-service resort and Tillamook's finest accommodations. Moderate.

Food

Hadley House, 2203 Third Street; 842–2101. Across the street from the courthouse. Lunch and dinner daily. Hearty soups, salads, deli-style sandwiches, burgers, and traditional sandwiches. Dinner menu offers a half-dozen appetizers—including Tillamook cheese—charbroiled steaks, and house specialties such as sauteed chicken livers, finger steaks, fried chicken, and veal cutlets. Seafoods include baked or grilled salmon, razor clams, or Tillamook Bay oysters. Homemade pies. Moderate.

Shilo Inn, 2534 North Main; 842–5510. East side of U.S. 101, north of downtown. Breakfast, lunch, and dinner daily; brunch Sunday. Outstanding omelets and egg dishes, traditional breakfast fare with a flair. Super luncheon salads, including crab or chicken cobb, fresh spinach salad, and several house-specialty salads. Tillamook cheese and fruit board, seafood fettuccine, tortellini Alfredo, and great deli-style sandwiches, such as Tillamook cheese and crab or Old English prime rib—charbroiled and served on grilled sourdough bread. Dinner offerings include London broil, Cajun chicken sauté, halibut fish and chips, and excellent prime rib. Cocktails, beer, and wine. Moderate.

Steffano's, 903 Main; 842–3244. East side of Main, downtown. Lunch and dinner daily. Italian restaurant and deli, offering hot or cold deli-style sandwiches, Italian salads, soups, and chowder. Appetizers include mushrooms stuffed with escargot, marinated crab, and steamed clams or mussels. Such dinner offerings as poached salmon, halibut with artichoke ragout, and all the Italian favorites. Imported and domestic beers and wines. Inexpensive to moderate.

Shopping and Browsing

Bear Creek Artichokes, 842–4501 (home) or 398–5411 (stand). East side of U.S. 101, 11 miles south of Tillamook. Summer: daily, 9:00 A.M. to 6:30 P.M. Off-season: daily, 10:00 A.M. to 5:00 P.M. Weekends only in November and December. Great fresh fruits and vegetables to complement the Oregon wines and Tillamook cheeses. Succulent artichokes in season. You-pick or they-pick veggies, fresh herbs, honey, and homemade jams and jellies.

Tillamook County Creamery Association (The Cheese Factory), P.O. Box 313; 842–4481. East side of U.S. 101, north end of town. Daily, 8:00 A.M. to 6:00 P.M. The finest of cheeses—cheddars, Swiss, Monterey Jack, low-fat, cheese curds, and special extra sharp cheddars—available here. Daily factory tours. Retail sales and large gift-shop area, includes wine shop, candies, and ice cream. A *must see* for every traveler. Gift packs and mail-order catalog available.

Museum

Tillamook County Pioneer Museum, 2106 Second Street;

Tillamook

842–4553. Northbound U.S. 101 at Second. Daily, 8:30 A.M. to 5:00 P.M.; Sunday, noon to 5:00 P.M. October 1 to May 1, closed Mondays. Clearly the largest and best museum of its kind on the coast. It is located in the old county courthouse, built in 1905, and offers three full floors of topflight exhibits. In the basement are the last Tillamook-to-Yamhill stagecoach, a 1902 Holsman Horseless Carriage, a 1909 Buick, an old wagon, canoes, antique cameras and typewriters, washing machines and kitchen items, cheesemaking equipment, and nautical and logging displays. On the main floor are displays of toys and musical instruments, Indian baskets and artifacts, china and glassware, a fine gun collection, and an interesting display of items from the old Naval Air Station and blimp hangars. Second-floor displays include extensive collections of rocks, minerals, and fossils and a surprisingly large natural-history exhibit of more than 500 specimens. With more than 35,000 artifacts and antiques on display, this museum is classified *must see.*

Beaches, Parks, Trails, and Waysides

Three Capes Loop will take you west-northwest along Tillamook Bay to the Bayocean area and **Cape Meares** and **Cape Lookout State parks,** where there are hiking trails, picnicking, camping, and beach access. The scenic highway then continues south to Oceanside, Netarts, and Pacific City, all of which provide access to great beach areas.

South of Tillamook is a county park that's worth a visit. Take U.S. 101 south about 6.7 miles and turn east at the sign for Munson Creek Falls. Follow the road 1.5 miles to a small parking area and turnaround (not recommended for large travel trailers). Two trails lead to the waterfall, which, at a height of 266 feet, is the highest waterfall in the Coast Range. The lower trail leads an easy quarter-mile along the creek to the base of the falls. The upper three-eighths-mile trail gradually ascends 250 feet and is well maintained. But canyon walls drop away abruptly in places, so this is no place for small children. The view from the upper trail is spectacular and well worth the little extra effort the hike takes.

Water Sports and Activities

It's said that *Tillamook* is an Indian word meaning "land of

114

many waters," which is appropriate for an area with the second largest bay in the state, many rivers and creeks, and miles of beaches nearby. The most popular forms of recreation here are associated in some way with water.

Tillamook Bay provides year-round recreation for residents and visitors alike. Anglers take bottomfish all year. Perch fishing is good from late winter through the summer months. Spring chinook show up in April and are present into early summer. In August the first fall chinook and coho begin arriving in the bay. July and August are also good months for sea-run cutthroat.

Crabbing on the bay is good all year, particularly in the Crab Harbor area on the west side. The best crabbing is during the fall and winter.

Tillamook Bay is probably second only to Coos Bay as a clam-digging area. The bay is rimmed with beds that give up limits of horseneck, hard-shell, littleneck, soft-shell clams, and cockles.

The Tillamook River, which enters the bay from the south, is a short stream of only 14 miles. Summer fishing is mainly for stocked rainbow and native cutthroat trout. Angling for sea-run cutthroat is good from midsummer to early autumn. Fall chinook move into the river in September and October and coho usually in November.

The 50-mile-long Trask River is a favorite for sea-run cutthroat from midsummer to early fall. It gets good runs of spring and fall chinook and both summer and winter steelhead. The Trask enters the south end of the bay just south of the Wilson River.

State Route 6 follows the Wilson River for much of its course through the **Tillamook State Forest.** The popular river gets runs of summer and winter steelhead, spring and fall chinook, and sea-run cutthroat. Each year the Wilson gives up some big steelhead and salmon. Best bank access is upriver, while the lower 10 miles is favored by drift-boat fishermen. The Wilson also has some excellent fly-fishing waters upstream.

Dean's Guide Service, P.O. Box 199; Netares 97143; 842–7107. Drift-boat fishing trips on the Trask and Wilson rivers.

Rick Howard's Guide Service, 52122 Southeast Third Place; Scappoose 97056; 543–7372. Drift-boat fishing for salmon and steelhead on Tillamook Bay and Tillamook-area rivers. Everything furnished.

Tillamook

Tours and Trips

Oregon Coastline Express, 4000 Hangar Road; 842–2768. Board at the depot on Third Street in town. Travel by train in completely refurbished observation cars along scenic Tillamook Bay. The Coastline Express made its maiden run in May 1989 and continues to operate from Tillamook to Garibaldi, Rockaway Beach, and Wheeler, making two trips a day during the week and three trips a day on weekends from May to October and on special weekends during the off-season. Discounts for seniors and children three to twelve. Children under three travel free.

Events

March Midwinter Festival, 842–7525
June Dairy Parade and Rodeo, 842—7525
August Tillamook County Fair, 842–2272
September Car Club Auto Fun Run, 842–4066

Travel Information

Tillamook County Chamber of Commerce, 3705 U.S. 101 North; 842–7525

A sign maker gone mad in Garibaldi

Garibaldi/Rockaway Beach, Oregon 97118/97136
Population: 1,070/906

Location: *Garibaldi is on U.S. 101, 9 miles north of Tillamook, 5 miles south of Rockaway Beach, at the north end of Tillamook Bay; Rockaway Beach is on U.S. 101, 5 miles north of Garibaldi, 10 miles south of Nehalem*

If fishing and allied water sports are not the only attractions in Garibaldi, they are certainly the main ones. The town is home port to a large commercial fishing fleet, which makes fresh seafood readily available to local markets and restaurants. The harbor has boat-launching and mooring facilities and a fleet of modern character boats. You can crab from boats or docks and piers and dig clams on minus tides at nearby flats.

Overnight lodging is slim in town; ample accommodations

117

can be found at nearby Rockaway Beach, where there are more than three hundred lodging units as well as a fine broad beach.

Lodging

Beach House Bed & Breakfast, 115 North Miller Street; Rockaway Beach; 355–8282 or 355–2411. West of U.S. 101 and railroad tracks, downtown. Single, double, and queen beds in 4 guest rooms. Traditional seventy-eight-year-old beach house with 2 shared baths. Common living room with cable TV. Breakfast served across the highway at Beach Pancake House. Inexpensive to moderate.

The Captain's Lady Bed & Breakfast, 127 South Miller Street; Rockaway Beach; 355–2966. West of U.S. 101 and railroad tracks, in town. Victorian beds and antiques in 5 rooms. Two shared baths, cable TV, and VCR tapes. Full breakfast features homemade pastries, jams, and fresh fruits. Deli plates and homemade pies available for evening snacks. Moderate.

Hill Top House Bed & Breakfast, 617 Holly Avenue; P.O. Box 538; Garibaldi; 322–3221. East of U.S. 101 on Seventh to Holly and up the hill to the highest street in town. Has 3 guest rooms with private and semi-private baths; 1 with double and single beds; 1 with queen bed; and master suite with king bed, whirlpool tub, and private balcony. Cedar inside and out. Furnished with antiques and original paintings. Hot tub, decks, and one of the most spectacular views in the area, encompassing Garibaldi, the waterfront, the bay, the ocean, the city of Tillamook, and Cape Meares. Moderate to expensive.

Silver Sands Motel, P.O. Box 161; Rockaway Beach; 355–2206. Queen beds in 64 units with cable TV and Showtime. Beachfront, ocean-view rooms and suites, some with kitchens, some with fireplaces. Covered and heated pool, sauna, whirlpool. Coffee and newspapers in rooms. Accommodations for up to six persons. Moderate.

Campgrounds and RV Parks

Barview Jetty County Park, 322–3522. West of U.S. 101 at Barview, 2 miles north of Garibaldi. Has 250 sites: 40 full-hookup,

20 electric-hookup, 190 tent. Showers, tank dump, picnic tables, fire rings, and jetty access. Inexpensive to moderate.

Jetty Fishery, 27550 U.S. 101 North; Rockaway Beach; 368–5746. West side of U.S. 101, 3 miles north of Rockaway Beach. Has 15 RV sites with electric and water hookups. Showers, store, boat rental, moorage, ice, propane, gas, and oil. Good spot for those who plan to fish, crab, and dig clams on Nehalem Bay and lower Nehalem River.

Shorewood Travel Trailer Park, 17600 Ocean Boulevard; Rockaway Beach; 355–2278. One mile south of Rockaway Beach, west of U.S. 101 less than a quarter mile. Has 105 RV sites with full hookups, cable TV, HBO, and picnic tables. Showers, tank dump, firewood, laundry, playground, gasoline, and propane. Beautiful setting, on the beach. Moderate.

Food

The Beach Pancake House, 202 U.S. 101 North; Rockaway Beach; 355–2411. East Side of U.S. 101, downtown. Breakfast, lunch, and dinner daily. Breakfast includes pancakes, waffles, and egg dishes—served all day. Chicken, fresh seafood, and Mexican food. Chicken and dumplings a house specialty. Carryout. Moderate.

The Troller Restaurant & Lounge, Garibaldi; 322–3666. On Mooring Basin Road, west of U.S. 101. Open twenty-four hours from June 1 to October 1. Breakfast, lunch, and dinner daily. Traditional and unusual, including oysters and eggs, or trout and eggs. Burgers and other sandwiches, such as shrimp or crab and cheese, Bay City oysters, and albacore tuna. Fish and chips, clam strips, steamer clams, and more. Prime rib, steaks, chicken, surf 'n' turf, and fresh local seafood. Moderate.

Water Sports and Activities

Garibaldi Charters and Seafood Market, 606 South Commercial Street; P.O. Box 556; Garibaldi; 322-0007. Salmon trips of five to six hours leaving twice daily. Eight-hour bottomfishing trips. Light-tackle rockfish angling and, weather permitting, trips to deep offshore reefs for big lingcod and yelloweye and canary rockfish. Custom smoking and canning.

Garibaldi/Rockaway Beach

Jetty Fishery, 27550 U.S. 101 North; Rockaway Beach; 368–5746. West side of U.S. 101, 3 miles north of Rockaway Beach. Bait, tackle, fishing licenses and tags, boat and motor rental, gas and oil, moorage, dock crabbing, crab ring rental, fish-cleaning station, and clam-digging gear. Also 15 RV spaces. On Nehalem Bay.

Siggi-G Ocean Charters, P.O. Box 536; Garibaldi; 322–3285. At the Garibaldi boat basin, west of U.S. 101. Salmon, bottomfish, and combination trips include bait, tackle, cleaning, ice, and bags. Specializes in long-range, deep-water fishing for big bottomfish when weather cooperates. Also offers crabbing, whale-watching, and birdwatching trips.

Troller-Garibaldi Deep Sea Fishing, P.O. Box 605; Garibaldi; 322–3343. West side of U.S. 101, at Fisherman's Wharf, in the boat basin. Large fleet of charter boats available for bottomfish, salmon, combination, and long-distance offshore trips as well as scuba-diving and whale-watching trips.

Events

February	Crab Feed and Crab Races, Garibaldi, 322–0301
March	Blessing of the Fleet, Garibaldi, 322–0301
May	Kite Festival, Rockaway Beach, 355–8108
June	Rockaway Beach Birthday Celebration, 355–8108
July	Garibaldi Days Festival, 322–0301
August	Arts & Crafts Fair, Rockaway Beach, 355–8108
November	Old Fashioned Christmas, Rockaway Beach, 355–8108

Travel Information

Garibaldi Chamber of Commerce, 202 U.S. 101; 322–0301

Rockwork along U.S. 101, north of Manzanita

Nehalem/Manzanita, Oregon 97131/97130
Population: 258/443

Location: *Nehalem is on U.S. 101 and the Nehalem River, 10 miles north of Rockaway Beach; Manzanita is just west of U.S. 101, 2 miles north of Nehalem, 14 miles south of Cannon Beach*

Nehalem (nee-*hay*-luhm) is believed to be a Salish Indian word meaning "place where people live." While not all that many people live here, it is a gathering place for shoppers and browsers, as well as those interested in fishing and allied sports on Nehalem Bay and Nehalem River.

Named for a small shrub that grows wild along the coast, Manzanita is a quiet little village next to the ocean on the south slope Neahkahnie (nee-uh-*kah*-nee) Mountain. The mountain stands 1,795 feet above sea level and is the most imposing headland on the north coast.

121

Nehalem/Manzanita

Indian legend has it that there's buried treasure on the mountain—booty from a Spanish galleon that went aground here, long before white men settled the land. Treasure seekers have made many futile hunts over the years, but nary a doubloon has been unearthed.

Lodging

The Inn at Manzanita, 67 Laneda Avenue; Manzanita; 368–6754. A half-mile west of U.S. 101, on the north side of the street. Beautiful cedar two-story bed-and-breakfast inn. Four guest rooms, each with a whirlpool spa and fireplace or wood stove. Queen beds, wet bars, refrigerators, and cable TV. Separate house accommodates up to eight persons. Continental breakfast brought to the room. Expensive.

The Manzanita Inn, 476 Laneda Avenue; Manzanita; 368–5499. Located 0.2 mile west of U.S. 101 on the south side of the street. Large, comfortable inn accommodates up to eight persons. Smaller cottage accommodates six persons. Whirlpool spa on deck. Barbecue, kitchen-dining area for use by guests. Rates include breakfast and newspapers. Inexpensive to moderate.

Sunset Surf Motel, 248 Ocean Road; P.O. Box 458; Manzanita; 368–5224. On Manzanita Beach, just north of Laneda Avenue. Queen and king beds in 41 units with cable TV, HBO, and Showtime. Pool, beachfront units, most with ocean view, 30 with kitchens, some with fireplaces. Moderate to expensive.

Campgrounds and RV Parks

Nehalem Bay State Park, 368–5154 (booth); 368–5943 (manager's residence). Located 1.5 miles west of U.S. 101, 1 mile north of Nehalem, 1 mile south of Manzanita. Has 292 RV sites with electrical and water hookups, picnic tables, and fireplaces. Showers, tank dump, and firewood. Hiker/biker camp. Horse camp with picnic tables, fire rings, restrooms, and tie stalls for eighteen horses. Hiking, biking, and horseback-riding trails. Access to miles of broad beach. The park is a 5-mile spit that separates Nehalem Bay from the ocean. Inexpensive.

Oswald West State Park, 368–5943. West side of U.S. 101, 4 miles north of Manzanita, 10 miles south of Cannon Beach. Foot access only to 36 tent sites. Wheelbarrows for hauling gear to campsites. Ample parking on both sides of the highway. Camp on a beautiful headland amidst the tall timber of a rain forest. Picnic tables, fireplaces, firewood, restrooms, and water. Hiking trails. Inexpensive.

Food

The Uptown Supper Club, 165 Laneda; Manzanita; 368–6189. Located 0.4 mile west of U.S. 101 on the north side of the street. Dinner daily. Seafood appetizers, soups, salads, chicken, steaks, and seafoods. Breast of chicken stuffed with shrimp and Swiss cheese, then breaded and baked. Shrimp fettucine, halibut fish and chips, scampi, halibut amandine, seafood platter. Cocktails, beer, and wine. Moderate.

The Wooden Ladle Restaurant, 822 U.S. 101; Manzanita; 368–6111. West side of U.S. 101 at the Manzanita junction. Wednesday through Sunday: breakfast, lunch, and dinner. Features homemade breads and pies, clam chowder, steaks, and seafoods. Breakfasts for large and small appetites, three-egg omelets, large list of burgers and traditional sandwiches. Steaks, chicken, veal, and seafoods. Moderate.

Shopping and Browsing

Beverage Bin & River Gallery, P.O. Box 142; Nehalem; 368–5295. West side of U.S. 101, in town. Good selection of wine, coffee beans, and teas on one side; superb marine and wildlife art on the other. Great reproductions of old signs for sale here—perfect for decorating home or business.

Nehalem Bay Trading Company, P.O. Box 31; Nehalem; 368–5181. East side of U.S. 101, in town. Daily, 10:30 A.M. to 5:00 P.M. The main shop here offers reproductions of antique oak furniture, as well as brass and pewter items. Other shops on premises offer a variety of country and gift items.

North Coast Basket Studio, P.O. Box 83; Nehalem; 368–6147. Southeast corner of Nehalem Bay Trading Company, on east side of U.S. 101. Open "most days" in summer, weekends in winter. Many beautiful and unusual handmade baskets in all shapes and sizes. Also information and instructions on basket weaving, as well as supplies. Workshops offered.

The Peacock Gallery, 35955 Seventh Street; P.O. Box 67; Nehalem; 368–6924. East side of U.S. 101, downtown. Daily, 10:00 A.M. to 5:00 P.M. A large, pleasing gallery offering original art, prints, gift items, and kitchenware.

Water Sports and Activities

Nehalem Bay is popular for crabbing and clam digging. Crabbing is good from boats much of the year, but it's best from fall through winter. The most abundant clams are soft-shell and little-neck.

Bay fishing is good for perch and flounder from early spring to the first rains of autumn. Chinook and coho salmon move into the bay in August and are caught into November. This is also a good area for sea-run cutthroat trout, which are present most of the year but most abundant in late summer. Winter months produce steelhead in the upper bay.

The Nehalem River is one of the longest coastal rivers, extending more than one hundred miles through the Coast Range. It provides a fall chinook and coho fishery, winter steelhead angling, and year-round cutthroat fishing in the lower river.

Rentals

Manzanita Fun Merchants, 186 Laneda Avenue; Manzanita; 368–6606. A half-mile west of U.S. 101 on the south side of the street. Sells and rents Funcycles—three-wheel recumbents.

Events

March	Canoe Races, Nehalem, 368–5338
May	Oregon North Coast International Raft Race, Nehalem, 368–5338
July	Nehalem Arts Festival, 368–5295
August	Nehalem Bay Blackberry Festival, 368–6924
September	Nehalem Bay Salmon Days, 368–6864
	Northwind Music Festival, Manzanita, 368–6468
October	Manzanita Kite Fly, 368–5492

November "Home for the Holidays" Christmas Market, Nehalem, 368–5002

Travel Information

Manzanita Merchants Association, P.O. Box 164; Manzanita

Downtown Cannon Beach

Cannon Beach, Oregon 97110
Population: 1,187

Location: *West of U.S. 101, 14 miles north of Manzanita, 9 miles south of Seaside*

A month after Lewis and Clark settled for the winter of 1805–1806 near Astoria, Oregon, William Clark led a small party 20 miles south to a headland overlooking a "butifull Sand Shore." No doubt, his coign of vantage was Tillamook Head, and what he described, most believe, is the expanse of beach stretching southward to what is now the city of Cannon Beach.

The beach here is wide; the backdrop of craggy headlands is impressive. Adding to the area's visual appeal are the many sea stacks just offshore. Most prominent, and certainly the most photographed, is Haystack Rock, one of two on the coast and three in the state so named. The one here stands 235 feet high, 92 feet

126

shorter than the one south of Cape Kiwanda, but nonetheless interesting for its surroundings.

The cannon after which Cannon Beach was named is from the U.S. Naval Survey schooner *Shark*, which broke up on Clatsop Spit at the mouth of the Columbia River on September 10, 1846. Part of the ship, including the cannon and capstan, washed ashore south of Tillamook Head. One of the area's early settlers hauled the cannon and capstan away and set them in concrete. They now stand on the east side of U.S. 101, just south of Cannon Beach. Cannons near the Cannon Beach exits on U.S. 101 are fair copies, made in 1953.

The architecture in Cannon Beach is an odd but interesting admixture of the quaint and the contemporary, the curious and the traditional. Structures range from beachy little bungalows to hilltop manors, mostly glass and weathered wood, and a lot of shingles, shakes, and shutters. The strict building codes are kind to the eye and environment.

After a glimpse, it's not surprising to learn that Cannon Beach is an artsy little community and the cultural center of the north coast. A number of artists live and work in the area and sell their works at local galleries. A thriving repertory company keeps the theater arts alive and lively, and an annual arts program revitalizes residents and visitors every year.

Lodging

The Argonauta Inn, P.O. Box 3; 436–2601 or 436–2205. On the beach, next to The Waves Motel. Not an inn, per se, but several houses or cottages on the beach that accommodate two to six persons and feature queen beds, fireplaces, kitchens, antiques, fine-art prints, nautical items, ocean view, cable TV, whirlpool, hot tub, and more. Walk to shops and restaurants. Expensive.

Best Western Surfsand Resort Hotel, P.O. Box 219; 436–2274; Oregon, 1–800–452–4470; elsewhere, 1–800–457–6100. West side of Hemlock, south of downtown. Queen and king beds in 72 units, 30 with kitchens. Heated indoor pool, whirlpool spa, ocean view, fireplaces, cable TV, HBO, beach access. Walk to shops. Superb ocean-view restaurant and comfortable lounge on the premises. Moderate to expensive.

Tern Inn Bed & Breakfast, 3663 South Hemlock; P.O. Box

Cannon Beach

952; 436–1528. South of town on east side of Hemlock at Tyee Street. Two guest rooms with either a fireplace or sun-room, goose-down quilts, private baths, and cable TV. Breakfast includes home-made baked goods. Short walk to the ocean. Two nights minimum summers and weekends. Moderate.

Tolovana Inn, P.O. Box 165; Tolovana Park 97145; 436–2211 or 1–800–333–8890. On South Hemlock, 2 miles south of down-town Cannon Beach. Queen beds in 96 studio, 1- and 2-bedroom units with kitchens, fireplaces, and cable TV. Heated indoor pool, two saunas, whirlpool, and game room. Nonview rooms available. On the beach. Walk to Daggett's Restaurant. Moderate to expensive.

The Waves Motel, 224 North Larch; P.O. Box 3; 436–2205. On the beach, downtown, at Larch and Second. Twin, double, and queen beds in 37 units with cable TV. A variety of accommodations, including cottages and rooms with and without ocean views, kitchens, and fireplaces. Oceanfront spa. Easy beach access. Moderate to expensive.

Campgrounds and RV Parks

RV Resort at Cannon Beach, 345 Elk Creek Road; P.O. Box 219; 436–2231; Oregon, 1–800–452–4470; elsewhere, 1–800–547–6100. East of U.S. 101 at the third exit if traveling north, second exit if traveling south. Has 100 drive-through sites with full hookups and cable TV. Heated indoor pool, spa, showers, picnic area, hiking and biking trails, horse trails, recreation center, convenience store, laundry, propane, gas, and ice. Expensive.

Food

Bill's Tavern, 188 North Hemlock; 436–2202. West side of street, downtown. Lunch and dinner daily. Burgers and deli-style sandwiches, including chili burgers, bacon cheeseburgers, shrimp and cheese, BLT, as well as hot dogs and chili dogs. Excellent selection of wines, imported and domestic beers. Six brews on tap, including Widmer Ale, Guinness Stout, Smith & Reilly. Beer garden, darts, pool table. Nifty tavern. Moderate.

Cafe de la Mer, 1287 South Hemlock; 436–1179. East side of Hemlock, south of downtown. Dinner daily in summer, Thursday through Sunday in winter. A special dining spot serving such appetizers as smoked salmon pâté, crab Dijon, mussels, and steamer clams. Dinner offerings include bouillabaisse, sole and crab in parchment with light curry sauce, oysters tarragon, seafood pasta moutarde, veal with Oregon blue cheese and cream, and rack of lamb with homemade chutney. Moderate.

Dooger's Seafood Grill, 1371 South Hemlock; 436–2225. East side of the street, south of downtown. Breakfast, lunch, and dinner daily. Great breakfast menu includes hobo scramble, steak and eggs, Hangtown fry, Belgian waffles, pancakes, biscuits and gravy, and wonderful three-egg omelets. Lunch includes burgers, chowder, and seafood specials. Dinners are mostly great seafood— calamari, fish and chips, halibut, oysters, steamer and razor clams, crab legs, prawns, lobster, and more. Peanut butter pie, lemon cheese pie, deep-dish apple pie, chocolate fudge cake, and other desserts. Beer, wine, and nonalcoholic wine. Moderate.

Lazy Susan Cafe, 126 North Hemlock; 436–2816. West side of the street, behind Fair Winds and The Wine Shack. Breakfast and lunch daily in summer, closed Tuesday and Wednesday in winter. Poached egg specialties include eggs with Tillamook cheese and eggs Benedict. Oatmeal waffles, seven omelets. Lunch includes broiled shrimp sandwich, quiche of the day, various salads and sandwiches. Daily specials. Moderate.

Shopping and Browsing

Country Shores, 123 South Hemlock; P.O. Box 910; 436–2935. At Ecola Square, east side of Hemlock, downtown. Daily, 10:00 A.M. to 6:00 P.M. A charming shop chock-full of gifts in the country motif, including folk art, quilts, dolls, and collectibles.

Fair Winds, 120 North Hemlock; P.O. Box 642; 436–1201. West side of Hemlock, downtown. Daily, 10:00 A.M. to 6:00 P.M. in summer; closes 5:00 P.M. in winter. January to March, closed Tuesday. A small shop full of nautical items: brassware, scrimshaw, ships' clocks, weather instruments, limited-edition prints, and marine artifacts.

A Great Shop, 436–1129. At Sandpiper Square, west side of North Hemlock, downtown. Daily, 10:00 A.M. to 6:00 P.M. in summer, closes 5:00 P.M. in winter. Interesting and practical items, travel aids, jigsaw puzzles, and the best refrigerator magnets available anywhere.

Haystack Gallery, 183 North Hemlock; P.O. Box 12; 436–2547. At Cannon Beach Mall, east side of Hemlock, downtown. Daily 11:00 A.M. to 5:00 P.M. A fine, large gallery featuring original paintings, limited-edition and open-edition prints, sculpture, pottery, and more. Good collection of marine and wildlife art. Custom matting and framing, packaging, and shipping.

The Northwest Shop, 436–0402. At Sandpiper Square, west side of Hemlock, downtown. Daily, 10:00 A.M. to 6:00 P.M. Many interesting and unusual items here—especially fine wood products, pottery, and artwork.

The Wine Shack, 124 Hemlock; P.O. Box 652; 436–1100. West side of Hemlock, between Fair Winds and Lazy Susan Cafe. Daily, 11:00 A.M. to 6:00 P.M.; Saturday, until 7:00 P.M. Closed Tuesday and Wednesday in winter. Well stocked with imported and domestic wines, Oregon wines, collector's wines, and items of interest to wine fanciers.

Beaches, Parks, Trails, and Waysides

Beaches sweep north and south past the city of Cannon Beach, and most lodging facilities here are right on the beach or within a short walk of it. These are broad beaches with hard-packed sand near the surf line for easy hiking. Low tide exposes tide pools in rocky areas.

Hikers will find beautiful trails at **Oswald State Park** and **Neahkahnie Mountain** to the south. Just north of Cannon Beach is **Ecola State Park,** with picnic facilities, great views of Cannon Beach and the coastline, and trails for hiking and biking. The **Tillamook Head Recreation Trail** winds north from here to Seaside and affords the best view from land of **Tillamook Light.**

More than a mile off **Tillamook Head** is **Tillamook Rock,** atop which stands Oregon's northernmost lighthouse, completed in 1881. Although Tillamook Light ceased operating in 1957, its light and foghorn warned mariners of danger for seventy-six years. After selling several times to private parties, the neglected light deteriorated badly. Its current owners, Eternity at Sea, made extensive repairs, and Terrible Tilly, as the old light was widely known, now functions as a columbarium—a repository for ashen remains of the cremated.

Rentals

Manzanita Fun Merchants, 1235 South Hemlock; 436–1880. South of downtown. Sells and rents Funcycles—three-wheel recumbents.

Mike's Bike Shop, 248 North Spruce; 436–1266. One block east of Hemlock, downtown. Sells, services, and rents bicycles and Funcycles—three-wheel recumbents.

Other Attractions

Coaster Theater, 108 North Hemlock Street; P.O. Box 643; 436–1242. West side of the street, across the courtyard from Fair Winds nautical shop. June through August, tickets at the box office or order by phone. February through May and September through December, buy tickets at Fair Winds, 11:00 A.M. to 5:00 P.M., or phone 436–1201. A busy theater and repertory company offering a summer stock program June through August. Other plays, concerts, and children's programs offered the rest of the year.

Events

April Kite Festival, 436–2623
May Sandcastle Day, 436–2627
June Children's Parade, 436–2623
November Stormy Weather Festival, 436–2623
December Christmas Celebration, 436–2627
Dickens Christmas Play, 436–1242

Travel Information

Cannon Beach Chamber of Commerce, 201 East Second, 436–2623

Haystack Program in the Arts, Portland State University; Division of Continuing Education; 464–4812; Oregon, 1—800–452–4909, ext. 4812; elsewhere, 1–800–547–8887, ext. 4812

Downtown Seaside

Seaside/Gearhart, Oregon 97138
Population: 5,580/967

Location: *On U.S. 101, 17 miles south of Astoria, 9 miles north of Cannon Beach, 79 miles northwest of Portland*

Unquestionably the premier resort destination of the north coast, Seaside has become a year-round destination, especially on weekends. Since 1938, Portlanders have poured into town on weekends, via U.S. 26, also known as the Sunset Highway. When summer vacationers join the throngs, the city fairly bulges.

On U.S. 101 at Broadway is the visitor information center, which is classified a *must stop* for any visitor to Oregon's north coast. This is the biggest and best source of travel information on the Oregon coast and is staffed by friendly and knowledgeable people who are eager to answer your questions and make your coastal stay a pleasant one.

Broadway is Seaside's main east–west street, extending through town from U.S. 101 to the turnaround on the promenade, next to the Shilo Inn. Park on Broadway or any nearby perpendicular or parallel street to visit the many shops, restaurants, galleries, arcades, and attractions of the downtown area. Enjoy the unfettered pace and relaxed atmosphere, akin to the festive air of a carnival midway.

Lodging

The Boarding House Bed & Breakfast, 208 North Holladay Drive; 738–9055. On the Necanicum River, one block west of U.S. 101, two blocks from downtown. Erected in 1898, lovely old Victorian-style boardinghouse with 6 guest rooms, each with private bath, cable TV, twin or queen beds, and down quilts. Decorated with wicker, wood, and family heirlooms. Continental breakfast served in the dining room. River cottage accommodates up to six persons. Moderate.

Gearhart By-The-Sea, P.O. Box 2700; 738–8331; Oregon, 1–800–452–9800; Washington, 1–800–547–0115. Half-mile west of U.S. 101 on North Marion, at the golf links. Queen beds and sofa beds in 80 condominium units with cable TV. One-bedroom, 2-bedroom, and 3-bedroom suites. Fireplaces, ocean view, heated indoor pool, spa, laundry, coffee shop, restaurant, and lounge. Walk to beach, pro shop, and golf course. Expensive.

Gilbert Inn Bed & Breakfast, 341 Beach Drive; 738–9770. West of U.S. 101, one block from the beach, downtown. Built in 1892. Three rooms and 2 suites with queen beds, down quilts, period furniture, private baths, and cable TV. Full breakfast. Moderate.

Riverside Inn Bed & Breakfast, 430 South Holladay; 738–8254. One block west of U.S. 101, two blocks south of Broadway, on the east bank of the river. Has 11 rooms, each with separate entrance, private bath, cable TV. Kitchen units available. Continental breakfast. Moderate.

Shilo Inn, 30 North Prom; 738–9571 or 1–800–222–2244. On the Prom at the turnaround, west end of Broadway. Has 112 deluxe units with cable TV and Showtime. Accommodations range from comfortable east rooms with queen beds to ocean-view rooms and suites with queen or king beds. Fireplaces and kitchens available. Heated indoor pool, sauna, steam room, whirlpool, and exercise room. Located at the center of Seaside's downtown area, near shops and galleries, on the beach. Superb restaurant and lounge on premises. Moderate to expensive.

10th Avenue Inn Bed & Breakfast, 125 10th Avenue; 738–0634. West of U.S. 101, on the beach and promenade at the north end of town. Has 3 rooms, each with queen bed, cable TV, and private bath. Electric typewriter and copy machine available. Full breakfast. Moderate.

Victoriana Bed & Breakfast, 606 12th Avenue; 738–8449. Located one and a half blocks west of U.S. 101, two and a half blocks east of the beach. Has 2 guest rooms with private half baths and shared full bath. Continental breakfast. Inexpensive to moderate.

Campgrounds and RV Parks

Bud's Campground & Groceries, 4412 U.S. 101 North; P.O. Box 2525; 738–6855. West side of U.S. 101, about a mile north of Gearhart. Has 24 RV sites with full hookups and a half-dozen tent sites. Cable TV, showers, laundry, picnic tables, horseshoe pits, store, beer and wine, bait and tackle, gifts, propane. Moderate.

Riverside Lake Resort, Hamlet Route; Box 255; 738–6779. West just off U.S. 101, 1.5 miles south of Seaside. Has 40 spaces available on seventeen wooded acres on the Necanicum River. Showers, full hookups, cable TV. Beautiful setting with year-round fishing. Moderate.

Food

Channel Club, 521 Broadway; 738–8618. Located one and a half blocks west of U.S. 101, downtown. Breakfast, lunch, and dinner daily. Great breakfasts include eggs with New York steak, prime rib, fillet of sole, fillet of salmon, grilled oysters, or razor clams. Also omelets, pancakes, and more. Lunch features chowder, salad bar, burgers, sandwiches, and seafood entrees. In addition to steak and prime rib, dinners include seafood prepared a variety of ways: baked, pan-fried, deep-fried, and sautéed. All the usual local seafoods, as well as frog legs, trout, sea bass, shark, and mahi mahi. Cocktails, beer, and Northwest wines. Moderate.

Doogers Seafood Grill, 505 Broadway; 738–3773. South side of the street, downtown. Lunch and dinner daily. Seafood sandwiches—crab, oyster, halibut. Daily lunch specials served until 4:00 P.M. Dinners served all day, including halibut fish and chips, calamari, oysters, petrale sole, razor clams, salmon, steaks, chicken, salads, and combo plate. Beer and wine. Moderate.

Shilo Inn, 30 North Prom; 738–8481. On the Prom at the turnaround, west end of Broadway. Breakfast, lunch, and dinner daily. Breakfast favorites include eggs Benedict, croissant Benedict, fresh fruits, hotcakes, Belgian waffles, crepes, seafood and vegetable omelets. Lunches include fish and chips, broiled halibut or salmon, chicken stir-fry, quiche, lunch-size salads, and sandwiches. Dinner menu features seventeen appetizers; seafood specialties such as seafood mixed grill or coast cioppino; such broiler dinners as rack of lamb or teriyaki sirloin, as well as Shilo specials: prime rib, veal, and roast pork tenderloin. New York steak or prime rib served surf 'n' turf style with choice of lobster, shrimp, scallops, or king crab. Moderate.

Shopping and Browsing

Sea Quest, P.O. Box 2476; 738–0819. In Gearhart on the west side of U.S. 101 at Pacific. Summer: Tuesday through Sunday, 11:00 A.M. to 5:00 P.M. Winter: Tuesday through Saturday, 11:00 A.M. to 5:00 P.M. Antiques, gift items, locally made craft items, cane, and wicker. An interesting and attractive shop worth a visit.

Wesrose's Antiques & Espresso Bar, 3300 U.S. 101 North; 738–8732. West side of U.S. 101, north end of town. Summer: daily, 11:00 A.M. to 6:00 P.M. Winter: Tuesday through Saturday, noon to 5:00 P.M. Closed Sunday and Monday. An interesting shop carrying some fine antiques and collectibles, including kitchenware, antique scales, old cash registers, furniture, glassware, china, and more. Espresso coffee and desserts in small cafe area.

The Wine Haus, 21 North Columbia; 738–0201. Just north of Broadway, across from Norma's Seafood Restaurant. Daily, 10:00 A.M. to 7:00 P.M.; Friday and Saturday until 8:00 P.M. Imported and domestic wines, more than forty brands of imported beers, domestic and imported tobacco products, coffees, and teas. Decanters, wine racks, glassware, and wine accessories. Daily wine tasting.

Museum

Seaside Museum and Historical Society, 570 Necanicum Drive; P.O. Box 1024; 738–8320. West of U.S. 101, four blocks north of the convention center on the west bank of the river. Daily, 10:30 A.M. to 4:30 P.M. Displays of Indian artifacts, fire equipment, printing equipment, early photographs, and other exhibits depicting the history of Seaside and vicinity.

Beaches, Parks, Trails, and Waysides

Atlantic City has its boardwalks, Seaside its promenade, or prom, as it's known locally. This broad concrete walkway, with its decorative seawall and lampposts, was built in 1920. It parallels the beach for nearly 2 miles and is perfect for strolling or biking, day or night.

The west end of Broadway meets the promenade at the turn-around. There a plaque commemorates trail's end for the Lewis and Clark expedition. Several members of the expedition spent some weeks in the Seaside area during the winter of 1805–1806.

December 28, 1805, only twenty days after Lewis and Clark established their winter headquarters at Fort Clatsop, the captains dispatched five men to the coast to find a suitable site for a salt-works. Five days later, the men, having traveled 15 miles, arrived near what is now Seaside.

The water was sufficiently high in salinity to make three or four quarts of salt a day. Between their arrival and their departure on February 20, 1806, they used five brass kettles to render 1,400 gallons of sea water into three and a half bushels of salt for the expedition's return trip. Visit the reconstructed salt cairn by turning west off U.S. 101 on Avenue G, then south on South Beach Drive to Lewis & Clark Way. Just follow the signs.

Tours and Trips

North Coast Pedi-Cabs, 1021 Broadway; 738–0433. West of U.S. 101, downtown. Quiet Pedi-Cab trips around town or along the promenade. Radio-dispatched, open-air cab service to and from shops, beach, motels, condos, and bed-and-breakfast inns. Hourly and trip rates.

Golf

Gearhart Golf Links, 738–5248. On North Marian at 10th Street, a half-mile west of U.S. 101. This public course is the oldest course in Oregon or Washington—established in 1892. Has eighteen holes, pro shop, resident pro, cart and club rental. Sandtrap Restaurant and Lounge, open for breakfast, lunch, dinner, and drinks. Adjoining rental condos at Gearhart-By-The-Sea.

The Highlands Golf Course, 738–0959. A half-mile west of U.S. 101, 1.3 miles north of Gearhart. Watch for the signs. Public, 9-hole, 1,880-yard, par-32 course. Clubhouse with snacks, coffee, soft drinks, beer, and wine. Pro shop. Equipment sales and rentals.

Rentals

Manzanita Fun Merchants, 332 South Columbia; 738–3733. Two blocks from the beach, south of Broadway. Sells and rents Funcycles—three-wheel recumbents.

Prom Bike Shop, 325 South Holladay Drive; 738–8251. One block east of U.S. 101. Rents bicycles and tandems.

Seaside Arco, 231 South Holladay Drive; 738–7105. One block east of U.S. 101. Year-round moped rentals. Open daily.

Events

For information about events listed without a phone number, contact the Seaside Chamber of Commerce (see Travel Information).

February	Trail's End Marathon
	Beachcomber Festival
July	Fireworks on the Beach
	Miss Oregon Pageant, 738–8326
August	Dahlia Festival
	Volleyball Tournament on the Beach
	Seaside Beach Run
September	Cruisin' the Turnaround
	Oktoberfest
October	Great Pumpkin Party
November	Christmas Gift Fair
December	Yuletide at Seaside

Travel Information

Seaside Chamber of Commerce, 7 North Roosevelt Drive (U.S. 101 at Broadway); 738–6391

Astoria Toll Bridge

Astoria, Oregon 97103
Population: 9,998

Location: *At the junction of U.S. 101 and U.S. 30, on the Columbia River and near its mouth, 17 miles north of Seaside, 95 miles northwest of Portland*

Astoria is America's oldest West Coast city. In fact, it's the oldest continuously occupied settlement west of the Mississippi River, situated on a river that is second in size only to the Mississippi.

The Columbia River heads in British Columbia and flows south and west in a ragged route toward Oregon. The Snake River joins it near Pasco, Washington, just before the Columbia bends westerly. As it approaches Astoria, the great river broadens into an estuary more than 5 miles wide in places. At the mouth of the Columbia, 1,243 miles from its headwaters, the river's average discharge is 262,000 cubic feet of water per second.

138

Naturally, Astoria and the nearby environs are steeped in history. Here's where Captain Robert Gray discovered the Columbia River in 1792 and claimed it for the Americans. Here's where Lewis and Clark's Corps of Discovery spent the winter of 1805–1806. Here's where John Jacob Astor founded a fur-trading post in 1811. Here's where the first pioneer families arrived in the 1840s, and the first post office west of the Mississippi was established in 1847. Here's where coastal fortifications were built toward the end of the Civil War as protection against possible British invasion, via Canada, should the British side with the Confederacy.

Many of Astoria's fine old homes were built in the latter half of the nineteenth century. Some are still private residences; others, beautifully preserved or restored, are bed-and-breakfast inns; one of the most famous, the Flavel House, is a museum.

The Maritime Museum, located on the south bank of the Columbia River in downtown Astoria, stands as a monument to the area's maritime history. The maze of pleasingly displayed, beautifully restored or preserved, and expertly lighted treasures from the sea and river includes artifacts from shipwrecks, a great collection of ship models, whaling and commercial fishing exhibits, and much more—so much, in fact, that this is considered one of the finest museums of its kind.

Moored nearby is Lightship No. 604, *Columbia*—a 128-foot, 617-ton vessel built in East Boothbay, Maine, and launched in 1950. After serving for thirty years off the mouth of the Columbia, she was decommissioned, acquired by the Maritime Museum, and is now open for public tours.

The most prominent modern landmark in the area is the graceful Astoria Toll Bridge, also known as the Astoria-Megler Bridge. Built by Oregon and Washington states in the early 1960s to span the Columbia and join the two states, it was opened to traffic in 1966. It's the world's largest continuous-truss bridge, with a main span of 1,232 feet, overall length of 4.1 miles, and main-span height of 198 feet above the low-water mark, sufficient to allow passage of the Navy's largest ships at high tide.

Lodging

Franklin House Bed & Breakfast, 1681 Franklin Avenue; P.O. Box 804; 325–5044. Franklin at 17th, three blocks south of eastbound U.S. 30. Queen beds in 5 rooms with private baths. Gift shop on premises. Full breakfast, including homemade pastries, served in the main dining room. Near museums and shops. Moderate to expensive.

Franklin Street Station Bed & Breakfast Inn, 1140 Franklin Street; 325–4314. Between 11th and 12th, three blocks south of eastbound U.S. 30. Queen beds in 5 rooms with private baths. Full breakfast served at this charming Victorian inn. Moderate to expensive.

Grandview Bed & Breakfast, 1574 Grand Avenue; 325–0000 or 325–5555. Three blocks south of Marine Drive, between 15th and 16th. Double and queen beds in 7 attractively decorated rooms. Private and shared baths. Continental breakfast includes choice of five coffees, five teas, hot chocolate, milk, juices, and two or more kinds of fresh muffins. Grand view is no exaggeration. Moderate.

Rosebriar Inn Bed & Breakfast, 636 14th Street; 325–7427. Franklin at 14th, three blocks south of eastbound U.S. 30. Twin and queen beds in 9 rooms. Private and shared baths. Full breakfast. Moderate to expensive.

Campgrounds and RV Parks

Fort Stevens State Park, 861–1671. Four miles west of U.S. 101, between Warrenton and Hammond. Oregon's largest state park with more than 600 campsites: 213 full-hookup, 130 electric-hookup, and 262 tent. Showers, tank dump, and many activities for visitors to the great coastal park, including hiking, biking, swimming, fishing, photography, and beachcombing. A historical fort with interpretive displays to explore and study. Moderate.

Food

Pier 11 Feed Store Restaurant & Lounge, 325–0279. At Pier 11 mall, one block north of U.S. 30, between 10th and 11th. Lunch and dinner daily. Lunch features deli-style sandwiches, omelets, crepes, salads, soups, and seafood luncheon plates. Dinners include steaks, chicken, and large seafood menu: oysters, prawns, crab, and razor clams. Daily specials. On the river with a great view. Full bar. Moderate.

Ship Inn, 1 Second Street; 325–0033. Just north off U.S. 30 on Second Street, on the river. Lunch and dinner daily. Fish and chips and more, done to perfection. Halibut, cod, prawns, scallops, oysters, or a combination plate of all five, as well as squid, steamer clams, or sole mornay available as a half order, full order, or dinner. Half and full orders include fries, cole slaw, and tartar sauce. Dinners come with soup, salad, fries, tartar sauce, beverage, and ice cream. Appetizers and sandwiches available, as well as pork sausages and Cornish pasties. Cocktails, wine, and a large selection of domestic and imported beers. Watney's Red Barrel and Guinness Stout on tap. Great view. Moderate.

Shopping and Browsing

Josephson's Smokehouse & Dock, 106 Marine Drive; P.O. Box 412; 325–2190; Oregon, 1–800–828–3474; elsewhere, 1–800–772–3474. Monday through Saturday, 8:00 A.M. to 6:00 P.M. One of the best seafood markets on the coast. Finest fresh-smoked salmon, halibut, tuna, scallops, and oysters, as well as cold-smoked Nova-style lox. Fresh seafoods of all sorts in season, including crawfish. Gift packs of canned, smoked, and pickled salmon, tuna, shark, and more. Mail-order catalog available.

Michael's Antiques & Art Gallery, 1007 Marine Drive; 325–2350. South side of U.S. 30 at 10th and Marine. Daily, 10:30 A.M. to 5:00 P.M. A fine assortment of antiques and collectibles, including furniture, porcelain, silver, carpets, tapestries, glass, brass, paintings, and books.

Museums

Columbia River Maritime Museum, 1792 Marine Drive; 325–2323. North side of U.S. 30, on the river. Daily, 9:30 A.M. to 5:00 P.M.; closed Monday, October through April. A truly superb museum with an extensive maritime collection: entire boats, a steamboat pilothouse, the bridge of a World War II destroyer, operating submarine periscopes for viewing river traffic, ship models, numerous historical displays, photographs, and shop with maritime gifts and books. A *must see.*

Flavel House, 441 Eighth Street; 325–2563. Just south of U.S. 30, downtown. Follow the signs. Daily, 10:00 A.M. to 5:00 P.M. Situated in a beautiful Queen Anne mansion, once the home of Captain George Flavel. Exquisite architecture and ornamental interior complement the historical exhibits.

Heritage Carter Museum & Art Gallery, 1618 Exchange; 325–8395. Exchange at 16th. Daily, 10:00 A.M. to 5:00 P.M. Astoria's old city hall houses the Clatsop County Historical Society's permanent and rotating exhibits, including artifacts from the *Peter Iredale* shipwreck and from other historical sites.

Beaches, Parks, Trails, and Waysides

Miles of beach extend southward from the south jetty at the mouth of the Columbia River. To reach the beach, head for **Fort Stevens State Park,** which lies 4 miles west of U.S. 101, between Warrenton and Hammond. In addition to the fine beach areas, there are 8 miles of bike trails, 5 miles of hiking trails, picnic areas, and old fortifications and gun emplacements with interpretive displays.

Fort Stevens was built in 1865. In 1897 it underwent extensive refortification to improve harbor and coastal defenses. It had eight concrete batteries and armaments including 10-inch rifled cannons capable of lobbing 617-pound projectiles 9 miles.

The greatest activity at the fort was during World War II when 2,500 men were stationed there. New 6-inch guns were installed, which had a range of 15 miles.

On June 21, 1942, the fort had the distinction of being the first American fort to be fired on by a foreign enemy since the War of 1812. The Japanese submarine making all the noise did no damage, and, because the sub was out of range, the fort did not return fire. In fact, in the fort's history, the guns were never fired in anger.

Fort Stevens was deactivated after World War II and used by the Corps of Engineers for some time. The state leased the land in 1976 and has since operated it as Oregon's largest state park.

On October 25, 1906, the *Peter Iredale*—home port Liverpool, England—was twenty-eight days outbound from Salina Cruz. An iron-and-steel, four-masted bark under full sail, she was standing off the mouth of the Columbia when fierce winds and treacherous currents drove her aground on Clatsop Beach. Despite a furious surf, tangles of rigging and debris, and steel masts that, according to the ship's captain, "snapped like pipe stems," all hands escaped safely to shore. Time and tide have taken their toll, but the mighty ship's rusting skeleton remains visible on the beach for visitors to examine and photograph.

The Corps of Volunteers for Northwest Discovery, led by Captains Meriwether Lewis and William Clark, came within sight of the Pacific Ocean in November 1805. Within a month, the party established its winter headquarters in northwest Oregon and built a small fort they named after the friendly local Clatsop tribe.

A reconstructed fort, built by local citizens in 1955, now occupies the same spot. It's managed by the National Park Service and is open all year. During the summer months, park rangers dressed in period costume portray life as it was here for Lewis and Clark and their party of explorers. They demonstrate the use of flintlock rifles, candlemaking techniques, buckskin sewing, woodworking, and canoe building. The **Fort Clatsop National Monument** lies 3 miles east of U.S. 101, just south of Astoria.

In town the Astoria Column provides the best vantage for panoramic views and photography. It stands atop **Coxcomb Hill,** which rises 635 feet above the Columbia River. To reach it, turn south off U.S. 30 at 12th downtown and follow the signs up the hill, through a lovely residential area. Climb the 166 steps to the observation platform, and you will be able to see and photograph great expanses of Oregon and Washington, Astoria, the Columbia River estuary, bridges, jetties, ships, Youngs River and Youngs Bay, the ocean, and mountains. This is a great place to enjoy a sunrise breakfast or to watch a Pacific sunset.

Water Sports and Activities

Fishing is the main water sport in this area, and the fishing centers on the lower Columbia and nearby offshore areas, although surf fishing is seasonally good and the jetties can be productive.

Salmon angling is predominantly an offshore summer fishery. Charter boats are available in Astoria, Warrenton, and Hammond. Anglers who tow their own craft will find launching and mooring facilities in the same areas, but a note of caution is in order. The Columbia bar is dangerous. It did not earn the nickname "Graveyard of the Pacific" for its gentle waters and ease of navigation. Only experienced boaters with craft built for heavy seas should navigate these waters. Even experienced boaters with adequate boats should check on conditions with local boaters, marina owners, and the Coast Guard before venturing out.

Sea-run cutthroat fishing is good from midsummer to early autumn in the lower river and a number of the Columbia's tributaries. Fishing for salmon and steelhead in the lower river can be quite good, but it is affected by the usual fisheries-management concerns, as well as various Indian treaties and the governments of two states. Regulations are abundant and abundantly abstruse. Read them carefully; then check with locals for translation.

One of the top angling attractions of the lower Columbia is the sturgeon fishery. Although these prehistoric fish are available all year, the best fishing here is in the summer, when great runs of forage fish move into the river. Some charter operators offer sturgeon trips. If you try it on your own, check with tackle-shop proprietors for the latest information.

The ocean beaches in this area are the best in Oregon for digging razor clams. There's a midsummer closure along the beaches north of Tillamook, so check the regulations before going.

Executive Charter, 352 Industry Street; 325–7990. One block north of U.S. 30, west of the toll bridge. Operates Wednesday, Friday, and Saturday, 7:00 P.M. to 9:00 P.M. Evening cruises on the Columbia. Guides describe the area and relate its history.

Warrenton Deep Sea, 45 Northeast Harbor Place; Route 1; Box 486; Warrenton 97146; 861–1233. On the Warrenton waterfront, about 3 miles west of U.S. 101. Six-passenger and twelve-passenger boats. Salmon and steelhead trips. Anglers take limits nearly every day during summer and fall. Ocean and river fishing. Columbia River sturgeon fishing. All gear and bait furnished.

Tours and Trips

Astoria is a city for explorers, so get off the highways and get into the residential areas. Check out downtown sights. Walk the waterfront. Pick up a copy of a booklet entitled "Walking Tour of Astoria," available at the museums and visitor center, or buy the sixty-minute cassette tape, "Little San Francisco—The Pirate Town," which comes with a tour map and is available at the same outlets.

Historical Tours of Astoria, 612 Florence, 325–3005. West end of town, three blocks east of Business 101. Personalized small-group tours. Visit Astoria Column, Heritage Center, Flavel House, Fort Astoria, old Clatsop County Jail, Maritime Museum, Lightship *Columbia,* Shallon Winery, Josephson's Smokehouse, Fort Clatsop, Fort Stevens, Victorian homes, historical churches, and more. Tour includes coffee, juice, and muffins at Astoria Column and lunch at Fort Clatsop.

Events

April   Greater Astoria Crab Feed and Seafood Festival, 325–6311

May   Maritime Week, 325–2323

June   Scandinavian Midsummer Festival, 325–6311

August   Clatsop County Fair, 325–4600

            Astoria Regatta, 325–6311

October   Oregon Dixieland Jubilee, 325–6311

            Great Columbia Crossing Bridge Run, 994–3070 or 1–800–452–2151

November Santa Lucia Festival of Lights, 325–6311

December Fort Clatsop National Memorial Holiday Program, 861–2471

Weather and Tide Information

U.S. Coast Guard, Ilwaco; recorded message, 1–206–642–3565

Travel Information

Greater Astoria Chamber of Commerce, 111 West Marine Drive; P.O. Box 176; 325–6311

Washington

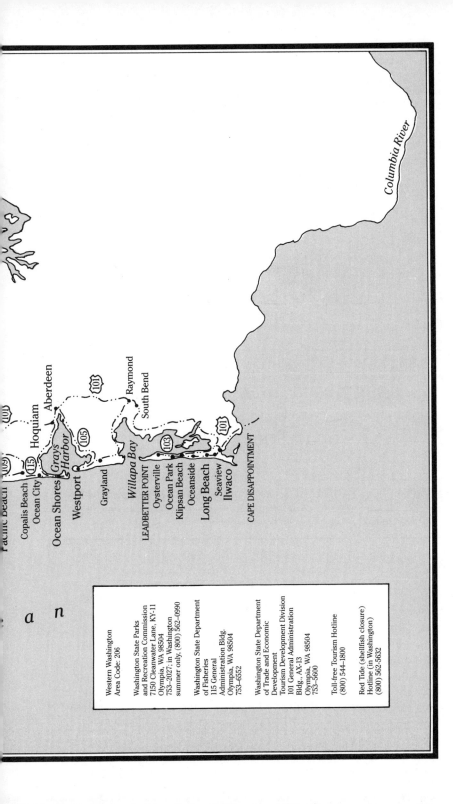

Fort Columbia State Park

Long Beach/Ilwaco, Washington
98631/98624
Population: 1,199/604

Location: *Long Beach is 2 miles north of the U.S. 101 junction at Seaview on State Route 103; Ilwaco is on U.S. 101, 2 miles south of Seaview, 11 miles northwest of the Astoria Toll Bridge over the Columbia River*

Pointing northward from Cape Disappointment and the mouth of the Columbia River is a long finger of surf-lined sand, shrubs, and scrub forest that separates the Pacific Ocean from Willapa Bay. Strung along the peninsula are seven tiny towns that offer visitors a wide range of attractions.

Chief among these in the south are Long Beach and Ilwaco, with Seaview in between. Ilwaco is a waterfront community where commercial, sport, and charter boats are moored a short distance from the Columbia River bar. Long Beach is a resort community with an abundance of travel accommodations and access to its namesake beach.

The peninsula's climate is ideal for growing cranberries, which are a major cash crop, with 465 acres in production. The Ocean Spray cooperative here has produced as much as 3.7 million pounds of berries in a single year.

On the bay side of the peninsula, oysters are big business. Willapa Bay oysters, shipped throughout the country and to many foreign destinations, add an estimated $18 million to the region's economy. All the oyster beds on the bay are privately owned, so there is no public harvest. Fresh oysters are available at local seafood markets, and most area restaurants serve them.

About 13.5 miles north of Long Beach is a community that was established because of the area's abundant oyster beds. Oysterville was founded in 1854 by I. A. Clark and R. H. Espy, grandfather of poet, author, and language maven Willard R. Espy. The town, once the county seat, now dozes on the bay shore, home to fewer than fifty year-round residents.

Oysterville was placed on the National Register of Historic Places in 1976. A number of its buildings, standing since the 1860s and 1870s, have been restored, making the idyllic town a worthwhile spot to visit. Stop by the church to pick up a walking-tour guide and map.

Lodging

Chautauqua Lodge Motel, 304 14th Northwest; P.O. Box 757; Long Beach; 642–4401. Located fourteen blocks north of Long Beach city center. Twin, double, and queen beds in 180 units with cable TV. Fireplaces and ocean-view rooms available. Indoor pool, whirlpool, sauna, and recreation room. Near the golf course. Potlatch Restaurant & Lounge on premises, open daily for breakfast, lunch, and dinner. Moderate.

Heidi's Inn, 126 East Spruce; P.O. Box 776; Ilwaco; 642–2387. On U.S. 101, one block east of the traffic light, downtown. Double and queen beds in 23 newly remodeled units with cable TV, in-room coffee and tea, and in-room refrigerators. Near port docks and charter operators. Inexpensive.

The Shelburne Country Inn & Restaurant, P.O. Box 250;

Long Beach/Ilwaco

Seaview 98644; 642–2442. In Seaview, 2 miles north of Ilwaco, on State Route 103 at North 45th. Has 17 guest rooms with private and shared baths, furnished with antiques. Established in 1896. Listed in the National Register of Historic Places. Room rates include an excellent country-style breakfast. Facilities for handicapped. Widely acclaimed Shoalwater Restaurant on premises. One-act plays in the lobby during the summer. Moderate to expensive.

Campground and RV Parks

Andersen's RV Park, Route 1; Box 480; Long Beach; 642–2231. Located 3.5 miles north of the Long Beach traffic light. Has 15 tent sites and 60 full-hookup RV sites with cable TV. Showers, laundry, playground, beach access. Propane available. Moderate.

Fort Canby State Park, P.O. Box 488; Ilwaco; 642–3029 or 642–3078. Has 250 campsites, 60 with full hookups. Each site has picnic table and stove. Restrooms accommodate the handicapped. Showers, tank dump, two boat ramps at Baker Bay, four hiking trails, two lighthouses, and interpretive center. Ocean view, beach access, summer interpretive programs. Store sells groceries, supplies, and fishing tackle. Reservations accepted. Moderate.

Ocean Park Resort, P.O. Box 339; Ocean Park 98640; 665–4585. At 259th and R Street, two blocks east of Pacific Highway. Has 140 RV sites with full hookups and cable TV. Showers, laundry, heated pool, spa, recreation room, horseshoe pits, volleyball court, wheelchair access. Moderate.

Food

Chuck's Restaurant & Lounge, P.O. Box 503; Long Beach; 642–2721. In north Long Beach. Breakfast, lunch, and dinner daily. Specializes in old-fashioned family dining. Chicken-fried steak with cream gravy, steaks, and seafood are specialties. Friday night prime rib. Cocktails, beer, and wine. Moderate.

Red's Restaurant & Lounge, 109 First Street; Ilwaco; 642–3171. Breakfast, lunch, and dinner daily. Traditional breakfast fare, charbroiled steaks, prime rib, seafood sauté. Friday seafood buffet. Cocktails, beer, and wine. Moderate.

Shoalwater Restaurant, P.O. Box 250; Seaview 98644; 642–4142. At the Shelburne Inn, on State Route 103 at 45th Street, 2 miles north of Ilwaco. Summer: lunch and dinner daily, Sunday brunch. Off-season: dinner daily, except Wednesday, Sunday brunch. Truly one of the Northwest Coast's finest restaurants, offering great soups and salads, including mussel chowder and seafood Caesar's salad. Tempting appetizers include smoked seafood mousse with local smoked oysters, or pâté Shoalwater—Oregon duck-liver pâté with homemade cranberry chutney. Homemade pasta dishes. Entrees, served with homemade bread and seasonally fresh accompaniments, include baked chinook salmon, grilled sturgeon, roasted stuffed quail, bacon-wrapped sirloin—most served with interesting and delicious sauces. Cocktails, beer, and wine. Moderate to expensive.

Uncle Bob's Crab Pot, 1917 Pacific Highway South; Long Beach; 642–2524. On State Route 103 in south Long Beach. Lunch and dinner daily. Specializes in fresh local seafood. Whole-crab dinners, steamer clams, fish and chips, chowder, and crab Louis. Fresh seafood market. Gift packs available. Beer and wine. Moderate.

Shopping and Browsing

Bergkvist Scandia Gifts, 504 Pacific Avenue South; Long Beach; 642–4306. On State Route 103 in South Long Beach. Monday through Saturday, 10:00 A.M. to 6:00 P.M.; Sunday, noon to 4:00 P.M. Scandinavian imports, wood items, quilts, flags, crystal, collectibles, and cards.

Marsh's Free Museum, Long Beach; 642–2188. On State Route 103, between South Fourth and South Fifth. Open daily, except Christmas. Antiques, shells, gifts, souvenirs, glass floats, and a variety of oddities.

Museum

Ilwaco Heritage Foundation Museum, 115 Southeast Lake; Ilwaco; 642–3446. At the convention center downtown, east off First, one block south of the traffic light. Daily, 9:00 A.M. to 5:00 P.M.; Sunday, noon to 4:00 P.M. Displays of western and Indian art, peninsula history, the Old West, and a 50-foot-long miniature landscape and model railroad. A surprisingly fine museum.

Beaches, Parks, Trails, and Waysides

The **Long Beach Peninsula** *is* beaches, parks, trails, and waysides. Along its ocean side is a broad beach of fine basaltic sands packed hard enough to drive automobiles on. It stretches north to south for 28 uninterrupted miles. On the bay side are salt marshes and a wildlife refuge that is home to hundreds of thousands of birds and mammals.

Two miles west of the Astoria Toll Bridge, on the south side of U.S. 101, is **Fort Columbia State Park.** Built at the turn of the century during an era of intensive coastal fortification, Fort Columbia was first occupied by a regular garrison of troops in 1904 and continued to operate through both world wars, though its guns were never fired at an enemy.

The fort is now one of the state's Heritage Sites. Its guns have been removed, but its batteries are open for tours. The enlisted men's barracks have been restored and now function as an interpretive center. The commandant's quarters are now a museum, and the Coast Artillery Hospital is a youth hostel.

Fort Canby, which lies about 3 miles west of Ilwaco, via North Head/Fort Canby Road off U.S. 101, was established in 1875. With its huge bunkers and gun emplacements, it functioned with Forts Columbia and Stevens to guard the mouth of the Columbia. It became a state park in 1957.

The park's 1,700 acres—with campgrounds, picnic areas, hiking trails, and miles of beach—are situated between North Head and Cape Disappointment, with a lighthouse at each end. The **Lewis and Clark Interpretive Center** is also in the park proper, with exhibits that depict the adventures and hardships of the famous Corps of Volunteers for Northwest Discovery.

Construction of the **Cape Disappointment Light** was completed in 1856, after many delays. Although its tower is only 53 feet tall, its light is 220 feet above the water, making it the highest on the Washington coast, as well as the oldest.

The **North Head Light,** built in 1898, has a tower that stands 65 feet tall, with its light 194 feet above the water, visible 20 miles out.

To view and photograph the lighthouse, follow the signs to Fort Canby and to each specific light. Easy hiking trails lead short distances from the parking areas.

At the extreme north end of the Long Beach Peninsula is **Leadbetter Point State Park,** 3 miles north of Oysterville on Stackpole Road. Small dunes, shrubs, grasslands, sparse forests, ponds, and marshes characterize the area. On the west side are beach and ocean; to the east is Willapa Bay.

Much of the south end of the bay, including a 6-mile-long island, is a wildlife refuge. At Leadbetter Point and throughout the wildlife refuge abundant birdlife resides all year with seasonal increases when migratory waterfowl use the area. Other residents include beaver, otter, raccoon, deer, elk, and black bear.

Water Sports and Activities

The great ocean beach that attracts so many beachcombers, hikers, and kite flyers to this area also provides some of the best razor-clam digging in the state. Clam diggers need a license to harvest these strictly regulated bivalves and should check regulations carefully before digging. The beaches are closed to digging much of the year, and spring and fall openings depend on how well the clam populations are faring.

Fishing along the ocean beaches is mainly for surfperch and seaperch, which are also taken from the bay shore as well as from the north-jetty area and Baker Bay, near Ilwaco. Jetty fishermen also take bottomfish and the occasional lingcod. Along the lower Columbia, shore anglers also take flounder and sole.

The fishery for Columbia River salmon and steelhead is heavily regulated, so be sure to check the regulations carefully before keeping any salmonids caught here. The main salmon fishery is offshore, and at times it can be excellent. Those who tow their own boats will find adequate launching facilities at Ilwaco, but keep in mind that the mouth of the Columbia is often treacherous and never a place for the novice boater.

The lower Columbia also offers some fine sturgeon fishing all year, but particularly during the late spring and early summer. Farther upriver, anglers take largemouth bass in the many sloughs and creeks. From midsummer to early fall, the same waters give up good catches of sea-run cutthroat trout.

A large charter fleet at Ilwaco is ready to serve anglers. These experienced skippers know the Columbia bar and where to find fish offshore. They fish the runs of coho and chinook salmon and

155

work the reefs for bottomfish. Some also offer river fishing for sturgeon.

Ilwaco Charter Service, Box 323; Ilwaco; 642–3232. At the Ilwaco waterfront. Salmon fishing, reef fishing for bottomfish, tuna trips, river sturgeon fishing. Cold storage available.

Pacific Salmon Charters, P.O. Box 519; Ilwaco; 642–3466 or 642–4322. At the Ilwaco waterfront. Modern fleet of charter boats. Salmon trips, bottomfish trips, and combination trips offshore. Sturgeon trips on the lower Columbia. Trips are six to eight hours. All gear furnished. Will arrange to have your catch canned, smoked, stored, or shipped.

Tours and Trips

Willapa Bay Tours, P.O. Box 22; Nahcotta 98637; 642–4892. Located 11 miles north of Long Beach on the east side of the peninsula. Rents kayaks for guided and unguided half-day, all-day, and overnight trips on Willapa Bay and the Columbia River.

Golf

Peninsula Golf, 642–2828. On State Route 103 at 97th, just north of Long Beach. A 9-hole course with putting green, clubhouse, snack bar, fountain, club and cart rental, and pro merchandise.

Events

April	Ragtime Rhodie Festival, Long Beach, 642–3166
	Loyalty Day Children's Parade, Ilwaco, 642–2400
May	Loyalty Day Parade, Long Beach, 642–2400
	10K and 20K Volksmarches, Long Beach, 642–2400
	Clam Diggers' Breakfast, Ilwaco, 642–2400
June	Annual World's Longest Beach Run, Long Beach, 642–4207
July	Fourth of July Fireworks, Long Beach, 642–4421
	Annual Sand Sations, Ilwaco, 642–2400
October	Cranberry Festival, Ilwaco, 642–3446
	Water Music Festival, Long Beach, 642–3040

Weather and Tide Information

U.S. Coast Guard, Ilwaco; recorded message, 642–3565

Travel Information

Long Beach Peninsula Visitors' Bureau, P.O. Box 562; Long Beach; 642–2400; Washington, 1–800–451–2542; Oregon, Idaho, Northern California, 1–800–451–2540

Refuge Manager, Willapa National Wildlife Refuge; Ilwaco; 484–3482

Westport and the waterfront

Westport, Washington 98595
Population: 1,954

Location: *West of U.S. 101, via State Route 105, 23 miles southwest of Aberdeen, 32 miles northwest of Raymond*

Since its earliest days, Westport has been a sea town, dependent on the ocean for its livelihood and for its connection with the rest of the world. It is situated on a small peninsula called Point Chehalis (chuh-*hay*-lis) that juts northward to within 2 miles of Point Brown on the opposite shore. The two points form the jaws of Grays Harbor, a large bay more than 12 miles wide in places and reaching inland more than 15 miles to the cities of Aberdeen and Hoquiam.

Grays Harbor was named after explorer and fur trader Captain Robert Gray. He crossed the bar and passed Chehalis Point in 1792 aboard his ship *Columbia Rediviva,* looking for Indians who would trade pelts for trinkets.

By the early 1900s, Westport had become an important whaling port. Ironically, vessels still depart the harbor and cross the bar in pursuit of whales that now get hurrahs instead of harpoons, as observers thrill to the sight and nearness of the huge mammals.

It's the smaller but more numerous denizens of the sea, however, that attract the great majority of visitors to Westport each year: chinook and coho salmon, rockfish and lingcod, flounder and halibut, tuna and shark. Anglers by the thousands converge on Westport each season. And there to serve them is not only the largest fleet of charter boats on the Washington coast, but also an entire city, with its motels and inns, campgrounds and RV parks, restaurants and taverns, delis and markets, tackle shops and cold-storage facilities poised for the purpose of making fishermen happy.

Lodging

Albatross Motel, 200 East Dock Street; P.O. Box 1546; 268–9233. Downtown, three blocks from the waterfront. Twin, double, queen, and king beds in 13 units with cable TV, some with ocean view. Near shops, restaurants, and charter operators. Inexpensive to moderate.

Chateau Westport Motel, P.O. Box 349; 268–9101. At West Hancock and South Surf streets, west of southbound State Route 105. Queen and king beds in 110 rooms, suites, and studios with cable TV. Heated indoor pool, sun deck, hot tub, ocean view, and fireplaces. Continental breakfast. Moderate.

Coho Charters Motel & RV Park, 2501 North Nyphus; 268–0111. One block from Float 12 in the boat basin. Has 28 rooms and 80 full-hookup RV sites with cable TV. Showers, laundry, fish-cleaning facilities. Booking office for Coho Charters. Moderate.

Glenacres Inn Bed & Breakfast, 222 North Montesano; P.O. Box 1246; 268–9391. On State Route 105. Situated on eight wooded acres. Has 8 rooms with private baths and antique furnishings. Deck, gazebo-covered hot tub, barbecue and picnic area, badminton and volleyball, horseshoe pit, horse-trailer space and corral. Continental breakfast. Also 4 guest cottages with full kitchens. Moderate.

159

Westport

Campgrounds and RV Parks

Grayland Beach State Park, 267–4301. Off State Route 105 in Grayland, 6 miles south of Westport. Has 60 full-hookup sites for RVs to 40 feet. Showers, picnic areas, self-guided interpretive trail. On 210 acres with beach access, beachcombing, kite flying, surf fishing. Moderate.

Ocean Gate Resort, P.O. Box 67; Grayland 98547; 267–1956. On State Route 105 in Grayland, 6 miles south of Westport. Has 20 tent and 22 RV sites with full hookups, showers, laundry, firewood, picnic tables, playground. Also 6 cabins with kitchens. Inexpensive to moderate.

Pacific Motel and Trailer Park, 330 South Forrest; 268–9325. On southbound State Route 105. Has 80 RV sites with full hookups, cable TV, showers, pool, recreation room, and barbecue. Also 11 motel rooms and an apartment. Moderate.

Twin Harbors State Park, 268–9565 or 753–4055. West of State Route 105, 2 miles south of Westport. Has 332 campsites: 49 with full hookups, picnic table and stove at each site. Kitchen shelter, showers, tank dump. Park is on 317 acres with 17,710 feet of ocean frontage. Moderate.

Food

Arthur's, 2681 Westhaven Drive; 268–9292. On the waterfront. Lunch and dinner daily, except Monday. Soups, salads, and sandwiches. Specialties include steaks, prime rib, fresh seafoods, cioppino, and pasta dishes. Homemade desserts. Cocktails, beer, and wine. Moderate.

Coley's Seafood, 2309 Westhaven Drive; 268–9000. On the waterfront. Breakfast, lunch, and dinner daily, 4:00 A.M. to 10:00 P.M. Fishermen's breakfasts and lunches to go—stuffed croissants, sandwiches, salads, fruits, cold cuts, and bread. Deli and hors d'oeuvre trays, smoked salmon, cracked crab. Moderate.

Shari's Continental House, 2581 Westhaven Drive; 286–9228. On the waterfront. Breakfast, lunch, and dinner daily. Sunday brunch. Early breakfast and box lunches for fishermen. Texas-style barbecue, steaks, fresh seafood, Mexican food, and pasta specialties. Full bar. Moderate.

Museum

Westport Maritime Museum, 2201 Westhaven Drive; P.O. Box 2201; 268–9692. At the old Coast Guard Station, on the waterfront. Summer: Wednesday through Sunday, noon to 4:00 P.M. Weekends in April and May. Winter by appointment. Displays of cranberry-industry and logging equipment. Indian artifacts, agates and other gemstones, shipwreck relics, Coast Guard memorabilia, and many historical photographs, all housed in a beautiful old Nantucket-style Coast Guard building. Also on the premises are reassembled skeletons of a sea lion, a porpoise, and a gray whale.

Water Sports and Activities

Westport is built for all kinds of saltwater angling. In the boat basin are docks, floats, ramps, and an arched bridge leading to a 1,000-foot-long fishing pier, from which sportsmen take crabs, perch, cod, rockfish, flounder, sole, lingcod, and even salmon.

Westport's huge charter fleet serves anglers, whale watchers, birdwatchers, and sightseers. Bottomfishing is good most of the year, weather and water conditions permitting. Salmon angling is a summer fishery offshore, with limit catches the rule rather than the exception. Albacore tuna show well offshore in July and through early fall. Several charter operators are now running shark trips and combination shark/tuna trips. Peak season for watching and photographing whales is from March to mid-May.

Many of the charter operators and other businesses have toll-free phone numbers for those phoning in Washington. These are seasonal phones, however, usually in service from late spring to early fall.

Cachalot Charters, P.O. Box 348; 268–0323. On the waterfront, across from Float 2. Fast, comfortable boats offering salmon, bottomfish, and tuna trips. Rental tackle available. Bait furnished. Free coffee and fish bags. Whale watching on weekends, March through May.

Deep Sea Charters, 268–9300; Washington, 1–800–562–0151. On the waterfront, across from Float 6. Half-day and full-day salmon trips. Bottomfishing trips every day for rockfish, lingcod, and others. Tuna trips 50 to 100 miles offshore. Whale-watching and estuary tours. Get on the "tuna call list" to be called when the albacore show.

161

Westport

Gull Charters, P.O. Box 351; 268–9186 or 268–9676; Washington 1–800–562–0175. On the waterfront, across from Float 3. Whale-watching and birdwatching excursions. Also shark-fishing trips for spiny dogfish as well as soupfin, blue, and thresher sharks, among others. Gear furnished. No license required. No limit.

Neptune Charters, P.O. Box 426; 268–0124 or 1–800–422–0425. On the waterfront, across from Float 14. Salmon, bottom-fishing, and tuna trips. Rental tackle and bait available. Two-day tuna trips—everything furnished. Whale-watching trips March 1 to May 15.

Northwest Educational Tours, P.O. Box 545; 268–9150; Washington, 1–800–562–0145. Whale-watching excursions scheduled for weekends, March through May. Special family rates.

Ocean Charters, 2315 Westhaven Drive; 268–9144; Washington, 1–800–562–0105. On the waterfront. Offers six-person boats for small parties or larger boats to accommodate up to twenty-five. Salmon, bottomfish, tuna, and shark trips. Overnight tuna/shark trips include food, bunk, bait, and tackle. Just bring a sleeping bag.

Salmon Charters, P.O. Box 545; 268–9150; Washington, 1–800–562–0145. On the waterfront. Ten modern and fast boats offering salmon trips, bottomfishing for rockfish and lingcod, tuna fishing, and whale watching. Tackle rental. Light-tackle angling.

Seahorse Charters, P.O. Box 327; 268–9100; Washington, 1–800–562–0171. On the waterfront, across from Float 5. Fast, modern boats offering salmon, tuna, and bottomfishing trips as well as whale-watching excursions. Tackle available for rent or sale. Free coffee.

Snider's Rainbow Charters, P.O. Box 585; 268–9182; Washington, 1–800–562–0165. On the waterfront. Salmon, tuna, and bottomfish trips. Also one-and-a-half-hour harbor tours.

Tours and Trips

Westport/Ocean Shores Passenger Ferry, 220 Dock Street; Float 4; 268–0047. Operates between Westport and Ocean Shores on weekends in May, daily June 1 to Labor Day. Departs Westport dock every one and a half hours from 8:45 A.M. to 7:15 P.M.

Other Attractions and Services

Coley's Seafood, 2309 Westhaven Drive; 268–9000; Washington, 1–800–562–0101. Will smoke, can, freeze, and store the fish you catch.

Westport Aquarium, 321 Harbor Street; 268–0471. Between Salmon Charters and Anchor Cannery, a half block from waterfront. Daily, 9:00 A.M. to 6:00 P.M. Displays local fish and shellfish.

Events

April   Crab Feed and Crab Races, 268–9422
June   Annual Kite Fly, 268–0877
July   Annual Fireworks and Dock Crunch, 268–9422
September Seafood Festival, 268–9422

Weather and Tide Information

U.S. Coast Guard, Westport; recorded message, 268–0622

Travel Information

Westport/Grayland Chamber of Commerce, 1200 North Montesano; 268–9422

When in port at Aberdeen, the brig *Lady Washington* is open for tours. (Photo courtesy Grays Harbor Historical Seaport)

Aberdeen/Hoquiam, Washington
98520/98550
Population: 17,010/9,010

Location: *On U.S. 101, 104 miles south of Forks, 83 miles north of Astoria Toll Bridge, 48 miles west southwest of Olympia*

Aberdeen was named after a city in Scotland. The Gaelic word means "the meeting of two rivers," which is appropriate for this Washington town established at the confluence of the Chehalis (chuh-*hay*-lis) and Wishkah (*wish*-kah) rivers. The name Hoquiam (*hoh*-kwee-uhm) derives from the Indian term *ho-qui-umpts,* meaning "hungry for wood," which referred to the abundance of driftwood at the mouth of the Hoquiam River. The term would also aptly describe the side-by-side cities today, with their sawmills, wood-products factories, and lumber-laden ships bound for the Orient.

164

This is an area mainly dependent on logging and the manufacture and shipping of lumber and wood products. Aberdeen's first sawmill was built in 1884. The shipbuilding industry flourished until the 1920s, followed by the establishment of plywood, shake, and pulp mills as well as furniture and other wood-product factories. The area, like so many of its kind, shows some wear from years of industrial use and scars from a recent recession and slumps in the wood-products industry.

Nevertheless, the Aberdeen/Hoquiam area is of interest to travelers and promises to offer even more in the near future. It has long been a favorite stopover for travelers heading north to the Olympic Peninsula and Olympic National Park or south to the beaches and parks of Washington and Oregon. The communities offer adequate eateries and overnight accommodations. For those with time to linger, there are three museums, some handsomely restored homes, and a number of annual events worth investigating.

This is also an important stopover area for nonhuman travelers. In April and May, the 98 square miles of Grays Harbor estuary, tidelands, and marshes attract shorebirds by the hundreds of thousands. They congregate here each spring to rest, feed, and store fat for their long journey north to arctic and subarctic nesting areas.

To reach the south shore areas and marshes on the estuary, take State Route 105 west off U.S. 101 in south Aberdeen, which leads to Westport. State Route 109, west off U.S. 101 in Hoquiam, follows the north shore all the way to the ocean.

No doubt, the greatest allure this area holds for travelers is the ambitious project launched in 1988 after many months of planning and fund raising. Called the **Grays Harbor Historical Seaport,** this major undertaking promises to be one of the most important and enjoyable maritime attractions on the Pacific Coast.

A topnotch maritime museum will display historical exhibits and nautical artifacts and will include rooms for classes and lectures, a library, and a gift shop. A new motel and convention center will complement the nearby seaport village with all its nautical shops and other attractions.

Two tall ships, built and launched in Aberdeen, will call this their home port. The *Lady Washington* and the *Columbia Rediviva*—square-rigged replicas of historically famous vessels

165

that plied the Pacific in the late 1700s—will be available for tours but will also be active sailing and training vessels, traveling with full crews and cadets to other ports.

The original *Lady Washington* sailed the Pacific in the 1780s and opened trade routes with the Orient. Captain Robert Gray, commanding the *Columbia Rediviva,* discovered the Columbia River and sailed into Grays Harbor in 1792. Both ships played significant roles in opening the Pacific Coast fur trade and establishing U.S. claims to the Oregon Territory, of which Washington was then a part.

The Historical Seaport will include boardwalks and viewpoints and should be a photographer's delight. Many special maritime events are planned, including tours of visiting ships, lecture programs, and a summer maritime festival.

Before you travel to this area, phone or write for the latest information on this exciting project.

Lodging

Lytle House Bed & Breakfast, 509 Chenault; Hoquiam; 533–2320. West of U.S. 101, next to Hoquiam's Castle. Two guest rooms with shared bath in a fine old Victorian home furnished with antiques. Full breakfast. Moderate.

Olympic Inn, 616 Heron Street; Aberdeen; 533–4200; Washington, 1–800–562–8618. On southbound U.S. 101, downtown. A modern motel with queen beds in 55 rooms, cable TV, in-room coffee, and in-room refrigerators. Laundry facilities. Kitchen units available. Moderate.

Food

Billy's Restaurant, 322 East Heron Street; Aberdeen; 533–7144. On southbound U.S. 101, downtown. Lunch and dinner daily. A newly restored saloon that serves tasty and hearty burgers and other sandwiches as well as salads, steaks, and seafood dinners. Full bar. Moderate.

Misty's, 116 North Heron Street; Aberdeen; 533–0956. On southbound U.S. 101, downtown, across from the Union 76 station. Lunch and dinner Monday through Saturday. Excellent appetizers, soups, salads, and sandwiches. Pasta dishes, stir-fry dinners, sumptuous desserts. A good selection of Washington wines and forty-eight imported and domestic beers, as well as four microbrews (made in small, local breweries) on tap. Moderate.

Museums

Aberdeen Museum of History, 111 East Third Street; Aberdeen; 533–1976. Four blocks east of northbound U.S. 101, between Broadway and North I Street. Summer: Wednesday through Sunday, 11:00 A.M. to 4:00 P.M. Winter: weekends, noon to 4:00 P.M. Situated in the old National Guard Armory. Pioneer, farm, logging, and other exhibits. Model of downtown Aberdeen before the destructive 1903 fire. Antique fire trucks, canoe collection, blacksmith shop, mercantile store, and more.

Hoquiam's Castle, 515 Chenault Avenue; Hoquiam; 533–2005. North of State Route 109, three blocks on Garfield. Summer: daily, 11:00 A.M. to 5:00 P.M. Rest of the year by appointment. State and national historic site, built in 1897 as the residence of timber tycoon Robert Lytle, and fully restored in 1971 by the Robert Watson family. A twenty-room mansion furnished with period antiques, cut-glass chandeliers, Tiffany lamps, stained glass, oak paneling. Everything here is top quality.

Polson Museum, 1611 Riverside Avenue; P.O. Box 432; Hoquiam; 533–5862. On U.S. 101. June through Labor Day: Wednesday through Sunday, 11:00 A.M. to 4:00 P.M. September through May: weekends, noon to 4:00 P.M. A beautiful twenty-six-room mansion that's now a national historic site, set amidst trees and rose bushes. Sawmill and logging exhibits, kitchen appliances and utensils, sports equipment and photographs, early fashions and furnishings, all pleasingly displayed.

Events

April	Rhododendron Show, Hoquiam, 532–9255
	Festival of Shorebirds, Aberdeen, 533–5228
	Rock and Gem Show, Aberdeen, 532–0564
July	Annual Americanism Days, Aberdeen, 532–1924
August	Bite of Grays Harbor, Aberdeen, 532–9253
September	Loggers' Playday, Hoquiam, 538–1147
October	Annual Octoberfest, Aberdeen, 532–1230

Aberdeen/Hoquiam

Weather and Tide Information

U.S. Coast Guard, Westport; recorded message, 268–0622

Travel Information

Grays Harbor Chamber of Commerce, 2704 Sumner Avenue; P.O. Box 450; Aberdeen; 532–1924

Grays Harbor Historical Seaport, 813 East Heron Street; P.O. Box 2019; Aberdeen; 532–8611

From Ocean Shores northward

Ocean Shores/Pacific Beach, Washington
98569/98571
Population: 2,175/1,200

Location: *Ocean Shores is west of U.S. 101, via State Route 109 and State Route 115, and about 20 miles west of Hoquiam; Pacific Beach is on State Route 109, west of U.S. 101, 16 miles north of Ocean Shores*

Several small communities lie along the Pacific, from Ocean Shores north. Ocean City (population: 500) is 8 miles to the north. Copalis Beach (population: 900) is 3.5 miles farther. Two miles above Pacific Beach is Moclips (population: 700). The village of Taholah is 9 miles north in the Quinault Indian Reservation, but there are no tourist facilities there, and the beaches are closed to the public.

At the southern end of this stretch is a peninsula that separates Grays Harbor from the ocean. The flat land here is charac-

169

terized by broad sweeps of sandy beach and prairies of beach grass, laced with narrow lakes and freshwater canals. Northward, lowlands give way to rocky bluffs, grasses succumb to shrubs, and highlands belong to timber.

Before 1960 the Ocean Shores area was a ranch owned by the Minard family. It was purchased for $1 million and subsequently developed. Today it is a residential and resort area of about 6,000 acres, with 6 miles of ocean beach where residents and visitors enjoy flying kites, riding horses, fishing, clam digging, hiking, and searching the surf and drift lines for seaborne treasures.

This is an active and artsy community that puts on an abundance of fairs, festivals, and shows each year. One event should provide visitors with insight into the pace of Ocean Shores and the seriousness with which residents perceive themselves and, perhaps, the outside world. "Undiscovery Day" is a celebration of that fateless event in 1792 when Captain George Vancouver sailed right by without discovering Ocean Shores.

Lodging

The Canterbury Inn, P.O. Box 310; Ocean Shores; 289–3317; Washington, 1–800–562–6678. Has 44 oceanfront condominiums with cable TV, HBO, Disney Channel, private balconies, and kitchens with microwave ovens and dishwashers. Heated indoor pool and spa. Moderate to expensive.

Iron Springs Resort, P.O. Box 207; Copalis Beach 98535; 276–4230. A longtime Washington coast favorite with 23 cottages (some duplexes) and 2 apartments with kitchens and fireplaces, accommodating two to ten persons. All linens and bedding furnished. Rental TVs available or bring your own. Heated, covered pool. On 100 beautiful wooded acres. Moderate to expensive.

Moonstone Beach Motel, P.O. Box 156; Moclips 98562; 276–4346. Queen beds in 8 oceanfront units with cable TV. Units sleep two to six persons. Only 40 feet from the beach. Wheelchair access. Inexpensive to moderate.

Ocean Crest Resort, Sunset Beach; Moclips 98652; 276–4465. One mile north of Pacific Beach, on State Route 109. Has 45 units with cable TV. Studios and 1- and 2-bedroom apartments accommodate two to six persons. Fireplaces and balconies. Kitchens available. Recreation center with exercise equipment, spa, sauna, heated indoor pool, tanning bed, and sun decks. Nightlighted beach and surf. Wooded setting. Children's play area. Beauty salon, gift shop, and gallery, as well as a fine restaurant on premises. Cocktail lounge with ocean view and entertainment. Moderate to expensive.

The Sandpiper Beach Resort, P.O. Box A; Pacific Beach; 276–4580. Located 1.5 miles south of Pacific Beach, on State Route 109. Twin and queen beds in 29 units with fireplaces and ocean view. Studios and units with 1 to 3 bedrooms. On the beach. Kite and gift shop on premises. No in-room phones or TV. Moderate.

The Sands Resort, P.O. Box 57; Ocean Shores; 289–2444 or 1–800–841–4001. On Ocean Boulevard. Cable TV and HBO in 80 units, some with kitchens. Heated indoor pool, sauna, whirlpool, hot tubs, game room, wheelchair access. Inexpensive to moderate.

Campgrounds and RV Parks

Ocean City State Park, 289–3553. Two miles north of Ocean Shores on State Route 115, on the ocean. Has 149 tent sites and 29 full-hookup RV sites for vehicles of any size. Picnic tables, fireplaces, showers, firewood in summer, kitchen shelter, tank dump. Wheelchair access. Inexpensive.

Pacific Beach State Park, 289–3553. Just off State Route 109 in Pacific Beach. Has 118 tent sites and 20 RV sites with water and electric hookups for vehicles to 45 feet. Picnic tables, showers, tank dump. On the beach. Inexpensive.

Food

Look's Village Chinese Restaurant, Point Brown Northeast; Ocean Shores; 289–2152. Lunch and dinner daily, closed Wednesdays in winter. Chicken chow mein, sweet-and-sour pork or chicken, barbecued pork or chicken wings, fried rice, fried wonton, egg rolls, deep-fried prawns, and more. Moderate.

The Polynesian Restaurant & Lounge, Ocean Shores; 289–3361. Breakfast, lunch, and dinner daily. Traditional and unusual breakfast fare. Large selection of seafoods, pasta dishes, and Polynesian cuisine. Full bar. Moderate.

Shopping and Browsing

Gallery Marjuli, Homeport Plaza; Point Brown Avenue; Ocean Shores; 289–2858. Daily, 10:30 A.M. to 5:00 P.M. Gifts and artwork. Limited-edition prints. Marine art. Unusual glassware, Mount St. Helens glass, vases, pottery, stationery, and more.

Ocean Shores Kites, Shores Mall; Chance A La Mer Boulevard Northwest; Ocean Shores; 289–4103. Daily, 10:00 A.M. to 5:00 P.M. Custom kites, windsocks, banners, flags, air toys, accessories, and kite repair. Largest kite shop on the Washington coast.

Tide Creations Gift Shop, P.O. Box 121; Ocean Shores; 289–2550. On Point Brown Avenue, south toward the marina. Daily, 10:00 A.M. to 5:00 P.M. A whacky shop full of gift items, T-shirts, sweatshirts, and wonderful homemade fudge—fifteen to thirty varieties.

Water Sports and Activities

Surf fishing is best along the ocean beach in the Ocean Shores vicinity and from the north jetty when water conditions permit. Surfperch and seaperch are the main species taken from the surf. The jetty gives up perch, rockfish, cabezon, lingcod, and salmon.

The beach from the jetty north to Moclips and beyond is good for digging razor clams in season. In fact, the motels and resorts along this stretch of coast fill up fast not only on weekends during the summer but also during minus-tide periods.

Duck Lake and Lake Minard and the 23 miles of interconnecting freshwater canals provide plenty of opportunities for canoeing, water-skiing, fishing, and exploring. The lakes are stocked with trout, but the best fishing here is for largemouth bass, with some big fish taken every year.

Those who tow boats on trailers or who arrive in the area by boat will find moorage at the marina. Some people fish and crab from the docks here, but there's much better dock and pier fishing and crabbing across Grays Harbor at Westport. During the summer, a passenger ferry travels between Ocean Shores and Westport.

172

Tours and Trips

Westport/Ocean Shores Passenger Ferry, Marina Store; Main Float; Ocean Shores; 289–3391 or 289–3393. Operates between Ocean Shores and Westport on weekends in May; daily, June 1 to Labor Day. departs Ocean Shores dock every one and a half hours, from 9:30 A.M. to 6:30 P.M.

Golf

Ocean Shores Municipal Golf Course, Albatross and Canal Drive; Ocean Shores; 289–3357. An 18-hole, 6,021-yard, par-71 course. Pro shop, cart and club rental and sales. Clubhouse with restaurant and lounge.

Events

March	Beachcombers' Fun Fair, Ocean Shores, 289–4552
	Dugan's Run, Ocean Shores, 289–2430
April	"Spring Fling of Kites" Festival, Copalis Beach, 289–4552
	Associated Arts Photo Show, Ocean Shores, 289–3857
	Undiscovery Day, Ocean Shores, 289–2451
	Casino Nite, Ocean Shores, 289–5781
May	Polly's Antique Flea Market, Ocean Shores, 289–4411
June	Woodcarving Show, Ocean Shores, 289–4411
July	Olympic Art Show, Ocean Shores, 532–2067
	"Color Over the Water" Kite Contest, Copalis Beach, 289–4552
	Annual Sand Sculpture Contest, Copalis Beach, 289–4552
	Annual Fire Over the Water, Ocean City, 289–4552
	Annual Kite-Flying Contest, Pacific Beach, 289–4552
August	Flatwater Canoe Races, Copalis Beach, 289–4411
	Polly's Antique Flea Market, Ocean Shores, 289–4411
September	Annual Kelper's Parade, Moclips, 289–4552
	Festival of Colors—Autumn at the Beach, Ocean Shores, 289–2451
	Associated Arts & Crafts Show, Ocean Shores, 289–3857
	"Splash 'n' Dash" 10K Run, Ocean City, 289–4552

Ocean Shores/Pacific Beach

October   Old Time Fiddler Fest, Ocean City, 289–4552
             Halloween Celebration, Ocean Shores, 289–3857
November Dixieland Jazz Festival, Ocean Shores, 289–2451
December Christmas Party, Ocean Shores, 289–4411

Weather and Tide Information

U.S. Coast Guard, Westport; recorded message; 268–0622

Travel Information

Ocean Shores Chamber of Commerce, Chance A La Mer Boulevard, Ocean Shores; 289–2451

Washington Coast Chamber of Commerce, P. O. Box 562; Copalis Beach 98535; 289–4552

Sekiu on Clallum Bay and Strait of Juan de Fuca

Neah Bay/Sekiu, Washington 98357-98381
Population: 2,594/600

Location: *Neah (nee-uh) Bay is on State Route 112, north of U.S. 101, 66 miles west-northwest of Port Angeles, 46 miles northwest of Forks; Sekiu (see-kyoo), also on State Route 112, is 15 miles east-southeast of Neah Bay*

Tucked away on the outer edge of Washington and the northwestern tip of the Olympic Peninsula, Neah Bay is home and home port to the Makah (muh-*kah*) Indians, a unique tribe unrelated to any others in the United States. These are a handsome, intelligent people who can trace their seafaring ancestry as far back as 1,000 B.C.

The Makahs have traditionally depended upon the sea for most of their food—today mainly as commercial fishermen and charter operators, in the past as fishermen, shellfish gatherers, and

175

whalers. As whalers, they showed unparalleled courage and skill, venturing forth in canoes to hunt their great quarry armed only with harpoons with points made of mussel shells.

About 500 years ago, a mud slide buried five Makah houses at the village of **Ozette,** 12 miles south of Cape Flattery. The clay earth encapsulated these houses and suspended them in time. By 1970, tides had eroded away enough earth to begin exposing the long-entombed Makah artifacts. In April of that year, a team of archeologists, headed by Richard Daugherty from Washington State University, began a dig that was to last eleven years and produce more than 55,000 wonderfully preserved artifacts, representing 97 percent of all Northwest Coast Indian artifacts found to date. The best of these are on display at the $2.5 million **Makah Museum** in Neah Bay.

The Makahs are friendly people who have a fascinating history on a spectacular part of the Washington coast. Best of all is their willingness and eagerness to share their culture and knowledge with the rest of us. In their own language, the name for their tribe means simply "people of the cape." The Salish name for them, however, was *Makah,* meaning "generous people."

Sekiu is an Indian word meaning "quiet waters." The tiny town of that name is situated on the west shore of Clallum Bay on the Strait of Juan de Fuca. The community of Clallum Bay (population: 600) is about 2 miles east of Sekiu. Here and elsewhere along State Route 112, sport fishing is the main attraction, with hiking, beachcombing, photography, and wildlife watching other popular attractions.

Lodging

Curley's Resort, P.O. Box 265; Sekiu; 963–2281. Has 22 units to accommodate up to six persons. Cable TV, some kitchens. Also 13 RV sites, full hookups, and showers. Boat and motor rental, launching and moorage, bait, tackle, and ice. Inexpensive to moderate.

Thunderbird Resort, P.O. Box 218; Neah Bay; 645–2450. Has 26 rooms and kitchen units with cable TV. Wheelchair access. Also 40 RV sites with full hookups. Showers. Boat launching and moorage. Bait, tackle, and ice. Inexpensive to moderate.

Tyee Motel & RV Park, P.O. Box 193; Neah Bay; 645–2223.

Has 18 rooms and kitchen units with cable TV. Also 30 RV sites, full hookups, showers, and laundry. Propane available. Inexpensive to moderate.

Campgrounds and RV Parks

Coho Resort, Sekiu; 963–2333. One mile east of Sekiu, on State Route 112. Has 108 RV sites with picnic tables, full hookups, showers, and laundry. Tent sites available. Boat launching and moorage, 800-foot breakwater, rental boats and motors, bait, tackle, gas, ice, and fish storage. Charters available. Also motel units with kitchens. Inexpensive.

Van Riper's Resort Motel & RV Park, P.O. Box 246; Sekiu; 963–2334. North off State Route 112 on Front Street. Has 80 RV sites with full hookups. Showers. Firewood available. Boat moorage, boat and motor rental, tackle rental, bait, tackle, and ice. Charter service. Also 10 motel units with kitchens. Moderate.

Westwind Resort, P.O. Box 918; Neah Bay; 645–2751. Has 10 tent sites and 26 full-hookup RV sites with picnic tables. Showers, laundry, and ice. Boat launching and moorage. Charter service. Also 4 cabins available. Moderate.

Museum

Makah Cultural and Research Center, P.O. Box 95; Neah Bay; 645–2711. Summer: daily, 10:00 A.M. to 5:00 P.M. September 15 through May 31, closed Monday and Tuesday. An exquisite, pleasingly designed museum exhibiting well-preserved artifacts from the famed Ozette dig and other archeological sites. The 23,000-square-foot museum has 10,000 square feet of gallery and 200 square feet of wall space for traveling or temporary exhibits. Also on display are many fine photographs depicting the Makah culture, full-scale reproductions of canoes, and a longhouse large enough for several families. Many handmade replicas on exhibit are for actual hands-on examination. Classified *must see.*

Beaches, Parks, Trails, and Waysides

Neah Bay lies just east of Cape Flattery, the most northwesterly point of land in the continental United States. To reach the cape, drive west from Neah Bay 8.5 miles on a good gravel road; then hike the half-mile trail for a view of the Pacific, the **Strait of Juan de Fuca,** and **Tatoosh Island.** The trail is partly planked, but it can be quite muddy after a rain. So don appropriate footwear and watch your step, even on the planks, which get slippery when wet.

The road to Cape Flattery also leads to **Koitlah Point,** which is 2.7 miles west of Neah Bay. There is an excellent view of the strait, **Vancouver Island,** and **Neah Bay.**

Hobuck Beach is 4.1 miles southwest of Neah Bay by paved and gravel roads. This is a good spot for a picnic and for hiking and photography. Just 2 miles beyond Hobuck Beach is a 3-mile trail leading to **Shi-Shi Beach;** a half-mile beyond is the **Makah National Fish Hatchery,** which is open to visitors.

When hiking on beaches in the Makah Reservation, respect the Makahs' wishes, and leave all shells and shellfish where they are.

Water Sports and Activities

Fishing is the main activity along State Route 112, and the productive Strait of Juan de Fuca is the reason. Chinook and coho salmon are the species most sought, but these waters also give up some huge halibut and lingcod as well as many other species.

Seasons vary, so check regulations. Phone charter operators and resort owners to check on local conditions and season openings.

The chinook season opens as early as February 22 in the Sekiu area, with fish then running between six and twenty pounds, occasionally to thirty or more. Bigger fish begin showing in May. Cohos follow in mid-June, with the biggest fish taken from mid-August through September.

Most bottomfish can be taken any time of the year, weather and water conditions permitting. There are special seasons for halibut, and both halibut and lingcod are regulated in the Neah Bay region.

Anglers find good freshwater fishing in the streams and lakes of this area, particularly for rainbow and cutthroat trout. On the Makah Reservation, two rivers and several lakes are open to the public for angling by permit. Freshwater and saltwater fishing permits are usually available at several places in Neah Bay.

Kingfisher Charters, Sekiu; 457–1935. Docked at Olson's Resort. King (chinook) salmon and bottomfishing trips. Morning and afternoon trips daily in season.

Westwind Resort Charters, P.O. Box 918; Neah Bay; 645–2751. At Westwind Resort on State Route 112, in town. Salmon, bottomfish, halibut, and combination trips. Special Canadian halibut trips. Four boats, 30 to 40 feet, fish six persons each. Phone ahead for halibut information and seasons.

Events

July   Clallum Bay/Sekiu Fun Days, Sekiu, 963–2526
August   Makah Days, Neah Bay, 645–2201
September Fall Salmon Derby, Sekiu, 963–2526

Travel Information

Clallum Bay/Sekiu Chamber of Commerce, P.O. Box 355; Clallum Bay 98236

Makah Fisheries Management Office (permits and information); 645–2201, ext. 423

Neah Bay Chamber of Commerce, P.O. Box 115; Neah Bay; 645–2211

Hurricane Ridge, Olympic National Park

Port Angeles, Washington 98362
Population: 17,400

Location: *On U.S. 101, 63 miles east-northeast of Forks, 48 miles west of Port Townsend, and 17 miles west of Sequim, on the Strait of Juan de Fuca*

Port Angeles is a shortening of the original name, for which we all can be thankful. In 1791 Spanish explorer Lieutenant Francisco Eliza named the natural harbor *Porto de Neustra Senora de los Angeles,* or "Port of Our Lady of Angels." Subsequently, the name was shortened to *Porto de los Angeles* and ultimately to its present form. Meanwhile, the city has grown to become the largest on the north Olympic Peninsula.

So many chambers of commerce tout their towns as "gateways" to one thing or another that the term has become a cliché. Nevertheless, it's difficult to resist discussing Port Angeles in such terms. For visitors arriving from Canada, the city is certainly their

180

gateway to the Pacific Coast and the rest of America. For those heading north, Port Angeles can be the gateway to Canada and Alaska. And for most, this is the threshold of **Olympic National Park,** with headquarters located in town.

For a variety of reasons, Port Angeles has become a popular retirement spot and is gaining favor among travelers. The climate is pleasant, and the rainfall is relatively low. The Olympic Mountains are only a few miles south, and the Strait of Juan de Fuca laps at the city's north limits. Naturally, opportunities for outdoor recreation abound.

The city is also emerging as the cultural center of the area. It supports an excellent historical museum and a fine-arts center. It has its own symphony orchestra, light opera company, and a theater group that offers a year-round program.

Although the waterfront area is heavily industrialized, improvements in recent years have made it kinder to the eye. The award-winning **City Pier** offers an excellent vantage point for the waterfront photographer. It has a picnic area, promenade deck, and observation tower. It also provides short-term moorage for boats and seaplanes. The Fiero Marine Laboratory is on the pier, and a sand beach is adjacent.

The Landing, an attractive mall, is just west of City Pier. HarborTowne Mall is across the street from it. The visitor center and Black Ball Ferry Terminal are nearby. Downtown shops, galleries, and restaurants are within walking distance.

Victoria, British Columbia—one of North America's most beautiful cities—is but 18 miles across the strait from Port Angeles. You can be there in ninety minutes via ferry, which docks in downtown Victoria, a short distance from the famed Empress Hotel. So plan to spend a day or more there, seeing the sights, many of which are within walking distance of the ferry dock.

Lodging

Glen Mar By The Sea Bed & Breakfast, 318 North Eunice; 457–6110 or 457–4686. North on Eunice off U.S. 101, east of downtown and ferry terminal. Two bedrooms and 1 suite, double and queen beds. All rooms with views of mountains or the strait. Full breakfast. Moderate.

Harbour House Bed & Breakfast, 139 West 14th Street;

Port Angeles

457–3424 or 1–800–654–5545. West 14th at Oak Street, south of downtown and waterfront. Cape Cod–style inn with 4 guest rooms. Continental breakfast. Moderate.

Harrison Beach Resort, 5930 West Lyre River Road; 928–3006. Located 20 miles west of Port Angeles, 5 miles west of Joyce, north on West Lyre Road off State Route 112. Spacious apartment with great view of the strait, furnished cabin, 3 trailers from 27 to 45 feet, and 6 campsites with water. Beautiful wooded setting. Beachcombing, rock hunting, clam digging, fishing, hiking, and photography. Inexpensive to moderate.

Lake Crescent Lodge, National Park Concessions; HC 62; Box 11; 928–3211. On the shore of Lake Crescent, 20 miles west of Port Angeles, via U.S. 101. Open May 15 to November 1. Choice of rooms with shared bath in main lodge, modern motor-lodge rooms with private baths, or cozy cottages with private baths and fireplaces. Excellent accommodations in a lovely setting on the largest and deepest lake in Olympic National Park. Lodge dining room serves breakfast, lunch, and dinner and will pack box lunches. Cocktail lounge and gift shop on premises. Moderate.

The Tudor Inn Bed & Breakfast, 1108 South Oak Street; 452–3138. Built in 1910 and completely restored and furnished with antiques. Has 5 rooms, 1 private and 2 shared baths. Full breakfast served. Winter cross-country ski packages offered. Summer salmon charters, backpacking, and bike rentals. Moderate.

Campgrounds and RV Parks

City Center Trailer Park, 127 South Lincoln; 457–7092. Lincoln at Second, downtown. Has 30 RV sites with full hookups, cable TV, showers, and laundry. Walk to shops, restaurants, and waterfront. Moderate.

Lyre River Park, 5960 West Lyre River Road; 928–3436. Located 20 miles west of Port Angeles, 5 miles west of Joyce, north on West Lyre River Road off State Route 112. Has 15 tent sites and 60 RV sites with full hookups, fire pits, showers, tank dump, firewood, store, propane, ice, groceries, and fishing tackle. Small rental boats available, or bring your own cartopper. Small-boat ramp. Saltwater fishing for perch, bottomfish, halibut, and salmon; freshwater fishing for trout and steelhead. Children's trout pond. Moderate.

Salt Creek/Tongue Point Recreation Area, 928–3441. Located 3.5 miles north of State Route 112, 19 miles west of Port Angeles and 1 mile east of Joyce. Has 80 campsites with picnic tables and fireplaces. Restrooms, showers, and tank dump. Firewood available. Hiking trails, World War II bunkers, beach, marine life sanctuary, sidewalks and stairs to tide pools. A beautiful setting and one of the finest county parks anywhere, on par with the best state parks. Inexpensive.

Food

C'est Si Bon, 2300 U.S. 101 East; 452–8888. North off U.S. 101, 4 miles east of Port Angeles. Dinner Tuesday through Sunday. Award-winning French restaurant, certainly the best on the Washington coast, some say the best in the state. Start with French onion soup or an appetizer of escargots or oysters in a special butter sauce. For dinner, select among roast duck, chicken breast in puff pastry, rack of lamb, New York steak, beef tenderloin, or other meat dishes prepared with fine and flavorful sauces. Seafoods include fresh salmon with Dungeness crab and leek sauce, prawns with garlic and tomatoes, scallops in champagne sauce. Specials every night are usually fresh seafood. Cocktails, beer, and wine. Moderate to expensive.

First Street Haven, 107 East First Street; 457–0352. Downtown. Breakfast and lunch Monday through Saturday, breakfast all day Sunday. Specializes in creative and unusual breakfasts, including blintzes, huevos rancheros, and a variety of egg dishes. Well known for homemade baked goods, such as cinnamon rolls, sour-cream coffee cake, raspberry bran muffins, and apricot walnut scones—all baked fresh daily. Serves fresh-squeezed orange juice and gourmet espresso coffees. The changeable menu might include such entrees as artichoke stuffed with dilled shrimp salad, cheese enchiladas, chicken fajitas, or fettuccine primavera. Or maybe a lunch-size salad of fresh spinach, crisp vegetables, bacon, Swiss cheese, and slivered almonds. Moderate.

The Landing Fish & Burger Bar, 115 East Railroad Avenue; Suite 101; 457–6768. On the waterfront, next to the Black Ball Ferry Terminal. Breakfast, lunch, and dinner daily. Burgers and other sandwiches, soups, chowders, and salads. Fish baskets with fries and coleslaw, as well as other baskets: oysters, clams, calamari, shrimp, scallops—even catfish. Kids' baskets, carry-out service. Beer and wine. Inexpensive to moderate.

Shopping and Browsing

Arlene's Gift & Wine Shoppe, 122 West Boulevard; 457–4564. At Oak Street and West Boulevard, south of downtown, via Lincoln Street. Daily, 10:00 A.M. to 6:00 P.M. Specializes in Washington wines and other products made in Washington. Daily wine tasting.

Hog Haven Antiques, 222 North Lincoln Street; 457–1904. At HarborTowne Mall, across from the City Pier, one block east of the Black Ball Ferry Terminal. Monday through Saturday, 9:30 A.M. to 5:30 P.M. Estate jewelry, sterling silver, tools, knives, fishing tackle, glassware, and collectibles.

Joyce General Store, State Route 112; Joyce 98343; 928–3568. Located 20 miles west of Port Angeles on State Route 112 in Joyce. Not much changed since the early 1900s—false front, oiled wood floors, same fixtures. A true old-fashioned general store, stocking everything from groceries, bait, and fishing tackle to clothing, hot food, souvenirs, and Indian arts and crafts.

Port Angeles Antiques and Collectibles, 220 West Eighth Street; 452–5411 or 452–2582. Between Oak and Cherry streets, downtown. Monday through Saturday, 11:00 A.M. to 5:00 P.M. Depression glassware, jewelry, clocks, prints, English and American furniture, and a good variety of other antiques and collectibles.

Museums

The Museum of the Clallum County Historical Society, Fourth and Lincoln streets; 452–7831, ext. 364. Downtown. June through August: Monday through Saturday, 10:00 A.M. to 4:00 P.M. Rest of the year, Monday through Friday. Historical collection housed in a 1914 Georgian-style courthouse. Exhibits of logging and fishing industries, agriculture, pioneer settlement, and Indian artifacts.

Port Angeles Fine Art Center, 1203 East Eighth Street; 457–3532. Thursday through Saturday, 11:00 A.M. to 5:00 P.M. Exhibits the works of prominent Northwest artists. Wheelchair access.

Beaches, Parks, Trails, and Waysides

The natural, deep-water harbor at Port Angeles was formed by a long spit, known as Ediz Hook. It was created centuries ago by silt and sand washed downstream by the Elwha River, west of town. The spit is popular with joggers, bikers, and fishermen. To reach it and **Ediz Hook Park,** follow Marine Drive west and north around the port.

Of course, the main attraction of the area is **Olympic National Park,** with 900,000 acres of mountains, meadows, forests, rivers, creeks, lakes, and rugged Pacific coastline, and containing seventeen campgrounds within its boundaries.

South of Port Angeles, at 3002 Mount Angeles Road, is the **Pioneer Memorial Museum and Visitor Center,** which houses park exhibits and a small theater for programs on the park. This is also the place to get park maps and literature. It has a good selection of books on the park, peninsula, and coast.

The road to mile-high **Hurricane Ridge** extends into the park 17 miles from Port Angeles. As the road climbs through forested mountains, a number of parking areas offer splendid views of the alpine country and the Strait of Juan de Fuca.

Hurricane Ridge Lodge serves sandwiches and light meals and beverages. There's also a small gift shop on the premises. The lodge is open daily from Memorial Day through September, weekends through mid-October. In winter, when the area opens for skiing, the lodge opens on weekends and holidays. For the shooshing set, there are ski rentals, rope tow, and Poma Lift.

West of Port Angeles, access to the park is along the Elwha River and in the Lake Crescent area. To the northwest, a road leads southwest off State Route 112 to the village of **Ozette** and parklands along the coast. Farther along U.S. 101, a number of roads lead into the park west and south of Forks.

The park offers hikers and backpackers more than 600 miles of trails in varied terrain. Those most easily reached from Port Angeles are in the Hurricane Ridge, Elwha River, and Lake Crescent areas.

Abundant wildlife in the park includes many species of songbirds and raptors as well as small mammals, amphibians, and reptiles. Rest easy—there are no poisonous snakes in the park.

Large mammals include black-tailed deer, Roosevelt elk,

mountain goat, cougar, and black bear. Bears can be dangerous and should be avoided. Even those that don't pose a threat can be a nuisance to campers who don't take the necessary precautions to hang food in trees, well out of the reach of bears.

The park service offers naturalist programs in the summer at Hurricane Ridge Lodge and elsewhere. Check site bulletin boards for details. Seminars are offered through the Olympic Park Institute. Get information at visitor centers or park headquarters.

Water Sports and Activities

Olympic National Park offers outstanding trout fishing in its many lakes and streams. Although no license is required in the park, a salmon and steelhead punch card is necessary in waters where those species are taken.

Rainbows are the most popular and abundant trout in the park. Cutthroat and brook trout are other park residents. Lake Crescent is the only place on the planet where anglers can catch Beardsley trout, a race of rainbow, and Crescenti, a race of cutthroat trout.

Minutes from port, saltwater anglers can catch coho and chinook salmon as well as halibut, lingcod, rockfish, Pacific cod, and other species of bottomfish. From shore, fishermen take perch, greenling, cabezon, rockfish, sole, flounder, and lingcod, as well as salmon, steelhead, sea-run cutthroat, and Dolly Varden.

Olympic Raft & Guide Service, Elwha Resort & Cafe, 464 U.S. 101 West; 457–7011. Eight miles west of Port Angeles on U.S. 101. River rafting trips down the Elwha River from its headwaters at Lake Aldwell. Cabins, RV sites with full hookups, fishing tackle, boats, gas, propane, groceries, beer, and wine. Some of the best fly-fishing on the peninsula.

Port Angeles Charters, 1216 Marine Drive; 457–7629 or 622–6893 (toll-free Seattle). Fleet of seven modern, well-equipped boats offer year-round, uncrowded fishing with everything furnished—tackle, bait, salmon punch card with stamp, fish bags, and coffee. Start fishing ten minutes from the dock.

Satin Doll Charters, P.O. Box 2108; 457–6585. Salmon and bottomfish trips out of Port Angeles and Neah Bay aboard the 38-foot *Satin Doll* or 43-foot *Satin Doll II.* All tackle and bait furnished.

Thunderbird Boathouse, P.O. Box 787; 457–3595. Located 1.5 miles east of the Crown Zellerbach mill, next to the Coast Guard Station on Ediz Hook, via Marine Drive. Boat and tackle rental, tackle shop, fresh and frozen bait, free boat launch, snack bar, gas, oil, propane.

Tours and Trips

Black Ball Transport, (ferry to Victoria); 457–4491. On the downtown waterfront at the foot of Laurel Street. Four trips every day in the summer, once a day in winter, to Victoria, British Columbia. Trip takes about ninety minutes aboard the 342-foot, twin-diesel MV *Coho,* which carries 100 cars and 1,000 passengers.

Golf

Peninsula Golf Course, 105 Lindberg Road; 457–7348 (clubhouse) or 457–6501 (pro shop). Lindberg Road off Golf Course Road, behind the Plaza Shopping Center, south off U.S. 101, east of town. An 18-hole course with driving range, complete pro shop, and resident pro.

Other Attractions

Arthur D. Fiero Marine Laboratory, 452–9277. On the Port Angeles City Pier at the downtown waterfront. Summer: daily, 10:00 A.M. to 8:00 P.M. Winter: weekends, noon to 4:00 P.M. A working lab used in local high school and college marine biology courses and research. More than eighty species collected from nearby waters live here, including sculpins, wolf eels, octopi, sea slugs, anemone, tube worms, sea stars, crabs, and sea urchins. Touch tank for hands-on examination.

Events

May   Community Concert, 457–7793
July   Antique Show & Sale, 457–4862
August Clallum County Fair, 457–3963

Port Angeles

Arts & Crafts Show, 457–7793
Joyce Daze Blackberry Festival, 928–3568
September Annual Salmon Derby, 457–4971

Weather and Tide Information

U.S. Coast Guard, Ediz Hook; recorded message, 457–6533

Travel Information

Park Superintendent, Olympic National Park, 600 East Park Avenue; 452–4501

Port Angeles Chamber of Commerce, 121 East Railroad Avenue; 452–2363

John Wayne Marina

Sequim, Washington 98382
Population: 3,180

Location: *On U.S. 101, 17 miles east of Port Angeles, 31 miles west of Port Townsend*

Sequim (*skwim*) grew out of a small cluster of farms in the Sequim/Dungeness Valley, some of which date as far back as 1851. The area is known for its unusually warm, dry climate, so dry in fact that pioneers found cacti growing on the lowlands. They couldn't raise crops without irrigation provided by the Dungeness River. While western portions of the Olympic Peninsula get drenched each year with as much as 140 inches of rain, the Sequim/Dungeness Valley lies in the dry shadow of the Olympic Mountains and gets a mere 10 to 18 inches.

The pleasant climate and nearby recreational opportunities have recently attracted enough new residents to make this one of

189

the fastest-growing areas on the peninsula. But it's largely a retirement community that doesn't court tourists. The town, itself, doesn't have much in the way of accommodations for travelers, but it bears mentioning for several reasons, not the least of which are an outstanding seafood restaurant north of town and a lovely marina and beautiful state park east of town.

Lodging

Dungeness Bay Motel, 569 Marine Drive; 683–3013. On Dungeness Bay, 7 miles north of Sequim. Four kitchen units with views of the bay and mountains. Near golf courses, wildlife refuge, and a superb seafood restaurant. Moderate.

Great House Motel, P.O. Box 85; 683–7272. North side of U.S. 101, in town. Twin, double, and queen beds in 20 rooms with cable TV and HBO. Inexpensive to moderate.

Campgrounds and RV Parks

Diamond Point RV Park & Campground, 137 Industrial Park Way; 683–2284. Three miles north of U.S. 101, via Diamond Point Road, between Sequim Bay and Discovery Bay. Has 25 tent sites and 32 RV sites with full hookups, showers, tank dump, laundry, kitchen shelter, beach access, and boat ramp. Breakfast served on weekends in summer; dinner served on Saturday nights— usually salmon dinner and dessert, all you can eat for a modest charge. Hiking trails, ten minutes to the beach. Fishing, beachcombing, and clam digging. Moderate.

Sequim Bay State Park, 1872 U.S. 101 East; 683–4235. West side of U.S. 101, 4 miles southeast of Sequim. Has 60 tent sites and 26 RV sites with full hookups, showers, and tank dump. In a beautiful wooded setting with hiking trails. Picnic area with 4 kitchen shelters, tennis courts, playground, horseshoe pits, and ball field. Boat launch, mooring floats and buoys, and loading dock. Fishing, crabbing, clam digging, scuba diving, and water-skiing are main attractions. Inexpensive.

Food

The 3 Crabs Restaurant & Lounge, 101 Three Crabs Road; 683–4264. Located 4.5 miles north of U.S. 101 on Sequim-

Dungeness Way, then right on Three Crabs Road a half-mile. Lunch and dinner daily. Award-winning seafood restaurant, among the best on the Washington coast. Start with oyster shooters, smoked-salmon appetizer, or jumbo-prawn cocktail. Then feast on such house specialties as crab Louis, crab sandwiches, crab and shrimp omelets, cracked crab, oysters, scallops, prawns, salmon, or halibut. Cocktails, beer, and wine. Moderate.

Museum

Sequim-Dungeness Museum, 175 West Cedar; 683–8110. One block north of U.S. 101. May 1 to October 1: Wednesday through Sunday, noon to 4:00 P.M. Rest of the year: weekends, noon to 4:00 P.M. A variety of historical exhibits. Some excellent old photographs depicting the settlement of the Sequim/Dungeness Valley. Most fascinating is an interpretive exhibit of mastodon remains discovered on a nearby farm.

Water Sports and Activities

John Wayne Marina, 615 West Sequim Bay Road; 683–9898. North off U.S. 101, east of Sequim. A beautiful marina, first envisioned by actor John Wayne and built mainly on land donated by the actor's family. Will eventually have a capacity of 422 moorage slips, protected by a gracefully curved breakwater that blends well with the environment. Showers, laundry, boat ramps, fuel facilities, public beach, and picnic areas. True Grits Restaurant on premises.

Golf

Dungeness Golf Course, 491-A Woodcock Road; 683–6344. North of U.S. 101, west end of town. An 18-hole course with driving range, pro shop, clubhouse, resident pro, and restaurant on premises.

Sunland Golf & Country Club, 109 Hilltop Drive; 683–6800. North of U.S. 101, between Sequim and Dungeness. An 18-hole course with driving range, pro shop, and coffee shop.

Sequim

Events

For information on those events listed without phone numbers, phone the Sequim Chamber of Commerce (see Travel Information).

February	Have a Heart For the Arts, 683–8364
April	A Night on the Town
May	Annual Irrigation Festival
	Annual Music Festival
	Sequim Bay Yacht Club Boating Events
	Exhibition of Fine Arts, 683–8364
July	Rotary Arts & Crafts Fair
	Show Your Stuff
	Small-Boat Regatta
August	Rotary Salmon Bake
September	Sequim Bay Yacht Club Fall Regatta
November	Christmas Bazaar, 683–4862
	Holiday Ball
	Winner Circle Art Exhibition, 683–8364
December	Christmas Concert

Travel Information

Sequim Chamber of Commerce, 720 East Washington; 683–6197

Starrett House Inn, Port Townsend

Port Townsend, Washington 98368
Population: 7,000

Location: *13 miles northeast of U.S. 101, on State Route 20; 48 miles east of Port Angeles, 31 miles east of Sequim, and 6 miles, via ferry, west of Whidbey Island*

Port Townsend, located on the northeast tip of the Quimper Peninsula, grew from a single log cabin (built in 1851) to a Victorian-era boomtown in the 1880s. It flourished as Washington's "Key City" and swelled with a population of 20,000. It functioned as the Port of Entry for Puget Sound, its waterfront a dense forest of great sailing-ship masts.

The city's prosperity and promise were both real and antici-pated, its future dependent upon the railroad. Townspeople, busi-nessmen, and speculators assumed that Port Townsend would become the northwestern terminus of the transcontinental railway

193

system. But their dreams were dashed when the rails stopped at Seattle, assuring that town's future as Washington's capital of commerce. By 1893 Port Townsend had gone bust and would languish where it lay for more than half a century.

In the 1960s Port Townsend's Victorian charm was rediscovered, and since then many of its beautiful old brick buildings have been restored and now house interesting shops, galleries, taverns, and restaurants. Most of its stately old houses and mansions also have been refurbished; a number of them function as bed-and-breakfast inns.

In some communities the terms uptown and downtown are used interchangeably, and the districts aren't always easy to distinguish. In others downtown is the business district, uptown the residential area. Port Townsend is both typical and unique. Downtown is clearly the lower section, comprising the waterfront and Water and Washington streets, as well as the streets connecting them. Uptown is situated on a bluff overlooking downtown and is mainly residential. Amidst the uptown houses and churches, however, another small business district grew in the latter part of the nineteenth century, so the wives and daughters of the town's menfolk would have a place to shop and stroll without having to associate with sailors, prostitutes, and other denizens of the waterfront. So uptown has its own downtown.

The rabble and riffraff are long gone, and nobody hesitates going to the waterfront now. In fact it's one of Port Townsend's main attractions: a shaped-up, compact area that is perfect for walking. It's the town's main shopping area, with a variety of stores, antique shops, and art galleries. Here, too, are the favorite eateries and watering holes, some with splendid waterfront views.

State Route 20 carries travelers right into downtown and to the ferry terminal. Motels and marinas are nearby, uptown inns only a short distance away, with shopping centers and drive-in restaurants on the outskirts.

Port Townsend Paper Company, a kraft-paper mill, is a major contributor to the town's economy, as are the many marine services and facilities located along the waterfront. Boatbuilding and repair are big business here. So are commercial fishing and fish processing.

Water sports and recreation are important, too. Port Townsend bills itself as the "Wooden Boat Capital of the World" and hosts an annual festival during which visitors can see wooden boats of all kinds and sizes, from skiffs to schooners. The three-day event attracts thousands of people with its boats and booths of nautical hardware and abundant literature and information on boatbuilding and allied topics.

Although food and lodging are a bit more expensive here than elsewhere on the Olympic Peninsula, prices aren't outrageous, as they often are in the larger metropolitan areas. And the Port Townsend people are a friendly lot who welcome travelers. So Washington's Victorian Waterfront, as it's known, is certainly worth a visit.

Lodging

A.Y.H. Hostel, Fort Worden State Park; 385–0655. North of downtown—follow the signs off State Route 20. Closed Thanksgiving and December 15 to January 3. Men's and women's bunkrooms, 2 family rooms, showers, and kitchen. Inexpensive.

Inn Deering Bed & Breakfast, 1208 Franklin; 385–3239. Three blocks above Water Street at Fillmore and Franklin. Three guest rooms, 1 with private bath, TV, refrigerator, and balcony; 2 with shared bath and whirlpool tub. Also a private guesthouse with kitchen, TV, and great view. Continental breakfast. Moderate.

James House Bed & Breakfast, 1238 Washington Street; 385–1238. One block above Water Street, overlooking the harbor and ferry dock. A fine Victorian mansion, built in 1891, with 12 guest rooms and suites furnished with antiques. Private and shared baths. Walk to shops and restaurants. Continental breakfast. Moderate to expensive.

Manresa Castle, P.O. Box 564; 385–5750; Washington, 1–800–732–1281. At Seventh and Sheridan, west off State Route 20, on a hill overlooking the city and waterfront. Turreted castle built in 1892 as a private residence but abandoned when the local economy slumped. Now a restored Victorian-style hotel with 41 rooms and suites with private baths, cable TV, and HBO. Double, queen, and king beds. Dinner restaurant on premises. Moderate to expensive.

Palace Hotel, 1004 Water Street; 385–0773. Downtown. A fine old Victorian inn, built in 1889 and fully restored. Has 15 Victorian units, from bedrooms with shared baths to suites with kitchens and private baths. Cable TV, in-room coffee and tea, continental breakfast. Moderate to expensive.

Starrett House Inn Bed & Breakfast, 744 Clay Street; 385–3205. At Adams and Clay streets, four blocks above the waterfront. Eight guest rooms in a fine example of classic Victorian, stick-style architecture in a stunning 1889 building with interior wall and ceiling frescoes, octagonal tower, and spiral staircase. View rooms available. Open for tours. Full breakfast. Moderate to expensive.

James G. Swann Hotel, P.O. Box 856; 385–1718. On Water Street at Monroe. Four cozy cabins with queen beds and private baths. Three sailors' suites are inexpensive sleeping rooms with shared bath. Boat launch across the street. Walk to downtown shops and restaurants. Inexpensive to moderate.

The Tides Inn, 1807 Water Street; 385–0595. On the waterfront, downtown. Used in the filming of the 1981 smash hit *An Officer and a Gentleman.* Has 21 rooms with queen and king beds, private decks and patios, cable TV. Waterfront view, whirlpool, and continental breakfast. Kitchen units available. Moderate to expensive.

Vacation Housing, Fort Worden State Park; 385–4730 or 464–7542 (toll-free Seattle). At the northern city limits—follow the signs off State Route 20. Offers 23 refurbished and unrefurbished houses with completely furnished kitchens, linens and towels provided. The houses, built at the turn of the century for commissioned and noncommissioned officers, have from two to six bedrooms. Most have fireplaces. One of the best family or group lodging values on the coast. Reservations essential, booked a year in advance. Moderate.

Campgrounds and RV Parks

Fort Worden State Park, P.O. Box 547; 385–4730 or 464–7542 (toll-free Seattle). About 1.5 miles from downtown—follow the signs off State Route 20. Has 3 tent sites and 50 RV sites with tables, stoves, firewood, full hookups, showers, kitchen shelter, boat launch, mooring floats and buoys, beach access, hiking and biking trails, and tennis courts. Reservations accepted all year. Moderate.

Food

Lido Inn & Restaurant, 925 Water Street; 385–7111. Downtown. Lunch and dinner daily. Seafood appetizers, more than a half-dozen salads, burgers, and deli-style sandwiches, fish and chips, cioppino, quiches, crepes, pasta, and seafood entrees round out an ambitious lunch menu. Dinner hors d'oeuvres include scallops, clams, or mussels, oysters, escargots, crab or shrimp cocktail, and calamari. Featured dinners include pastas, steaks, prime rib, and chicken dishes. Large selection of seafood, such as stuffed salmon, halibut with cucumber dill sauce, and clams or mussels steamed in wine and butter. Cocktails, beer, and wine. Fine waterfront view. Moderate.

Maestro Burger, 600 Sims Way; 385–5499. On State Route 20, next to Safeway. Lunch and dinner daily. Great burgers, hot dogs, chili, fish and chips, fries, shakes, and sundaes. Phone ahead and pick up at the drive-by window. Inexpensive.

Water Street Deli, 926 Water Street; 385–2422. Downtown. Lunch and dinner daily. Clam bisque, soups, specialty sandwiches, make-your-own sandwiches, daily lunch specials. Such homemade desserts as coconut macaroon pie, bread pudding, and chocolate fudge cake. Wine and eighteen different beers. Moderate.

Shopping and Browsing

Bergstrom's Antique and Classic Autos, 809 Washington; 385–5061. One block above Water Street, downtown. Open Monday, Thursday, Friday, Saturday, and sometimes Sunday 10:00 A.M. to 5:00 P.M. Historic garage built in 1917 and formerly used as Ford and Buick dealerships, now used for restoring vintage and classic cars and trucks.

Captain's Gallery, 1012 Water Street; 385–3770. Downtown. Daily, 10:00 A.M. to 5:30 P.M. Original artworks, limited-edition prints, posters, collectibles, gifts, and cards. A good selection of marine art.

Earthenworks, 1002 Water Street; 385–0328. Downtown. Daily, 10:30 A.M. to 5:00 P.M. A pleasing gallery displaying wood sculptures, carvings, pottery, kaleidoscopes, wall hangings, jewelry, and limited-edition prints.

Port Townsend Antique Mall, 802 Washington Street; 385–

Port Townsend

2590. One block above Water Street, downtown. Daily, 10:00 A.M. to 5:30 P.M. Large selection of antiques and collectibles, including oak furniture, Victorian furniture, clocks, lamps, guns, decoys, nautical items, dolls, glassware, baseball cards, musical instruments, and old paintings.

Sabo's, 1042 Water Street; 385–3350. Downtown. Daily, 9:30 A.M. to 5:30 P.M.; Sunday, 11:00 A.M. to 4:00 P.M. Outdoor outfitter offering a full range of gear and clothing for hikers, backpackers, anglers, skiers, runners, and other active people. Good source of information on local angling, hiking, and other outdoor activities.

Tibbals, 1010 Water Street; 385–0773. Downtown. Daily, 10:00 A.M. to 6:00 P.M. Kaleidoscopes, pottery, sculpture, jewelry, limited-edition prints, original art, and collectibles—all tastefully displayed.

The Wine Seller, 940 Water Street; 385–7673. Downtown. Daily, 10:30 A.M. to 6:00 P.M.; Sunday, 11:00 A.M. to 5:00 P.M. Good selection of wines and beers, case-lot discounts, coffees, teas, cheeses, chocolates, wine tasting, and espresso bar.

Museums

Commanding Officer's House, Fort Worden State Park; P.O. Box 574; 385–4730. North of town—follow the signs off State Route 20. April to October: daily, 10:00 A.M. to 5:00 P.M. Phone for winter hours. A two-and-a-half story, fully restored Victorian structure with cross-gabled roof and great veranda. Has 5,979 square feet of living space, all beautifully decorated with period furnishings and memorabilia.

Jefferson County Historical Museum, 210 Madison Street; 385–1003. Downtown. Daily, 11:00 A.M. to 4:00 P.M.; Sunday, 1:00 to 4:00 P.M. Located in the rear of Port Townsend's city hall, built in 1891. A fine museum on four levels, displaying Indian, military, pioneer, and maritime artifacts. Early firefighting equipment, Victorian furnishings, toys, collections, and more than 6,000 cataloged photographs. Don't miss the city jail on the lower level—a chamber of horrors where author Jack London is said to have spent a night on his way to the Klondike gold fields in 1897.

Rothschild House. At Taylor and Jefferson, two blocks above Water Street. Daily, 11:00 A.M. to 4:00 P.M. A family house built in 1868 and maintained by the State Parks and Recreation Commission. Contains many original family furnishings, original carpeting, and even original wallpaper. Fine craftsmanship. Many interesting antiques.

Beaches, Parks, Trails, and Waysides

Port Townsend is the seat of a county that has 271 miles of saltwater shoreline. Visitors to the area should have no difficulty finding beaches to hike. Near town, **Point Wilson** and **Fort Worden State Park** offer beaches and trails to hike and a former military reservation to explore.

At the tip of Point Wilson is the beautiful Point Wilson Light with an octagonal tower that stands 46 feet tall. This lighthouse, with its beacon flashing alternating red and white signals, is critically important to Puget Sound shipping and navigation. It also warns mariners away from nearby shoals and serves as a guide light to the Port Townsend harbor.

Fort Worden occupies lands adjacent to Point Wilson. This is one of three forts built at the turn of the century as part of a major coastal-fortification effort to guard the entrance to Puget Sound. The other two are **Fort Flagler on Marrowstone Island** and **Fort Casey on Whidbey Island.**

The fort was first occupied on May 3, 1902, by the 126th Coast Artillery Company and was deactivated in 1953. Counting the gun emplacements, Fort Wordon has ninety-nine buildings on 339 acres. Many of its buildings have been refurbished. Some are used as dormitories and vacation housing. Others are used for conferences. A few hold local businesses.

The fort is now a beautiful, immaculately maintained state park that certainly ranks as a *must see* attraction. First-time visitors may attribute any déjà vu to the popular movie *An Officer and a Gentleman,* which was filmed here and starred Richard Gere, Debra Winger, and Louis Gossett, Jr. To get to Fort Worden and Point Wilson, simply follow the signs off State Route 20.

Water Sports and Activities

Calm Sea Charters, P.O. Box 930; 385–5288. Point Hudson Marina, at the northeast end of Water Street. Sunset cruises, fishing trips, whale-watching and birdwatching excursions, trips to the

Port Townsend

San Juan Islands, and custom charters aboard a comfortable, modern craft licensed for forty-nine passengers.

Sea Sport Charters, P.O. Box 805; 385–3575. At the Port of Port Townsend Boat Haven, Washington Street at Benedict. Salmon and bottomfish trips with gear and bait furnished, marine wildlife excursions to Protection Island, evening dinner cruises, and special charters aboard the 42-foot *Cheyenne.*

Golf

Chevy Chase Golf Course, 7041 Cape George Road; 385–0704. North off State Route 20 at Four Corners Grocery. A 9-hole course with pro shop, club rental, pull-cart rental, and snack bar with beer available.

Port Townsend Golf Course, 1948 Blaine Street; 385–0752. Off State Route 20 on Kearney to Blaine, in town. A 9-hole course with driving range, pro shop, resident pro, rental carts and clubs. Clubhouse restaurant and lounge. Full breakfast and lunch menu. Beer and wine.

Events

May	Rhododendron Festival, 385–5028
	Historic Homes Tour, 385–4400
June	Port Townsend Theater Festival, 625–9779
July	Festival of American Fiddle Tunes, 1–800–742–4221
	Jazz Port Townsend, 625–9779
August	Jefferson County Fair, 385–1013
	Theater Festival, 625–9779
	International Folk Music Festival, 1–800–742–4221
September	Wooden Boat Festival, 385–3628
	Historic Homes Tour, 385–2722
October	Great Port Townsend Kinetic Sculpture Race, 385–2722

Travel Information

Port Townsend Chamber of Commerce, 2437 Simms Way (State Route 20); 385–2722

Admirality Head Light at Fort Casey State Park

Oak Harbor/Coupeville,
Whidbey Island, Washington 98277/98239
Population: 13,400/1,006

Location: *Whidbey Island is 6 miles, by ferry, northeast of Port Townsend. Coupeville is about 4 miles north of the ferry landing, via county road; Harbor lies 10 miles north of Coupeville, via State Route 20*

Whidbey Island is the largest of more than 600 islands that punctuate the Washington coastline. At 40 miles tip to tip, it's also the longest island on the West Coast.

The island's pleasing climate and relatively low annual rainfall first attracted the Northwest's greatest concentration of Indians and later led to settlement of the island. While Seattle gets about 36 inches of rain a year, and more than 100 inches drench western portions of the Olympic Peninsula, south Whidbey Island gets only

201

about 25 inches, and a mere 18 inches dampen the central and north island.

Oak Harbor is Whidbey's largest city. From the mid-1800s to the turn of the century, this area was settled mainly by people of Irish and Dutch extraction. The same climate that attracted others also led the U.S. Navy to pick the Oak Harbor vicinity for a major air installation—the weather is good for flying.

The U.S. Naval Air Station Whidbey Island began as a seaplane base on the harbor in 1942, followed soon by the construction of Ault Field, 5 miles north. As the Naval installation grew to be the largest in the Northwest, Oak Harbor grew with it—from a town of 600 at the beginning of World War II to a community with a combined military and civilian population of more than 20,000.

Although no apologies are necessary, signs along the highway near the air station say: "Pardon our noise—it's the sound of freedom." Truth be known, most visitors probably enjoy the free air show, watching the sleek jets take off, land, and maneuver during training exercises. The planes you'll see most often are EA-6B Prowlers, which are tactical electronic-warfare aircraft, and A-6 Intruders, which are attack bombers.

The explorer Captain George Vancouver named Whidbey Island after shipmaster Joseph Whidbey of the HMS *Discovery*. Whidbey discovered Deception Pass and thereby proved this to be an island after all. Coupeville was named after another sea captain Thomas Coupe, who was the only man ever to sail a full-rigged ship through the pass.

Captain Coupe's house, built in 1854, still stands in Coupeville, as do a number of other historical buildings, many of which have been carefully restored. Downtown, Front Street is itself a historical area, with interesting shops, galleries, and restaurants situated behind Victorian facades. A "Walking Tour" brochure with a map of the historical buildings is available at the museum.

A trip to south Whidbey Island will take you through forests, meadows, and agricultural lands to a variety of parks, island hideaways, and some fine bed-and-breakfast inns. The southernmost community is Clinton, which is the western terminus of the Mulkiteo–Clinton ferry.

Langley lies on the southeast shore of the island, east of State Route 525, via Langley Road (4 miles north of Clinton) or Bayview Road (5 miles south of Freeland). This quaint and quiet village is a favorite stop for travelers. It's an artsy little hamlet with studios and galleries tucked among shops, restaurants, and taverns. It's also headquarters for the Island Arts Council and home to several theater groups that perform at the old Clyde Theater in town.

With its easy pace, rich history, miles of parklands, and interesting towns, as well as land-based and waterborne recreation, Whidbey Island is great for day trips, weekend getaways, or full and fulfilling vacations.

Ferries connect the island with Port Townsend in the west and Mulkiteo in the east. Those traveling I-5 should exit west at Mount Vernon and take State Route 536 to State Route 20, or near Burlington at State Route 20. From Bellingham, follow State Route 11 (scenic Chuckanut Drive) south to State Route 237 and on to State Route 20, which leads west and south to the island.

Lodging

Auld Holland Inn, 5861 State Route 20; Oak Harbor; 675–0724. Nine miles south of Deception Pass, north end of town. Queen and king beds in 52 rooms with cable TV. Kitchen units available in adjacent mobile park. Pool, sauna, whirlpool, tennis courts, basketball, playground, and laundry facilities. Varied decor. Rooms furnished with some antiques. Flowers in window boxes. Restaurant and lounge on premises. Moderate.

Captain Whidbey Inn, 2072 West Captain Whidbey Inn Road; Coupeville; 678–4097. Off Madrona Way, north of Coupeville, Twin, double, queen, and king beds in 30 rooms, suites, and cottages. Room rates include continental breakfast. Kitchen units available. Rustic inn built of madrona logs in 1907. Inn rooms with shared baths, antiques, and featherbeds. Lagoon rooms have private baths and waterfront views. Restaurant and lounge on premises. Expensive.

Eagles Nest Inn Bed & Breakfast, 3236 East Saratoga; Langley 98260; 321–5331. East off State Route 525. Three guest rooms with private baths, queen and king beds. Guest lounge and library. View of Saratoga Passage. Full breakfast. Coffee, tea, and cookies all day. Moderate.

Fort Casey Inn, 1124 South Engle Road; Coupeville; 678–8792. Next to Fort Casey State Park, less than a mile from Keystone Ferry Terminal. Ten duplex units are refurbished World War I officers' quarters with 2 bedrooms, living room, bath, and country-style kitchen, built in 1909. Fruit and cereal provided for breakfast; bring your own groceries for other meals. No radio or TV (bring your own). Two bikes provided. Trails to beach. Good location for walk-on ferry traffic. A good lodging bargain. Moderate.

Guest House Bed & Breakfast, 835 East Christenson Road; Greenbank 98253; 678–3115. West off State Route 525, 10 miles south of Coupeville, 1 mile south of Greenbank, 16 miles north of Clinton. Three cottages, a log lodge, and a suite in a 1920s farmhouse on twenty-five acres of meadow and woods. Private baths, fireplaces, stained glass, antiques, TVs, VCRs, outdoor pool, and spa. Full breakfast served at the farmhouse. Breakfast makings provided at cottages and lodge. Expensive.

Campgrounds and RV Parks

City Beach Park, City Beach Road; Oak Harbor; 679–5551. On the waterfront on 90th Street. Has 55 RV sites, plus overflow area. Bathhouse, swimming pool, tennis courts, playground, and ball fields. Good place for July Fourth fireworks. Moderate.

Deception Pass State Park, 5175 North State Route 20; 675–2417. Ten miles north of Oak Harbor on State Route 20. Has 246 campsites with picnic tables and stoves, as well as 5 primitive sites. Lake and saltwater fishing, boat launch, mooring floats and buoys, beach access, hiking trails, showers, wheelchair access. Moderate.

Fort Casey State Park, 1280 Fort Casey Road; Coupeville; 678–4519 or 678–5632. Three miles south of Coupeville, off State Route 20, adjacent to the Keystone Ferry Terminal. Has 35 campsites with picnic tables and 3 primitive sites. No hookups. Showers, firewood, restrooms, and wheelchair access. On the beach. Boat launch nearby. Underwater park for scuba divers. Old fort to explore. Inexpensive.

Fort Ebey State Park, 395 North Fort Ebey Road; Coupeville; 678–4636 or 678–3195. Eight miles south of Oak Harbor, off State Route 20. Has 50 campsites with picnic tables and 3 primitive sites. Showers. Inexpensive.

Island County Fairgrounds, P.O. Box 172; Langley 98260; 321–4677 or 321–4574 (caretaker). Has 50 RV sites with full hookups and an open tent area. Showers and tank dump. Near town. Closed mid-August to month end for county fair. Inexpensive.

Mutiny Bay Resort, 5856 South Mutiny Bay Road; Freeland 98249; 321–4500. West off State Route 525 on Fish Road. Has 30 RV sites with full hookups, 8 sites on the water. No tents. No pull-throughs. Fishing pier, gas dock, moorage, and dry storage for boats. Bait, tackle, firewood, and crab-gear rental. Moderate to expensive.

South Whidbey State Park, 4128 Smuggler's Cove Road; Freeland 98249; 321–4559. West off State Route 525 on Smuggler's Cove Road, 15 miles southwest of Coupeville, 7 miles northwest of Freeland. Has 54 campsites with picnic tables and stoves and 6 primitive sites. Showers, tank dump, and firewood. Inexpensive.

Food

Captain Whidbey Inn, 2072 West Captain Whidbey Inn Road; Coupeville; 678–4097. Off Madrona Way, north of Coupeville. Breakfast, lunch, and dinner daily. Great breakfasts include apple-nut pancakes or French toast with raspberry butter, biscuits and gravy, and Hangtown fry. Design your own omelets with a choice of forty fillings. Soups, hearty lunch salads, sandwiches, and such entrees as Cajun crab cakes for lunch. Appetizers include smoked salmon and onion cheesecake, smoked quail, and ginger-steamed mussels. Clam chowder. Warm duck salad. Entrees include New York pepper steak, pecan chicken breast, poached salmon or oysters, and blackened rockfish. Cocktails, Northwest and imported wines, and two dozen domestic and imported beers. Moderate to expensive.

Kasteel Franssen Restaurant & Lounge, 5861 State Route 20; Oak Harbor; 675–0724. Adjacent to Auld Holland Inn. Dinner daily. European-French cuisine. Start with Chuckanut Bay oysters, Penn Cove mussels, Zuiderzee herring, or any of a half-dozen other appetizers and soups. Dinners include steaks, veal, chicken, and seafoods such as mahi mahi, prawns, lobster, salmon, and halibut. Great desserts such as baked Alaska, peach melba, chocolate mousse, and English trifle. Piano bar and lounge. Moderate.

Mario's Pizza, 1153 Midway Boulevard; Oak Harbor; 679–2533. Advertises "old-fashioned" pizza and is certainly no exaggeration. Pizzas made from scratch and from the freshest ingredients. Fresh dough made daily. Free delivery. Moderate.

Shopping and Browsing

John Charles MacPherson Glassblowing Studio and Art Gallery, 4809 East State Route 525; P.O. Box 298; Clinton 98236; 221–3637. Daily, 9:00 A.M. to 5:00 P.M. A bright, airy gallery with artworks tastefully arranged. Sign says, "Browsers are welcome. Buyers are adored."

Whidbey's Greenbank Farm, 2832S 780th East; Greenbank 98253; 678–7700. Ten miles south of Coupeville on State Route 525, 18 miles north of Clinton Ferry Terminal. Daily, 10:00 A.M. to 4:30 P.M. A beautiful berry farm where Whidbey's Liqueur is made and sold, along with Chateau Ste. Michelle wines, jellies, and gifts. Self-guided tour and tasting room.

Museum

Island County Historical Museum, 902 North Main; Coupeville; 678–6854. Downtown. Summer: daily, noon to 4:00 P.M. Off-season: weekends, noon to 4:00 P.M. A small museum, depicting island history with exhibits of farming, logging, Indian, and maritime artifacts. A selection of literature about the island.

Beaches, Parks, Trails, and Waysides

Fort Casey State Park, adjacent to the Keystone Ferry dock, was one of three forts built in the area at the turn of the century to protect the Puget Sound entrance and to ward off foreign invasion of the Bremerton Navy Yard and other likely targets. Troops occupied the fort until shortly after World War I, when the installation was mothballed and its great 10-inch guns melted down for scrap. The fort was reactiviated as a training center during World War II, but it was again placed in caretaker status and ultimately sold to Washington State.

Visitors to the park are free to roam the concrete gun emplacements, and to the delight of most, there are guns to inspect that are similar to the fort's original artillery. In 1968 the park acquired two 3-inch rapid-fire guns and two 10-inch guns on disappearing carriages from the Philippines.

Also in the park proper is **Admiralty Head Light,** which was deactivated in 1927. The state acquired the land and converted the beautiful old lighthouse into an interpretive center. Shutterbugs will find this to be one of the most photogenic lighthouses remaining on the West Coast.

At the north end of Whidbey Island and the south end of Fidalgo Island is **Deception Pass State Park,** with 2,500 acres of forest and miles of hiking and biking trails. The park has a freshwater lake and saltwater beach. Trails lead to many spectacular vistas of mountains, islands, and Puget Sound.

Park and walk out onto **Deception Pass Bridge** for a dizzying view of the chasm that narrows to 200 yards. Watch tides boil and rip in an eight-knot current, and imagine Captain Thomas Coupe navigating the gorge under full sail.

Water Sports and Activities

With 135 miles of shoreline, Whidbey Island offers abundant opportunities for all kinds of water-related recreation. Fishing is a popular year-round sport, both from shore and boats, with chinook and coho salmon the most popular species. There is some clam digging on the island, and crabbing is good from docks, piers, and boats.

Sailing and island cruising are popular pastimes, and Whidbey Island serves as a good stopover port between Seattle and the San Juan Islands. Several marinas are here to serve those arriving by water and others who tow their boats and need launching facilities.

Cornet Bay Marina, 5191 North Cornet Bay Road; Oak Harbor; 675–5411. East off State Route 20, about 8 miles north of Oak Harbor. Fishing tackle, bait, ice, beer, licenses, fishing information, charter fishing, launching facilities, and moorage.

Deception Pass Charters, 565 West Cornet Bay Road; Oak Harbor; 675–9597 or 679–1043. East off State Route 20, about 8 miles north of Oak Harbor. Eight-hour salmon and bottomfish trips, five-hour sightseeing trips, extended fishing and island cruises, and custom charters aboard the modern, 34-foot *Irish Mist.*

Oak Harbor Marina, 8075 Catalina Drive; Oak Harbor; 679–

2628. East side of town, near the seaplane base. A full-service marina with 130 open and 183 covered slips for boats up to 50 feet, dry storage for 104 craft to 24 feet, largest launch ramp in the Northwest (usable on any tide), and 8,000-pound-capacity launching crane.

Events

January   Yacht Club's Annual Salmon Derby, Oak Harbor, 675–1314
February Whidbey Island Gem Show, Oak Harbor, 675–1989
April   Holland Happening, Oak Harbor, 675–3535
May   Bed & Breakfast Tour, Langley, 321–6765
              Memorial Day Parade, Coupeville, 678–5434
June   Annual Art Show, Oak Harbor, 679–1881
              Olde Fashioned 4th of July Celebration, Oak Harbor, 675–3535
July   Chochokum Arts Festival, Langley, 321–7494
August   Arts and Crafts Festival, Coupeville, 678–4606
              Island County Fair, Langley, 321–4677
October   Squash Festival, Coupeville, 678–5434
              Monster Manor, Langley, 321–6765
December Greening Day, Coupeville, 678–5434
              100 Bucks Flat Art Show, Langley, 321–6765
              Sinterklaas Fest, Oak Harbor, 675–3535

Travel Information

North Whidbey Island Chamber of Commerce, P.O. Box 883; Oak Harbor; 675–3535

Central Whidbey Island Chamber of Commerce, P.O. Box 152; Coupeville; 678–5434

Langley Chamber of Commerce, P.O. Box 403; Langley 98260; 321–6765

Clinton Chamber of Commerce, P.O. Box 317; Clinton 98236; 321–4545

Freeland Chamber of Commerce, P.O. Box 361; Freeland 98249; 321–4838

Bellingham is a veritable treasure trove for the collector and antique hunter.

Bellingham, Washington 98225-27
Population: 46,500

Location: *On I-5, 21 miles south of the Canada border, 89 miles north of Seattle, 26 miles north of State Route 20, via State Routes 237 and 11*

In 1904 a handful of communities scattered along the shores of Bellingham Bay were consolidated into one city and named after the bay. The city has grown and absorbed the individuality of the earlier towns and tied them together in an occasionally trouble-some tangle of thoroughfares.

One of the early townsites, Fairhaven, remains a relatively distinct district within the city. Its charming collection of old brick buildings and attractive Victorian houses will continue to attract visitors, so long as Fairhaven can resist the ravages of progress.

Like their neighbors to the southwest in Port Townsend, Fairhaven speculators, gambling that the area would become the

209

western terminus of the Great Northern Railroad, built the town in the 1890s. When the railroad went south, Fairhaven went bust. The area remained in a state of decline well into the twentieth century. In 1970 a developer bought a number of buildings and renewed Fairhaven's vitality.

Another historically significant area is the downtown Eldridge or "Old Town" district near the waterfront and Whatcom Creek. This is where the first white settlers came ashore in the mid-1800s and where Henry Roeder built a sawmill in 1853. A number of historical buildings still stand here, including the magnificent New Whatcom City Hall, which is now the Whatcom Museum of History and Art. Several interesting galleries, antique shops, and restaurants add to the enjoyment of an Old Town tour.

The Eldridge district's residential area is characterized by some fine old houses built in the late-nineteenth and early-twentieth centuries. In the Sehome district, near the Western Washington University campus, are more vintage houses and other buildings. "Walking Tour" guides and maps of all these areas are available at the visitor and convention bureau.

Arriving at and departing from Bellingham via the north, it's difficult to avoid I-5 and its frenetic freeway pace. But to the south, you have a much more pleasant and scenic alternative. A stretch of the old coast highway—State Route 11 (Chuckanut Drive)—clings to sheer coastal bluffs above Bellingham and Samish bays, commanding splendid views of Rosario Strait and the San Juan Islands.

You can pick up State Route 11 off I-5 south of Bellingham at Burlington. From Whidbey Island, take State Route 237 north 9 miles off State Route 20 to State Route 11. Chuckanut Drive leads into the Fairhaven district. From Bellingham head south on Chuckanut Drive, take Exit 250 west off I-5, and follow Old Fairhaven to Chuckanut.

Lodging

The Castle Bed & Breakfast, 1103 15th Street; Bellingham 98225; 676–0974. West of I-5 at Exit 250, west on Fairhaven/Valley Parkway, north on 14th, east on Knox. On a hill overlooking the Fairhaven district and Bellingham Bay. A 21-room Victorian mansion built in 1890 with 3 guest rooms furnished with antiques. Twin and queen beds, shared bath, full breakfast. Moderate.

Chuckanut Manor Bed & Breakfast, 302 Chuckanut Drive; Bow 98232; 766–6191. South of Bellingham, west of I-5, on State Route 11. One 2-bedroom suite for one to four persons, furnished with antiques. Kitchen, dining area, living room, and bath. Continental champagne breakfast. Restaurant on premises. Moderate.

DeCann House Bed & Breakfast, 2610 Eldridge Avenue; Bellingham 98225; 734–9172. About 3 miles west of I-5, via Lakeway and Holly Street, Exit 253. Two guest rooms with private baths, decorated with family heirlooms. Turn-of-the-century house overlooks Bellingham Bay and San Juan Islands. Moderate.

Heron Reach Bed & Breakfast, 1601 Fourth, Bellingham 98225; 671–2811. One mile west of I-5, Exit 250, Valley Parkway to Donovan and Fourth. Near Fairhaven district and Bellingham Bay. Two guest rooms. Limited boat and trailer parking available. Full breakfast. Inexpensive to moderate.

North Garden Inn Bed & Breakfast, 1014 North Garden Street; Bellingham 98225; 671–7828. West of I-5 at Exit 253, Lakeway to Holly, then left on North Garden. Ten guest rooms have a view of Bellingham Bay. Near the university, shops, and restaurants. Continental breakfast. Moderate.

Schnauzer Crossing Bed & Breakfast, 4421 Lakeway Drive; Bellingham 98226; 733–0055. Three miles east of I-5 at Exit 253. Inn overlooks Lake Whatcom and has 2 guest rooms. One room with private bath and queen bed. Master suite with king bed, private bath with whirlpool tub and double shower, sitting or child's room, and TV. Use of canoe and sailboat. Private tennis court. Sumptuous breakfasts of quiche, berries, muffins, fruit parfaits, bagels, and freshly ground coffee. Moderate to expensive.

Campgrounds and RV Parks

Larrabee State Park, 245 Chuckanut Drive; Bellingham 98226; 676–2093. Seven miles south of Bellingham on State Route 11. Has 61 tent sites, 25 RV sites with full hookups, and 3 primitive sites. Tables, stove, picnic area, kitchen shelter, showers, and tank dump. A beautiful park on 1,886 wooded acres with 3,600 feet of shoreline on Samish Bay. A great area for exploring tide pools at low tide. Good hiking trails. Fishing and scuba diving are other popular attractions. Inexpensive.

Sudden Valley Camping Park, 2145 Lake Whatcom Boulevard; Bellingham 98226; 734–6430. Eight miles southeast of Bellingham, 8.6 miles northeast of Alger. From the north, take Exit 253, from the south exit 240. Recreational complex with 89 campsites with full hookups, showers, tank dump, heated swimming pools, sauna, and tennis courts. Boat launch, moorage, and rentals. Championship golf course, restaurant, and lounge. Moderate.

Food

Bay Side Inn, 1801 Roeder; Bellingham 98225; 761–9988. In the Squalicum area, at the mall and marina on Bellingham Bay. Breakfast, lunch, and dinner daily. Breakfast includes pancakes, French toast, fresh-baked muffins, biscuits and gravy, homemade hashbrowns, and crab Benedict. Lunch favorites are fish and chips and variations with oysters, prawns, or halibut. Burgers and deli-style sandwiches. Chowder, soups, and salads. Steak, chicken, pasta, and seafood dinners. Children's menu. Homemade desserts. Beer and wine. Moderate.

Bullie's, 1200 Harris; Bellingham 98225; 734–2855. In the Eldridge district, Old Town. Breakfast, lunch, and dinner daily. Good tavern food here, including eighteen different burgers, soups, salads, chicken, and seafood. More than 200 beers, ales, and stouts available. More than two dozen on tap, including imported, domestic, and Northwest microbrews. Moderate.

Chuckanut Manor Restaurant, 302 Chuckanut Drive; Bow 98232; 766–6191. South of Bellingham, west of I-5, on State Route 11. Lunch and dinner Tuesday through Saturday, brunch and dinner Sunday. Friday smorgasbord includes all the roast chicken, beef, oysters, poached salmon, and salads you can eat. Sunday brunch features baked goods, fruit, eggs, quiche, oysters, omelets, and complimentary champagne or sparkling cider. Other house specialties include fresh Samish Bay oyster dishes, Penn Cove mussels, poached or grilled salmon, prime rib, veal, and New Zealand lamb. Good wine list, featuring Northwest and California wines. Offers more than seventy-five domestic and imported beers, including Northwest microbrews. Moderate.

Sadighi's, 921 Lakeway Drive; Bellingham 98226; 647–1109.

Off I-5, Exit 253, across from the Fred Meyer store. Lunch and dinner weekdays, dinner weekends. Carefully prepared international cuisine, some Cajun, some Chinese, some Northwest. Select from a half-dozen appetizers, including shrimp and avocado salad, hot spinach salad, and smoked salmon. Entrees include blackened New York steak, lamb chops, veal sautéed in butter and brandy, stuffed sole, seafood Creole, sockeye salmon fillet, and chicken Dijon fettuccine. Homemade desserts. Cocktails and domestic beers and wines. Moderate.

Shopping and Browsing

Bellingham Antique Mall, 202 West Holly; Bellingham 98225; 647–1073. West of I-5, Exit 253, West Holly at Commercial. Monday through Saturday, 10:00 A.M. to 5:30 P.M.; Sunday, noon to 5:00 P.M. Clocks, watches, tools, glassware, china, toys, trains, jewelry, furniture, Indian artifacts, and more.

Bellingham Fish Company, 1206 Central Avenue; Bellingham 98225; 734–5010 or 1–800–537–2699. Central at Chestnut, on the waterfront. Monday through Saturday, 8:00 A.M. to 5:30 P.M. Fresh salmon, sturgeon, halibut, perch, rockfish, lingcod, sole, cod, and sablefish. Fresh and smoked oysters. Crab, clams, shrimp. Gift packs of smoked salmon, salmon pâté, and whole salmon shipped anywhere.

Jody Bergsma Gallery, 1344 King Street; Bellingham 98226; 733–1101; Washington, 1–800–445–5639; elsewhere, 1–800–237–4762. East of I-5, next to the visitor information center, Exit 253. From January through May: Monday through Saturday, 10:00 A.M. to 6:00 P.M.; Sunday, noon to 5:00 P.M. June through December: Monday through Saturday, 10:00 A.M. to 9:00 P.M.; Sunday, noon to 5:00 P.M. Original artworks, plates, figurines, and limited-edition prints. Mail-order catalog available. Coffee shop on premises.

Granny's Attic & Pantry, 2711 Meridian; Bellingham 98225; 647–1374. Exit 256 off I-5, then 1.2 miles south on Meridian. Monday through Saturday, 10:30 A.M. to 5:00 P.M. Specializes in old and new collectible dolls and teddy bears. Also antiques and collectibles, toys, glass, and more.

Aladdin's Lamp Antique Mall & Cafe, 138 East Holly; Bellingham 98225; 647–0066. West of I-5 at Exit 253, Lakeway to East Holly. Monday through Saturday, 10:00 A.M. to 6:00 P.M.; Sunday, noon to 5:00 P.M. Oak furniture, glassware, pottery, dolls, comics, toys, jewelry, Victorian lampshades, and collectibles. Cafe on premises serves quiches, lasagna, salads, desserts, and coffee.

Indian Street Pottery, 1309 Indian Street; Bellingham 98225; 733–3432. West of I-5, Exit 253, Lakeway to East Holly to Indian Street. Wednesday through Saturday, 11:00 A.M. to 5:00 P.M. Large selection of pottery, raku, stoneware, lamps, masks, vases, planters, and wall hangings.

Museum

Whatcom Museum of History & Art, 121 Prospect Street, Bellingham 98225; 676–6981. West of I-5, via Exit 253. West on Lakeway to East Holly to Prospect. Tuesday through Sunday, noon to 5:00 P.M. An elegant Victorian building, erected in 1892, served as city hall until 1939, now houses permanent and changing exhibits of regional history and Northwest art. Exquisite, well-lighted interior complements displays of Indian artifacts, logging equipment, nautical items, and furnishings and fixtures from the Victorian era. Ranks among the best such museums on the coast. Classified *must see.*

Water Sports and Activities

Chuckanut Charters, P.O. Box 5361; Bellingham 98227; 733–2125. At No. 22 Squalicum Harbor Mall, on the waterfront. Sail the San Juan and Canadian Gulf islands aboard one of about twenty vessels from 27 to 50 feet in length. Fully crewed or bare-boat charters by the half day, day, weekend, or week. Learn-and-sail cruises. Sunset and dinner cruises. Custom cruises.

North Sound Tours, 1515 Cornwall Avenue; Bellingham 98225; 733–5888. West of I-5, Exit 255, Sunset to Cornwall. Sea-kayak trips throughout north Puget Sound. Evening sunset tours, full-moon tours, full-day and overnight trips, and extended excursions. No previous experience necessary. Competent guides and all gear furnished. Phone for reservations.

Rosario Princess, No. 5 Harbor Esplanade; Bellingham 98225; 734–8866. On Bellingham Bay waterfront. Whale-watching and nature excursions, as well as dinner cruises in the San Juan Islands aboard the 83-foot former Coast Guard cutter *Rosario Princess.*

214

Golf

Lake Padden Golf Course, 4882 Samish Way; Bellingham 98225; 676–6989. East of I-5, southeast of Bellingham, via Exit 252. An 18-hole, par-70, 6,123-yard course. Practice area, pro shop, and snack bar.

Sudden Valley Golf Course, 2145 Lake Whatcom Boulevard; Bellingham 98226; 734–6435. East of I-5, southeast of Bellingham. From the north, take Exit 253, from the south Exit 240. An 18-hole, par-72, 6,553-yard course.

Events

March	Jazz Festival, 676–3130
	Coin & Stamp Exhibition, 733–7724
April	Rock & Gem Show, 733–5764
May	Antique Show & Sale, 733–8304
	Opening Day Boating Season, Squalicum Harbor, 733–7390
	Home Tour, 671–7828
June	Boat Show, 734–1330
	Lummi Stomish Water Festival, 734–8180
July	Red, White & Hullabaloo, 734–1330
	Peace Arch Games, 676–6985
	Sudden Valley Summer Festival, 734–6430
August	Heritage Day Cup, 671–2325
	Maritime Festival, 671–2325
	Annual West Coast Chowder Challenge, 671–3990
	Art Day at the Bay, 676–6985
September	P.I.T.C.H. Regatta, 733–7390
	Children's Fair & Slug Race, 676–0760
	Fairhaven Fall Festival, 676–0760
October	Harvest Festival, 733–5432
November	Christmas Festival & Tree Lighting, 734–1330
December	Roeder Home Christmas Show, 733–6897
	The Children's Shop, 676–6985

Travel Information

Bellingham/Whatcom County Visitor & Convention Bureau, 904 Potter (I-5, Exit 253); Bellingham 98226; 671–3990

Semiahmoo Resort and Marina

Blaine/Birch Bay, Washington 98230
Population: 2,500/900

Location: Blaine is on I-5 at the Canada border, 21 miles north of Bellingham; Birch Bay is about 10 miles south of Blaine via county roads

Blaine is a border town, more border than town. It has a few eateries, watering holes, and overnight digs. Charter boats take anglers to nearby fishing grounds for salmon and bottomfish. **Peace Arch Park** has attractive formal gardens, a pleasant picnic area, and a picturesque arch standing between northbound and southbound lanes of I-5 as a monument to the peaceful border between the United States and Canada.

The area's main attraction, though, is a posh resort at the tip of Semiahmoo (seh-mee-*ah*-moo) Spit, across Drayton Harbor from Blaine. The $200 million complex includes an inn with three restaurants and 200 guest rooms, a 300-slip marina that's expand-

216

able to 800 slips, a golf course designed by Arnold Palmer, a complete fitness center, shops, homesites, and townhouse condominiums. To reach Semiahmoo, take Blaine Road south to Drayton Harbor Road, which follows the south shore and connects with Semiahmoo Drive.

South of Blaine, on the shores of Birch Bay, is a small resort community of the same name. This is a popular area for water sports and activities. The bay is shallow, and the summer sun warms its waters enough for wading and swimming. Because the bay is so shallow, minus tides expose miles of tide flats, making this one of the best areas on the Washington coast for digging big horseneck and hard-shell clams. Along the south shore of the bay is **Birch Bay State Park** with fine campgrounds, beautiful picnic area, and a long stretch of sandy beach.

Lodging

Driftwood Inn Resort Motel, 7394 Birch Bay Drive; 371–2620. Exit 266 west off I-5, then 8 miles to Jackson, north 2 miles to Birch Bay Drive, and left three blocks. Has 15 motel rooms, cottages, and condominium suites, 1 to 3 bedrooms, some with kitchens. Cable TV, heated pool, playground, bike rental, boat and canoe rentals, beach access. Moderate.

Jacobs Landing Rentals, 7824 Birch Bay Drive; 371–7633. Exit 270 west off I-5, 7 miles south of Canada border. One-, 2-, and 3-bedroom beachfront condominiums with cable TV, fireplaces, decks, living rooms, dining areas, and fully equipped kitchens. All utensils and linens supplied. Heated indoor pool, therapy spa, two racquetball courts, and two tennis courts. Moderate to expensive.

The Inn at Semiahmoo, 9550 Semiahmoo Parkway; 371–5100; United States 1–800–854–2608; Canada, 1–800–854–6742. A $33.5 million inn at the 800-acre resort complex. Washington's largest resort hotel with 200 rooms and suites featuring all the expected amenities, with view rooms and fireplaces available. Walk to shops, galleries, marina, charter craft, beach, and bike rentals. Fitness center includes indoor and outdoor pools, indoor and outdoor tennis courts, indoor track, squash and racquetball courts, fully equipped weight room, spa, saunas, steam rooms, and tanning booths. Also at the inn is a gourmet dining room called Stars

Blaine/Birch Bay

Restaurant, and, for more casual dining, the R & R Restaurant and Packers Oyster Bar and Lounge. Expensive.

Campgrounds and RV Parks

Birch Bay State Park, 5105 Helwig Road; 371–2800. Ten miles south of Blaine, via Blaine Road and Birch Bay Drive, or Exits 266 and 270 west off I-5. Has 147 tent sites and 20 RV sites with water and electric hookups, picnic tables, stoves, firewood, showers, tank dump, and picnic area along the bay. Access to a mile-long beach. Store and cafe nearby. Reservations accepted. Inexpensive.

Museum

Semiahmoo Interpretive Center, Semiahmoo County Park; 371–5513. On Semiahmoo Spit, west of town. Wednesday through Sunday 1:00 to 5:00 P.M. A fine little museum with displays of logging equipment, Indian artifacts, and superb exhibits of the salmon fishing and canning processes. Historical exhibits of the Alaska Packers Association operation that once dominated here. Small but interesting gift shop with artworks, craft items, and souvenirs at very reasonable prices.

Water Sports and Activities

Grayline Sportfishing & Water Sightseeing, Resort Semiahmoo; 371–5222. Or 500 Wall Street; Suite 218; Seattle 98121; 441–1887. Near the old cannery site, behind the inn. Salmon and bottomfish trips twice daily in the summer, once a day the rest of the year, to Boundary Bay and the Strait of Georgia, aboard the *Emerald Star.* Also, four-hour sightseeing cruises aboard the 80-foot *Star of Semiahmoo* to Clements Reef National Wildlife Refuge and Roche Harbor on San Juan Island, as well as Sucia, Speiden, Waldron, and Patos islands. Also sunset-cruise charters for private parties, and ninety-minute evening cruises in summer.

Jim's Charter & Marine, 65 Marine Drive; P.O. Box 464; 332–6724. At Blaine Harbor. Salmon-fishing trips aboard the fast, modern, 25-foot *Thunderbird.* All tackle, bait, licenses, fish cleaning, fish bags, and coffee furnished. Good chinook fishing in June, cohos all summer. Book at least two weeks ahead.

Semiahmoo Marina, 9540 Semiahmoo Parkway; 371–5700. A 300-slip marina that will eventually expand to 800 slips. Features yacht maintenance, thirty-five-ton haulout capacity, full hookups and phone lines, showers, laundry, boat repairs, and supplies. A short walk to the inn, shops, galleries, and restaurants.

Golf

Semiahmoo Golf and Country Club, Resort Semiahmoo; 371–7005. An 18-hole, par-72, 7,000-yard course, laid out in a beautiful forested setting. When course designer Arnold Palmer saw the finished course, he said, "It looks like it's been here for a hundred years." Complete facilities. A semiprivate course, open to the public. Phone for tee times.

Events

May	English High Tea, Semiahmoo Park, 371–5513
June	Peace Arch Celebration, Blaine, 332–4544
	Skywater Festival, Blaine, 332–4544
July	Fireworks Show, Blaine, 332–4544
	Annual Arts & Crafts Fair, Birch Bay, 317–7675
	Salmon Bake & War Canoe Races, Blaine, 371–5513
August	Two-nation Celebration, Blaine, 332–4544
	Kite Flying, Blaine, 371–5513
September	Semiahmoo Cup Windsurfing & Sailing Regatta, Blaine, 332–4544
November	Christmas Lighting Celebration, Blaine, 332–4544
December	Christmas Sail-by, Blaine, 332–4544

Travel Information

Birch Bay Chamber of Commerce, 4897 Birch Bay-Lynden Road; Birch Bay; 371–7675

Blaine Visitors Information Center, Peace Portal Drive; P.O. Box Q; 332–6484

Oregon Index

Oregon Index

Oregon Index

Oregon Index

Washington Index

Washington Index